D1270353

Born to Raise Hell

Born to Raise Hell

The Untold Story of Richard Speck

by

Jack Altman & Marvin Ziporyn, M.D.

Grove Press, Inc.
New York

Library of Congress Catalog Card Number: 67-27330

First Printing

Manufactured in the United States of America

Contents

A Routine Task

AT 12:30 P.M. ON THE 29TH DAY OF JULY, 1966, A YOUNG MAN was brought to Ward 1 of the hospital at Cook County Jail on Chicago's South-West Side. Under the supervision of the chief prison guard, David Brierton, a nurse and doctor helped the young man into bed number 11 in a corner of the narrow cream and olive-drab ward. Only ten of the twenty other beds were occupied. From one of them, four beds away, a Negro prisoner sat up and screamed at the newcomer: "I'll kill you, you bastard. I'll get you, sure as God." The rest of the patients stared in silence. The young man looked startled at the outburst, but said nothing. He turned and faced the brick wall, clenched his eyes tight and tried to sleep.

Chief Guard Brierton was posted at the foot of the young man's bed. A doctor approached the guard and asked to see the new patient. "I have to examine his heart," the doctor explained. Brierton replied that the special provisions for this prisoner required that the doctor show an identification card, even though he and Brierton had known each other for some time. Only a restricted number of authorized medical and prison personnel were allowed to approach the bed. The young man was Richard Speck, accused of murdering eight nurses.

The doctor duly identified himself as Dr. T. K. Anderson and began his examination of the prisoner. Elsewhere in the ward the routine was resumed, the momentary upset forgotten. The jail psychiatrist, Dr. Marvin Ziporyn, was making his regular rounds of the patients, chatting quietly, swapping wisecracks—what's known as maintaining rapport. He stopped by the newcomer's bed to exchange a few words with the chief guard.

The psychiatrist glanced down at Speck, who was propped up on two pillows. He lay there in a regulation white hospital smock, loose around the neck and revealing on his upper chest pockmarks like those that pitted the hollow cheeks of his pale, angular face. Beneath a mass of sandy hair slicked back from a high forehead, his watery blue eyes flickered apprehensively as Dr. Anderson moved around him with his stethoscope. His dry, colorless lips hung half-open. Speck looked haggard, tense, and considerably older than his twenty-four years. He had lost a lot of blood from cuts on his left wrist and the inner side of his elbow—the result of a suicide attempt. During treatment he had also suffered an inflammation of the heart sac. What strength his muscular body once had now seemed to have seeped entirely away.

Ziporyn walked away and was approached by the head nurse as he left the ward.

"Are you going to talk to him?" she asked.

"Speck? No, I don't want to jeopardize his rights," the psychiatrist replied. "He might say things to me that could hurt him." But the decision was not for Ziporyn to make, as he discovered a few minutes later in the office of the chief warden, Jack Johnson.

"Have you had a look at Speck?" the warden asked.

"No."

"Do you think he's suicidal?"

"No idea."

"Well, I think you should go down and see him. See whether he is suicidal and tell us what precautions we should take."

This was the bald assignment, in its way a routine task. A jail psychiatrist has to assure the minimal mental welfare of the prisoners, make sure they are equipped to withstand the rigors of prison life well enough to stand trial and well enough to serve their sentence. The jail psychiatrist must determine, if such is the sentence, that the prisoners are, psychologically speaking, fit to die. In Speck's case, the horror of the murders had immeasurably raised the stakes. He had already attempted suicide once since the murders. Warden Johnson, a man known for his progressive penological ideas—a holder of the Clarence Darrow Humanitarian Award and another from the American Civil

Liberties Union—was also a conscientious enforcer of strict jail discipline. He did not want Speck making another suicide attempt while in his custody.

The State's Attorney's office had made unusual efforts, following recent Supreme Court decisions on interrogation, to protect the prisoner's rights vis-à-vis the police and the judiciary. The warden was concerned with protecting the prisoner against himself. It was the psychiatrist's job to anticipate the risks.

This was the immediate task, but it did not represent the limit of Ziporyn's responsibility. Johnson had given him the broadest of mandates when he started work at Cook County Jail in 1965. For six years prior to take up the position of jail psychiatrist, Ziporyn had visited Cook County Jail four or five times a year to conduct diagnostic interviews of prisoners on behalf of their defense counsel, to assess a client's mental state and the possibilities of an insanity plea. In the course of these visits he made the acquaintance of the chief warden. On a visit in August 1965 Johnson stopped Ziporyn outside his office and told him: "I need a psychiatrist here. Our psychiatrist just quit. You wouldn't like the job, would you?"

Ziporyn said he might be interested but wanted to know what it would entail. The warden's answer could not have been more broad: "Come in a couple of days a week and take a look at whichever prisoners need looking at." Nothing more specific was said. They agreed on a salary and Ziporyn accepted the job on the spot, starting the next month.

Ziporyn was given absolute autonomy. The extent of Johnson's intervention was to ask that he see a particular prisoner, as he had done in the case of Richard Speck. Beyond that, Ziporyn worked out his own program: providing group therapy for women prisoners and individual therapeutic counseling for inmates in need of it, advising on whether they could benefit from activity in the prison's workshops for printing, carpentry, baking. He also prescribed medication and submitted diagnostic reports to the court when called for. He was required to make a report on each interview conducted with a prisoner, but the content of those interviews was left entirely to him.

In the case of Richard Speck, Ziporyn was to calculate the chances that the prisoner might try to commit suicide. This was not an area of investigation that could be neatly defined, and nobody could predict where such an investigation would end. Ziporyn would have to probe the thoughts, memories, worries and fears, and also the fancies and whims that made up the man Richard Speck. The methods that the psychiatrist would employ and the avenues he would explore were entirely his own responsibility.

Jails are not usually beautiful, and Cook County Jail is no exception. Situated just west of the Criminal Courts Building and a few yards north of Bridewell (the City of Chicago's House of Correction, where Speck was hospitalized after his arrest on July 17), the jail is a dirty gray-brown complex of eight blocks, set in pairs. Each block, lettered from A to H, contains either four or five numbered cell tiers.

The whole is fronted by a five-story administrative block that includes Warden Johnson's office. Behind blocks G and H is the exercise yard, including a basketball court, two baseball diamonds, a track area and a tennis court. It is surrounded by a 23-foot-high wall with the traditional watchtowers from which guards telephone the administrative block every half hour to show, among other things, that they have not dropped dead of a heart attack. A ground-floor corridor runs 200 yards from one end of the building to the other. This was the passage Ziporyn took to return to Ward 1, situated in block H.

Richard Speck was lying in bed reading *Look* magazine when the psychiatrist returned. It was hot, a sticky Chicago July afternoon. A large electric fan did little more than impose a constant reminder of its presence by its insistent whir from the corner opposite Speck's bed. It provided a background to the almost soundless shuffle of a nurse and doctor moving between the beds, broken only by an occasional half-hearted chuckle or a murmured exchange between the patients. None of them looked up as Ziporyn walked over to Speck's bed.

The chief guard, with whom Ziporyn had been chatting barely half an hour before, stopped the psychiatrist as he approached the bed. Brierton grinned sheepishly and said: "I'm afraid, sir, I have to ask you for your identification card. You understand—regulations."

Ziporyn smiled and took out his card accrediting him as psychiatrist to Cook County Jail, explaining at the same time that Warden Johnson had assigned him to see Speck. Brierton nodded and stood to one side to let Ziporyn pass. Speck was watching the interplay with the same nervous flicker of the eyes that Ziporyn had noticed when Speck was being examined by Dr. Anderson. He would glance up at Brierton and Ziporyn and then back to his magazine, without really seeming to comprehend, or wanting to comprehend, what was happening. As Ziporyn approached him, Speck stared fixedly at the magazine. Ziporyn coughed and said quietly: "Mr. Speck, my name is Dr. Ziporyn. I'm the jail psychiatrist and I've been asked to find out a little bit about you. Mind if we talk?"

Speck shrugged and continued looking at the magazine. He said nothing. The psychiatrist went on: "Do you like to read?"

Without looking up, Speck muttered, "Nope." He paused and added, still not looking at Ziporyn: "I don't read too well. I just like to look at the pictures."

"Can you read at all?" Ziporyn asked. "I'd like you to show me." He took the magazine and asked Speck to read an advertisement of the Chrysler Corporation. In a broad Texas drawl, stretching out each word in a halting rhythm that had nothing to do with the sense of what he was reading, Speck stumbled his way through two lines of text. The only words that came without difficulty were the familiar brand names of the automobiles. On the opposite page Speck read from an article about tropical birds. The title was "Prisoners of Paradise." The polysyllables were completely beyond him, but he remained unperturbed.

"You see?" he said blandly. "I just don't read well, do I?"

Speck's manner remained remote. Ziporyn felt he should try some formal mental-status tests. He asked Speck to name the year, the month, the day, where he was, who the President was, the Vice-President, the mayor of Chicago. The date, the place and Lyndon Baines Johnson he knew, but then he halted. Ziporyn followed up with two memory tests.

"I'm going to give you four numbers," he told Speck. "I want you to listen very carefully and then repeat them—41, 37, 16, 5."

Staring bleakly into space, Speck murmured: "41 . . . er . . . um. That's it. That's all I can remember."

The psychiatrist made no comment. There was always the possibility that Speck was faking, but only prolonged examination could reveal this. Ziporyn said he would read out a sentence which

Speck should memorize and repeat back. Slowly he intoned. "A cowboy from Arizona went to San Francisco with his horse and his dog to buy a saddle and a new suit of clothes."

Speck hesitated, then began: "A cowboy from San Francisco. . . ." He flushed, pursed his lips and stopped.

Given the careful warning that he would have to repeat the numbers and the sentence, a normal person could recite them back. Speck's failures of mental status and memory suggested possible brain damage. Ziporyn went on with a calculation test.

"Start with the number 100," he told Speck. "Then subtract by sevens until I tell you to stop."

"Subtract? You mean take away sevens? Well, I'm not sure. . . ."

Ziporyn interrupted. "Suppose you had 100 apples and you gave me 7. How many would you have left?"

"93."

"Then 7 more?"

Speck thought for perhaps thirty seconds and said "81."

Nonchalantly the psychiatrist continued: "Did you ever get hit on the head?"

"Plenty of times," said Speck, showing more interest in this than in the arithmetic questions. "When I was playing in a sandbox. I hit myself on the head with a claw hammer. Accidentally. I knocked myself out. Then, a few years later—I must have been about ten—I was playing with some kids. They chased me and I climbed into a tree. I hid there for a while, maybe ten feet from the ground, and lost my hold. I fell on my head. My sister found me. She thought I was dead. They told me I was out for about an hour and a half. When I came to, she was still screaming, 'He's dead, he's dead.' About five years after that, I did it again. This time I was running down a street and ran my head straight into a steel awning rod. I was knocked out again. That thing must have gone right into my brain. See that patch of light-colored hairs on my head? That's where it hit me. On top of that I've been pistol-whipped by cops and I've been beat up in bar fights. Hundreds of times."

Cause for brain damage seemed sufficient right there, but Ziporyn wanted to try another test to see whether Speck might be suffering from schizophrenia.

"You went as far as ninth grade, right? Did you ever have any history?" he asked.

"A little."
"Do you know who Captain Cook was?"
"A pirate?"
"No, a famous explorer. He went round the world on three separate trips and was killed. On which trip did it happen?"
Without hesitating, Speck replied: "Are you kidding? The third, of course."
Classic schizophrenics often say the first or second trip or excuse themselves from answering by saying something like: "I don't know about Captain Cook." The psychiatrist had deliberately chosen the most simplified tests. Anything more complex introduces the factor of the variable educational levels of patients, which would render analysis of the responses more difficult and less reliable.
Ziporyn decided to try one more standard primary test for schizophrenia. He began: "I read the other day they dug up a skull of an eight-year-old boy in Spain. They think it was Christopher Columbus. What do you think?"
Again Speck was scornful. "That ain't right. Columbus was an old man when he died."
The possibility of schizophrenia seemed increasingly unlikely. In this kind of questioning schizophrenics will often argue the pros and cons of the skull's possibly belonging to Columbus. Ziporyn was satisfied that Speck showed no cognitive or perceptive defects indicative of schizophrenia, but he needed evidence of a secondary nature, based on Speck's psychological history. Resuming a casual air, Ziporyn turned from the Captain Cook and Christopher Columbus quiz to ask: "Do you hear any voices?"
Speck blushed and did not seem to want to reply. Ziporyn waited. After a long pause Speck said, "Well, sometimes." He paused again and added, "When I take drugs." At the second hesitation, Ziporyn became puzzled. Hearing voices was a common symptom of schizophrenia. If Speck's hearing were not structurally impaired but occasionally functioned abnormally so that he heard voices, then he might be subject to schizophrenia, a functional psychosis. But his remark about drugs made it more likely that the voices were the result of an organic abnormality caused by the interaction of the drugs and the damage to the brain.
"Whose voices?" Ziporyn asked.

"You'll kind of think I'm silly, I mean it sounds ridiculous, but they're like my conscience talking to me. They warn me, tell me: 'Don't do it,' when I'm thinking of doing something bad." Speck was obviously embarrassed. With great deliberation he added: "But I want you to know, it only happens when I'm on drugs."

"What kind of drugs?"

"Yellow-jackets and red-birds.* Sometimes I shoot myself with inhalers. You know, Wyman's glue and stuff."

"And do you drink?"

"Boy, do I drink."

"What?"

"Anything I can lay my hands on—wine, beer, whisky, gin, you name it. I drink from the time I get up till I get drunk and fall back into bed. Sometimes it makes me feel real good. But sometimes it puts me in a real bad temper and then I get into fights."

Speck talked slowly, quietly, in a monotone. He was showing more interest in the psychiatrist's questions now that they were more directly related to his personal experience, but he still seemed listless. What part his real or apparent involvement in the murders was playing in creating his demeanor was not yet evident. It seemed an appropriate moment to approach the subject. Ziporyn took a deep breath and said: "Dick, you know that everybody is saying you killed these nurses. What happened?"

"I don't know anything more about it than you do."

"Did you do it?"

Speck sighed deeply and replied in a low voice, with a shrug of resignation: "Everybody says I did it. Must be so. If they say I did it, I did it."

This acceptance of guilt made it seem unlikely that he had earlier been feigning stupidity or deliberately dramatizing his brain injuries to pave the way for an insanity plea, but Ziporyn reserved judgment. It was still too early. He repeated his question:

"Did you do it?"

"Look, I was drinking that day. I told you how I drink. And I had six red-birds. To tell you the truth, I don't know nothing about anything from eight o'clock that night till I came to, about eleven o'clock the next day. All I remember is I met three sailors

* Sodium amytal and sodium seconal, both habituating barbiturates capable of causing hallucinations and bizarre actions.

in a tavern on the South Side in the afternoon. We had some drinks, then we went off some place and had a fix—a shot in the arm. I don't know what it was exactly, but it wasn't heroin. It was something in a blue bottle, I think. I don't remember a thing after that. I couldn't tell you or anybody else what any of those nurses looked like."

"You remember going into the building, the place where they lived?"

Speck hesitated. He smiled quizzically and looked around the room. Then he said: "You know, my lawyer told me not to talk about this to anybody."

"But this is part of the jail routine. You can tell me," said Ziporyn.

"Is it? Well, I guess it's okay then. Nope, I don't remember going into no building."

"What did you do when you came to, the next day?"

Speck snorted in a self-mocking tone and said: "Same thing I always do. Went out and got drunk again."

"Did you hear about the murders when you went out?"

"Yeah, I heard something about it."

"You didn't connect it with yourself?"

Speck considered the question and shook his head with a look of surprise on his face. It seemed to be striking him for the first time that his feeling of detachment was a little odd. "No," he said slowly. "No, I didn't make no connection, not till I heard my name on the radio."

"Were you frightened at all?"

"No. By that time I was too drunk again to feel anything."

"And how do you feel about it now?"

The tired air of resignation deepened in his voice. The nasals of his Southern twang added a harshness as he drawled, "Well, if I burn, I burn."

Ward 1 of Cook County Jail was silent on that hot summer afternoon. The other prisoner-patients could not hear the conversation going on in the corner, nor did they appear curious. The psychiatrist was just doing another routine interview. They read their magazines or stared vacantly at the ceiling. Speck and Ziporyn watched them for a while, and then Speck spoke again.

"When I heard what they said I'd done, on the radio, I just felt there was no point in living. If I was that kind of person then I was no good to anybody any more, no good to myself neither. First I tried a bottle of sleeping pills, a whole bottle, but that was no good. I had to do something, I had to find some way. I mean, what's the use of living, somebody like me? So then I tried cutting myself, with a blade, a razor blade. But that didn't work either, did it? I'm still here."

Ziporyn nodded. Speck's depression was deepening, and the psychiatrist decided to stop the interview. He took his leave of Speck and went to tell Warden Johnson what he wanted to know.

Yes, Speck was suicidal. He was emotionally unstable, impulsive, depressive. Throughout the sixty-five minutes of the interview his mood had shifted constantly—sometimes bland, then cheerful, then depressed, never the same for more than two or three minutes at a time. Ziporyn recommended standard psychiatric tests of Speck's condition—electroencephalogram, the Bender-Gestalt and Wechsler-Bellevue intelligence tests. And the usual practical precautions against suicide.

Ziporyn was assigned to see Speck on a regular basis. This meant he would see him whenever he came to the jail, which was usually twice a week.

The Available Facts

ZIPORYN WAS ABLE TO RECONSTRUCT MANY OF THE EVENTS OF mid-July that caused his new patient to be in Cook County Jail, but there were gaps. Police investigation had been quick and largely efficient. The surviving nurse furnished an account of the accused man's arrival on the scene and described the events that led to the murders. There was, however, no eyewitness to the crime, of which Speck professed total ignorance. The police had announced publicly, through Superintendent Orlando W. Wilson, that they were satisfied they had the right man, although many questions remained unanswered.

The scene of the murders was a sedate little neighborhood of some 7,500 people known as Jeffrey Manor, situated on the southeast edge of the city. The community is solidly white-collar middle-class, 40 per cent Jewish, with an average income of $8,000. The two-story family houses and rows of townhouses are neatly kept. Although Jeffrey Manor is close to Calumet Harbor and constantly attracts out-of-work seamen seeking jobs at the National Maritime Union on East 100th Street, no serious crime rate has developed. In the words of Sergeant Jack Crane, a veteran policeman on the Jeffrey Manor beat: "Bicycle thefts are a greater problem here than mugging or any kind of violence."

On the south side of East 100th Street, between Luella and Crandon Avenues, is a block of six simple two-story townhouses, with pastel-green wooden façades and buff brick walls. Three of the houses were rented by the South Chicago Community Hospital as a residence for 24 of their 115 student nurses. Behind the town-houses is a narrow parking lot that backs on Luella Park, a small recreation area with children's slides and swings. Across Crandon Avenue, on the southeast corner of East 100th, stands the red-brick branch office of the National Maritime Union.

The second week in July had been hot and humid. Wednesday night, the 13th, however, was cooler—as a neighbor of the nurses said, "the best for sleeping in a long while."

As she later told the police, Miss Corazon Amurao, a twenty-three-year-old Filipino exchange nurse living at 2319 East 100th, started to get ready for bed at about 10:30 P.M. with her two room-mates in their front bedroom on the second floor. At 11 P.M. they heard a knock on the door.

"I opened the door," Miss Amurao said in her statement, "and a man was standing there. The first thing I noticed about him was the strong smell of alcohol."

She described the man as aged about twenty-five, six feet tall, fair-haired, weighing about 170 pounds. He wore a black jacket, dark trousers and black shoes. According to the police version of her statement, he carried a small black gun in one hand and a knife in the other. He told her: "I'm not going to hurt you. I'm only going to tie you up. I need your money to go to New Orleans."

Motioning with the gun, he told Miss Amurao and the other two girls to go to a bedroom at the back of the house, where he found three more girls. He made all six lie on the floor. Repeatedly assuring them that he did not want to harm them, he took a sheet from one of the bunks, methodically tore it into strips and bound each girl.

At 11:30, Gloria Davy returned from a date and was met by the intruder. She was led to the back bedroom and was tied up along with the others. Half an hour later, Suzanne Farris came home with her friend Mary Ann Jordan. They were confronted by the man and taken to the bedroom. He asked them all where they kept their money. They gave him what they had.

Of the nine girls, six were senior nursing students and three were exchange nurses from the Philippines. Only eight of them actually lived in the house. The ninth, Mary Ann Jordan, was only intending to stay overnight with Suzanne Farris, who was engaged to be married the following spring to Mary Ann's brother, Philip. Mary Ann, twenty years old, lived at home with five brothers and sisters. Her father was a civil engineer employed by the city of Chicago. Suzanne Farris, a year older, was one of three children of a superintendent of the Chicago Transit Authority. She planned to specialize in pediatrics.

Nina Schmale, a twenty-four-year-old daughter of a cement mason in Wheaton, Illinois, had been a Sunday School teacher for four years and had worked as a volunteer nurse's aid at the Du Page Convalescent Home before coming to South Chicago Community Hospital. Patricia Matusek, aged twenty, was a local swimming champion and member of a water-ballet team. The daughter of a retail liquor dealer, she was to start work in the Chicago Children's Memorial Hospital when she finished her training in September. Pamela Wilkening, twenty, came from Lansing, Illinois, where her father was a steam fitter. Nursing had been her goal since early childhood. She was a sports-car enthusiast and had been promised a car for her twenty-first birthday, in nineteen days' time.

Perhaps the prettiest of the girls was Gloria Davy, a twenty-two-year-old brunette. She was one of six children of a steel-company foreman in Dyer, Indiana. She had worked for a year as a nurse's aid at Our Lady of Mercy Hospital in Dyer. President of the Illinois Student Nurses Association, she planned to join the Peace Corps after finishing her training.

The three girls from the Philippines—Merlita Gargullo, twenty-two, of Santa Cruz; Valentina Pasion, twenty-three, of Jones City; and Corazon Amurao, twenty-three, of San Luis Batanga—were all graduates of Manila nursing schools. They had arrived in Chicago the previous month for post-graduate training. Miss Pasion and Miss Amurao both attended the nearby Our Lady Gate of Heaven Catholic church. Now, they and the six American girls lay at the mercy of a stranger, a man who had, as the sole survivor was later to tell the police, "soft eyes, a very gentle appearance."

One by one, he took the girls out of the back bedroom. Each gave a muffled cry as she was led from the room, but otherwise, Miss Amurao related, there were no screams, no sounds of violence. At the time, she said, she had no idea of what was happening. During one of his absences from the room she was able to roll herself under one of the bunks set against the wall. She lay there, petrified, through the night. At 5:00 A.M., when the nurses regularly awoke to get ready for the hospital jeep that picked them up at 6:30, Miss Amurao heard an alarm clock go off in one of the other bedrooms. Apart from that, not a sound. Thinking the man might still be in the house, she lay still for another hour and then wriggled out from under the bed. She freed herself and crept out of the bedroom, along the hall to her own room at the front of the house.

As she went from room to room on the second floor, not daring to go downstairs, she found the bodies of her friends. She smashed the screen of her bedroom window and crawled onto the two-foot-wide ledge that ran along the front of the house, about ten feet from the ground. There she cowered, screaming for help.

At 6:00 that mild July morning, Jeffrey Manor's habitual calm was pierced by Miss Amurao's hysterical screams. "Help me, help me. Everybody is dead. I am the only one alive on the sampan." In her terror she imagined herself back in the Philippines.

Two houses away on the same block, Mrs. Betty Windmiller was standing on her back porch looking out at Luella Park. She heard the screaming and rushed round to the front, where she met a neighbor, Robert Hall, walking his dog. Together they ran to number 2319, where Miss Amurao was crouching on the second-story ledge, holding onto the screen she had smashed through and screaming: "My friends are all dead, all dead, all dead. I'm the only one alive, oh God, the only one. My friends are all dead." While other neighbors emerged and tried to calm Miss Amurao, Mrs. Windmiller and Mr. Hall went for the police.

Daniel Kelly, a policeman who had been cruising through the area in a patrol car, entered the house through the rear door, which he found open. One of four screen panels had been forced out of the door frame. Inside he found Gloria Davy lying naked, face down on a divan in the downstairs living room. He recognized Gloria Davy immediately as the sister of his former girl friend, Charlene. According to the published portion of Coroner Andrew Toman's autopsy, Miss Davy was strangled by a strip of clothing. A blood test conducted as part of the autopsy revealed that there were 111 milligrams of alcohol in her blood (the National Safety Council's measure for inebriation is 150 milligrams). An official police report stated that Miss Davy's anus was mutilated, perhaps as the result of a sexual assault, but the published autopsy did not refer to this.

The other bodies were upstairs. Patricia Matusek was found in the bathroom, choked to death. In the doorway of one front bedroom, through which Miss Amurao had crawled to scream for help, lay Mary Ann Jordan, stabbed in the heart, through her left breast, in the neck and in the left eye. Beside her was Suzanne Farris, lying on her back in torn underclothes. She had been stabbed several times in the back, slashed across the neck and chin and finally strangled. Pamela Wilkening was strangled with a strip of sheet and stabbed in the left breast. On the floor of the other front bedroom Valentina Pasion was found, dead of stab wounds in the neck, lying across the body of Merlita Gargullo, who had been strangled as well as stabbed in the neck. Nina Schmale, who had also been strangled and stabbed in the neck, lay on the bed. All the girls except Miss Davy and Miss Jordan were still bound. Miss Davy was the only one whom police described as having been left completely naked.

Over thirty fingerprints were found by police on the walls, the furniture and the girls' personal belongings. The only extraneous item reported at the time was a man's sweat-soaked T-shirt, lying on a desk in the living room. What appeared to be skidmarks from automobile tires were found on the lawn in front of the house.

Miss Amurao was taken to South Chicago Community Hospital, where she was placed under mild sedation while police interviewed her for two hours. By 8:30 on that Thursday morning the description of the intruder had been circulated to patrol cars touring the neighborhood. Twenty minutes later they learned that a man of that description had left two bags with an attendant at the gas station opposite, telling the attendant that he was seeking work at the National Maritime Union. At the N.M.U. office, police learned from an employee that a man had been there in the past few days looking for a job aboard a ship to New Orleans. They found his name on an application form discarded in a wastebasket: Richard Speck.

Speck had had a number of jobs as a seaman, and his photograph was filed with the U.S. Coast Guard. The police included the picture among 100 others of men with records of sex crimes to be shown to Miss Amurao at the hospital, but she was in too serious a state of shock to be disturbed. Meanwhile, it was decided to set a trap for Speck by having the N.M.U. offer him a job on a ship going to New Orleans. Detectives combing the area learned from one of his drinking pals, Robert (Red) Gerrald, a forty-eight-year-old merchant seaman, that Speck had been staying on the South Side, hopping from tavern to tavern. At 3:10 P.M. he telephoned the N.M.U. and was told of the job. The police waited for an hour but there was no sign of Speck. They traced the telephone call to the Shipyard Inn, a seamen's tavern and lodging house about a mile from the N.M.U. and the nurses' home. When they arrived there, they found he had left just five minutes after making the telephone call, taking a taxi to the North Side.

Speck's trail there led to the skid-row section of North Clark Street, where he had danced in the Twist Lounge with a blonde prostitute named Mary. He paid her $3 and took her to a cheap Clark Street hotel. He moved on.

At 8:15 on Friday morning, the manager of the Raleigh Hotel on North Dearborn Street telephoned the Near North Side 18th police district to report a Puerto Rican prostitute's complaint that the man she was with had a gun. Two patrolmen went to room 306 and found the man in bed. He said the gun belonged to the girl. He identified himself as Richard Speck, a twenty-four-year-old merchant seaman, and gave as his address the Chicago home of his sister, Mrs. Martha Thornton. The policemen confiscated the gun and six cartridges, filed a report, but did not arrest Speck. His description had not yet filtered through to the North Side district stations and his name was not matched with the man being hunted on the South Side. Speck left the hotel at noon, returned to collect some laundry and left again at 9:30 P.M., fifteen minutes before the police came rushing back for him.

The police had shown the collection of photographs to Miss Amurao, and she picked out Richard Speck as the man at the nurses' home. From the files of the Federal Bureau of Investigation in Washington, D.C., it was learned that Speck had a police record in Dallas and that among his identification marks was a tattoo on his left forearm with the words BORN TO RAISE HELL. At 7:30 P.M. his fingerprints arrived from Washington. By 4:30 on Saturday morning the Chicago Police Department's crime laboratory had established to its satisfaction that they matched with some of the thirty-odd fingerprints found at 2319 East 100th Street.

At 2:40 P.M. on Saturday, Superintendent Orlando W. Wilson made the following announcement: "The killer of eight nurses from South Chicago Community Hospital on Thursday, July 14, 1966, has been named and a warrant sworn out for his arrest. After a city-wide dragnet for clues, the murderer was identified as Richard Franklin Speck, white male, twenty-four, a seaman, also known by aliases as Richard Franklin Lindbergh and also Richard Benjamin Speck. Latent fingerprints taken at the scene of the mass killings identified Speck as the killer."

His statement went on: "Our detective division, aided by specialists from our crime laboratory, establishes the identity of a murderer and epitomizes the excellence of our personnel and their determination to seek out criminals of this nature without regard to personal hours spent in this grueling process. I commend all the detectives and officers who aided in the identification of this mass murderer, and I am hopeful for his immediate apprehension."

The Superintendent was widely criticized in the press for publicly calling Speck the killer before he had been brought to trial. No one, the critics said, had actually seen Speck commit the murders, nor had anyone who had seen Speck after the murders noticed any blood on his clothes, even though he had been reported wearing the same clothing Miss Amurao described. Wilson refused to retract his statement.

Meanwhile, the hunt continued. Speck's picture was flashed by every Chicago television station and published on the front page of every newspaper. Speck finally fell into the hands of the police without their realizing who he was. At midnight on Saturday he was lying on an uncovered mattress in room 584 on the fifth floor of the seven-story, 90-cents-a-night Starr Hotel on West Madison Street, in Chicago's sleaziest skid-row area. The room had been booked in the name of "B. Brian." On the bare cement floor beneath the bed lay a newspaper with the headline: POLICE SAY NURSE SURVIVOR CAN IDENTIFY SLAYER OF 8. The paper was soaked with blood that had run from cuts on his right wrist and inside his left elbow. Weakly, Speck called out to the man in the next room, George Gregorich: "Come and see me. You got to come and see me. I done something bad."

Gregorich tried to ignore him. "Leave me alone," he said. "You're a hillbilly, you just want to get at me. I don't trust no hillbilly."

Speck persisted. "I'm going to die if you don't come and see me."

Still Gregorich refused, and Speck staggered out of his room, covered with blood, to kick at Gregorich's door. As he did so, two men saw him and one of them shouted to the elevator operator, "Hey, this guy's bleeding himself to death." The desk clerk was alerted and he called the police.

Suicides are not uncommon on Madison Street, and the two patrolmen who answered the call to this typical flophouse regarded their task as strictly routine. They were not expecting to find anyone out of the ordinary, and they did not spare a second glance for the bleeding man they carried out on a stretcher to Cook County Hospital. At 12:30 A.M. they left him in the hands of Dr. LeRoy Smith, resident physician in the trauma unit of the hospital's Ward 32.

Dr. Smith looked down at the man thrashing his legs about on the bed. The name tag that the police had put on him read "B. Brian," but Smith thought he saw a resemblance to the picture of Richard Speck that he had seen in the newspapers. Beneath the caked blood on the left forearm the doctor could see the traces of a tattoo. He rubbed away some of the blood to reveal the letter B. He sent one of the nurses to bring a newspaper. To Smith's eyes the picture seemed to tally, but the nurse saw no resemblance at all. Smith rubbed away some more blood to reveal the letters B O R N. The doctor leaned over the man and asked: "What's your name?"

The man replied faintly: "Richard . . . Richard Speck."

Smith sent for the police.

Speck was weak from loss of blood—Smith estimated one and a half pints—from a nicked brachial artery in the left arm and lacerations of his right wrist. He was given five stitches in the arm and a transfusion of a quart of blood. As he was reviving, Speck looked up at Smith and said: "Do you collect the $10,000 reward?"

After the surgery, the police arrested him and placed him in legirons. Gasping faintly, "I'm scared . . . I'm scared," Speck was wheeled out of the County Hospital and driven in an ambulance to Bridewell prison hospital at 4 A.M. on Sunday morning.

In his third-floor room at Bridewell, Speck was placed under mild restraint—held spread-eagled in bed by leather thongs—the normal procedure for potentially suicidal patients. He was too weak on Monday from the loss of blood and prolonged sedation for the police to confront him with Miss Amurao. The next day she stood in the doorway of his room and looked at him lying beneath a sheet. She went out and told a detective: "That is the man." He was kept at Bridewell until he was considered fit enough, on July 29, to be transferred to Cook County Jail.

From police investigations of Speck's past, Dr. Ziporyn knew that his patient was born on the eve of the United States' entry into World War II, December 6, 1941, in Kirkwood, Illinois, about 180 miles southwest of Chicago. His father, a potter named Benjamin Speck, moved the family of three sons (one of whom died when Speck was thirteen) and five daughters to nearby Monmouth shortly after Richard's birth. They stayed in Monmouth till the father's death, in December 1947.

Speck then moved with his mother, Mary Margaret, to Dallas, Texas, where she remarried. Of his time at the J. L. Long Junior High School in Dallas, an eighth-grade teacher said: "He seemed sort of lost. It didn't seem like he knew what was going on. I wasn't able to teach him anything. I don't think I ever saw him smile. No one could get through to him. He was a loner. He seemed to be in a fog, sort of sulky. He didn't have any friends in class."

Speck went on to Crozier Technical High School and dropped out after one semester. During his teens in Dallas he ran up a record of ten arrests for trespassing, burglary and other misdemeanors. His police record was a handicap when looking for jobs, and he didn't last long as a laborer, garbage collector, truckdriver or carpenter.

He married a fifteen-year-old girl, Shirley Malone, when he was twenty. They separated in January 1966, and she retained custody of their three-year-old daughter. His mother told a reporter that the couple had both been hot-tempered and had fought throughout the marriage.

One of his sisters, Mrs. Carolyn Wilson, commented that Speck had been devoted to his daughter. "He took that little girl everywhere with him," she said. "He loved that baby so much—in fact, he loved all little children, but he loved that child." (At the time that Speck was taken to the County Hospital his wallet contained a color photograph of a little girl sitting on some steps in a bright dress, grinning up at the camera.)

Just four months before the murders, Speck returned to the scene of his early childhood, in Monmouth, Illinois. The local police chief, Harold Tinder, said Speck was arrested in March on a charge of disorderly conduct after a knife fight in Gulfport, thirty miles from Monmouth. He had stayed with some old friends of the Speck family and spent most of his time bar-hopping around town. At one of his favorite taverns, a fellow drinker later recalled: "He showed me a picture of a real nice-looking gal. He said she was his wife, and he was going back to Texas and kill her if it was the last thing he ever did."

He left Monmouth and found work in Michigan aboard a Great Lakes ore boat, working the waters of Keweenaw Bay, an inlet of Lake Superior. He was stricken with appendicitis and was rushed to St. Joseph's Hospital in Hancock, Michigan for an emergency operation. In May, while convalescing from his appendectomy, Speck befriended a twenty-eight-year-old nurse, Judy Laakaniemi. They went to dances together and took long walks along the beaches. She later described him as "quiet and gentle" at that time, but added that when he returned to see her toward the end of June "he had a hatred in him." He was fired from an Inland Steel Company ship, the *Randall*, for quarreling with one of the officers.

He came to Chicago at the beginning of July, seeking the help of his sister, Mrs. Martha Thornton, and her husband. On Sunday, July 10, they drove him to the National Maritime Union hiring hall, gave him $25 and left. For three days he tried without success to get work on a ship going to New Orleans.

On Tuesday, July 26, 1966, a grand jury indicted Richard Speck for the murder of Gloria Davy, Patricia Matusek, Pamela Wilkening, Mary Ann Jordan, Suzanne Farris, Valentina Pasion, Merlita Gargullo and Nina Schmale.

"I Hope They Catch the Son of a Bitch"

AFTER BREAKFAST ON THE MORNING OF AUGUST 1, SILENCE settled over the huge Cook County Jail. Every corridor of every tier was empty. There were no guards on patrol or prisoners going about their menial duties. Warden Johnson had ordered all activities stopped, all corridors kept clear. It was the day Richard Speck was to be taken to court for his formal arraignment, his first appearance in public since his arrest.

Johnson was taking no chances. One of the country's biggest men in sheriff's police uniform—Lee Collins, 6 feet 10 inches from his head to the toes of his gigantic boots—was assigned, with a hefty partner, Jerome Adasiak, to take Speck to court. Shuffling uneasily on his feet, with Collins and Adasiak gripping either arm, Speck was walked from his bed on Ward 1 along the 200-foot tunnel connecting the jail to the Criminal Courts Building. He was taken by elevator to a fourth-floor chamber adjoining the courtroom of Chief Judge Alexander Napoli.

There were ten cases to be heard before that of the People versus Speck. They were handled in routine fashion, and then the courtroom doors were locked. Standing guard that day were twenty-five sheriff's policemen and bailiffs. As the doors were locked, they herded the spectators and news reporters (cameramen were excluded) to one side of the courtroom and systematically overturned each bench to search for explosives or weapons. The spectators were then moved to the other side and the process was repeated. At the same time, each person attending the hearing was carefully searched for concealed weapons. (None of the half-dozen guards assigned to stand around the prisoner carried a gun—a precaution dating from a case some years back when a defendant wrestled a gun from one of his guards and attempted to escape.) The shooting of President John F. Kennedy's accused assassin by Jack Ruby was still fresh in the mind of every policeman and court official. There was to be no risk of a repetition.

Finally the courtroom was considered ready for the hearing to begin. Richard Speck was brought in. He wore an open-necked, short-sleeved white sportshirt which flapped over a pair of dark-blue slacks. There was no strength left in his legs after his fifteen days in bed. He swayed a little as he stood before Judge Napoli.

As the arraignment began punctually at 9:30 A.M., Public Defender Gerald W. Getty, who was assigned to Speck by the state, walked to the prisoner's side.

Judge Napoli began: "Are you Richard Franklin Speck?"

Speck, standing with his right hand in his pocket and staring fixedly at the floor, mumbled inaudibly.

"You'll have to speak up," Judge Napoli said.

Speck leaned forward to put his mouth close to a microphone on the bench in front of him and said, "Yeah."

In reply to the judge's questions as to whether he was able to hire his own lawyer, whether he had a bank account, real estate, stocks and bonds or other financial assets, Speck muttered simply, "Uh-uh."

Getty was duly appointed Speck's defense counsel and on Speck's behalf entered pleas of not guilty to each of eight indictments for the murder of the student nurses. Judge Napoli then assigned the case to his associate, Judge Herbert C. Paschen, who set the next court hearing for August 18. The arraignment had lasted only three minutes.

Getty told reporters after the arraignment that his client had been "confused and bewildered."

Speck's attitude of resignation and apathy continued at Ziporyn's second session with him, in the afternoon following the court hearing. The psychiatrist was finding it difficult to establish rapport. The only subject on which Speck cared to express himself forcefully was his distaste for the hospital ward. Herman Bernette, the prisoner who had vowed to kill Speck when he first arrived in Ward 1, was repeating his threat every day with growing vehemence.

"That guy bugs me," said Speck. "I want out of here. Why don't they put me in the isolation block?"

As he talked with Ziporyn he kept his back to the other prisoners. He showed no interest in any of them. Everything was bothering him. The hospital staff let him smoke but, Speck complained irritably, "they won't let me have the brand I like—Kools."

Ziporyn let him vent his irritation a while longer and then decided to bring him back to their conversation of three days ago. It was important not to let Speck control the direction of the interviews. At first, Speck claimed he could not remember anything of their previous conversation. He continued to sulk and refused to discuss any of the points he had brought up in the first interview. Ziporyn persisted. He wanted to examine Speck's attitude to the murders in relation to his general psychological condition.

"Do you remember how you said you often got into a real bad temper after a few drinks, a temper that made you violent? Is that what happened on the night the nurses were killed?"

"I don't know," Speck replied glumly.

"Let's suppose it was. What do you think the girls did to provoke your temper? What do you think made you do it?"

Suddenly Speck flared up angrily. "Me? I like girls—I wouldn't hurt *women*. Anyway, I don't remember a thing about that night. I never knew those girls."

He was becoming more and more morose and hostile, and Ziporyn saw little point in continuing the interview. He cut it short and prepared to leave. Speck leaned forward and gripped his arm as he rose. "Get me out of here, Doc, will you?" he said. "Out of this hospital, I mean, not the jail." For the first time the psychiatrist noticed Speck's hands as they held his arm. They were huge, powerful, with long fingers—a carpenter's hands, Ziporyn thought.

Speck was given three electrocardiograms a week at the jail hospital to make sure he had fully recovered from the heart-sac inflammation he had suffered at Bridewell. The doctors were satisfied with his progress and decreased his dosage of sedatives. He was responding relatively well, and by the time of his next session with Ziporyn he had recovered sufficiently from the effects of his suicide attempt to be moved to the isolation tier, in block H.

This maximum security section in the Cook County Jail consists of three cells cut off from the other tiers at the west end of the ground floor. It is usually reserved for prisoners under sentence of death or indicted on charges that carry the death penalty. At this time, however, Speck, who was assigned the middle cell, was flanked by Louis Stamos, for some reason better known as Tony Gambino, and by Mark Clancy, both in for armed robbery and placed in the maximum security block because of two escape attempts in January and February of 1966. The room next to the maximum security block, just a dozen paces from the door to Speck's cell, was the execution chamber, containing one of Illinois' three electric chairs. (The others are at Joliet and Menard.)

Maximum security was normally guarded by a single officer, seated at a desk facing the center cell. For Speck, a special second guard was assigned to visit the tier regularly on patrol. A round-the-clock vigil ensured that Speck would not hang himself. Suicide precautions did not include any special clothing, but the prisoner was to be shaved by the jail barber in order to keep razor blades out of his hands.

The cells in maximum security measure ten feet wide, ten feet long and twelve feet high, considerably larger than the cells in the rest of the jail. (The standard size is eight feet long, four and a half feet wide and eight feet high.) The bars to Speck's cell were painted a typical dark green, the green of a dusty rubber plant, as was the lower half of the cell's walls. The upper half and the ceiling were a dull, sickly cream color. The concrete floor was painted brick red. Speck's only furniture when Ziporyn first visited him was a low steel spring bed painted the same color as the ceiling, covered with white sheets, a dark gray blanket and two pillows. Hot-water pipes ran along the back wall, one set serving as a shelf above the radiator. Also on the back wall was a frosted window measuring about four feet by three, covered by a thick wire mesh and completely opaque. Behind it, but invisible, was another set of iron bars. A sink with hot and cold water and a toilet were set into the wall opposite the bed. The cell was lit by a hanging light bulb.

The grimness of the cell's interior made Ward 1 seem relatively bright, but this did nothing to diminish the relief and cheerfulness that Speck was apparently feeling now that he had left the hospital.

He greeted Ziporyn amiably from his bed. "Hi, Doc. How're you doing? Take a seat." There was no seat to take, so Speck swung his legs round from his reclining position to make room for the psychiatrist to sit next to him.

Speck offered Ziporyn one of his Kools—he was getting his favorite brand now—and a piece of his Baby Ruth candy bar. His sister, Mrs. Thornton, was sending him $10 a week with which he was able to buy coffee—he preferred Sanka—and cigarettes and candy from the jail commissary. Each day a guard brought around a list of items on which the prisoner marked what he wanted.

Speck walked over to the pipe-shelf arrangement above the radiator where he had neatly stacked his mail, in separate piles for letters and cards. He was receiving an average of three letters a day, in addition to a lot of "crank" mail which Warden Johnson kept back. Speck showed the letters, with some pride, to Ziporyn. "See what I got?" he said, grinning broadly.

Most of the letters were from religious people who quoted comforting or admonishing passages from the Bible and urged him to turn to Jesus. One of the tenderest notes was anonymous. In spidery printed letters it said:

> Dear Richard,
>
> Just a few lines to let you know how I feel about what has happened to you. I wish I could see you in person—but since I live in Connecticut that is pretty impossible. I wish I could let you know face to face that *if* you did what they blame you for—I can't believe you knew what you were doing. I'm with you—I'm not against you, and I hope God is with you. I pray every day & night that things will turn alright and the best for you. *If* you are guilty—it's not you that is to blame—I can't believe it was something you had intentions of doing.
>
> I'm no kid, Richard, I have a girl seven years old, and a boy almost a year. Why should I condemn you when I don't know how my son or daughter will grow up. As I said in the beginning—I wish I could let you know face to face that I am on your side. Right now you must think everyone is against you—*But I'm not*—please believe me. I'm keeping tract [sic] of what is happening—but I'm not going to write it here, as you must already know.

I will close for now Richard and keep my fingers crossed for you, and my prayers each day and night. God bless you and be with you. I can't sign this letter for obvious reasons, but I do hope you get it. God be with you, and please believe that I am with you, even though we are miles apart.

So long for now,
A friend you don't even know.

Another one, in similar vein, was signed "Love always, Lois." Speck said he did not know anyone by that name. He watched Ziporyn read the letters but made no comment. He gathered up the letters again and put them back in their tidy little piles, showing obvious pleasure at the attention he was receiving.

"Nice to get letters like that," Speck said finally. "You wouldn't think there was anybody around would bother writing like that. But I sure as hell don't like what the papers are saying about me. They been lying, every day. Like when they said I was sent to jail for assaulting a woman in Dallas. That's a lie. Fact was, it was just a drunken argument with an old whore."

Eager as he was to argue a nuance like this, Speck showed no inclination to refute his responsibility for the murders of the nurses, despite his repeated insistence that he remembered nothing about it. "You see," he said, resigned again, "everybody says it was me, so I guess I did it."

Suddenly he winced and gripped the back of his head.

"Headache, Doc," he explained. "I get them all the time. And I get dizzy at the same time. I get this haze in front of my eyes—it's like a white blank wall." He drifted off into silence and Ziporyn left him lying on his bed. Their relationship was improving. Speck was beginning to talk more freely, but Ziporyn did not want to force the pace. The measure of his success as a psychiatrist would be his ability to strip off the professional mask and act with Speck as one human being with another. At that point, Speck might feel sufficiently at ease to reveal his true self.

Ziporyn knew it would take him some time to win this alienated man's trust and that no deliberate plan of action was possible. The bulk of the work would have to be spontaneous and intuitive. Ziporyn was aiming at establishing rapport and an empathy with Speck that would encourage him to communicate his deepest emotions to the psychiatrist. Such a catharsis could greatly relieve Speck's depression and thus diminish his suicidal inclination. But beyond that, it would offer Ziporyn unique access to the prisoner's personality. Therefore, while other psychiatrists might argue that the approach could have been made in different or better ways, none of them could duplicate exactly Ziporyn's relationship with Speck. What Ziporyn would learn of Speck's personality depended very much on its interaction with his own. He was fond of quoting Karl Menninger's observation that "What a psychiatrist is, is infinitely more important than what he does."

Two days later, on August 8, Speck was still bothered by his headaches. He grimaced repeatedly and talked slowly, in depressed tones.

"All I'm interested in," he said, "is when they pull the switch. And if they don't do it, I'll find a way to do it myself."

"Why do you feel like this?" Ziporyn asked. "Have you been thinking about the murders again?"

"No. You see, I've been feeling like this a long time. This killing thing has nothing to do with it. Life just ain't worth living any more. When I tried to kill myself before they got me, it was because I didn't have nothing to live for. And then, when they said I killed those girls, what was the sense of it all?"

"But weren't you ever interested in anything?" Ziporyn asked.

"Nope, I ain't interested in nothing—don't care about nothing, either."

"How about your family . . . your daughter . . . your mother . . . your sisters, how about your wife?"

Speck shook his head and said nothing. He resisted all further attempts to draw him out on the reasons for his depression. He sat on the bed with his head down, arms resting across his thighs, the long hands clenching into tight fists and unclenching again to flap loosely between his legs. He looked up.

"You're asking me questions I can't answer," he blurted out, his temper rising. "Don't you see? I don't care a goddam thing about this world."

Ziporyn made no reply and got up to leave. Suddenly Speck softened.

"You're going? Do you have to?" he asked quietly. "Why don't you stay and talk some more?"

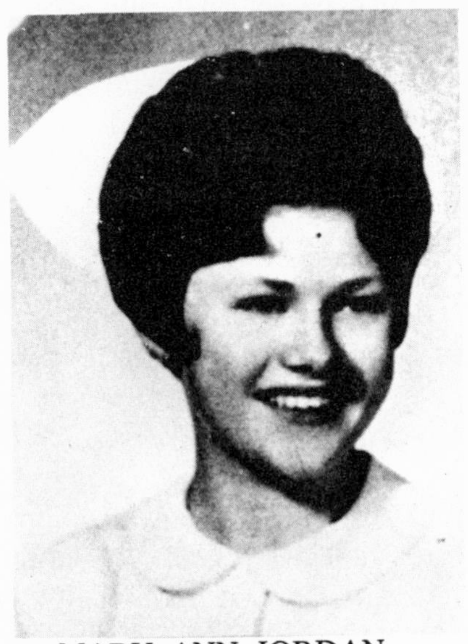

MARY ANN JORDAN

MERLITA GARGULLO

GLORIA DAVY

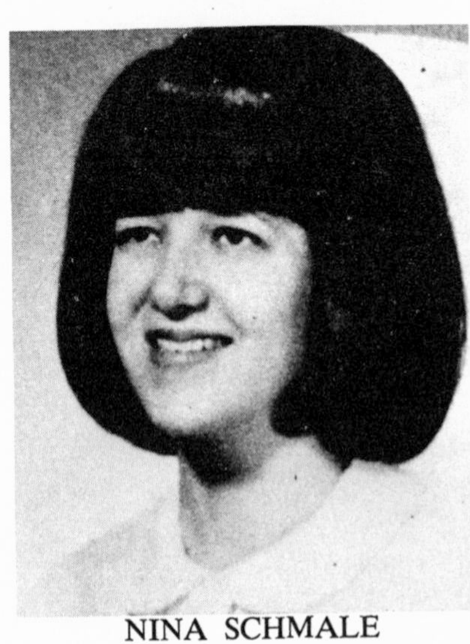

NINA SCHMALE

UPI Photos

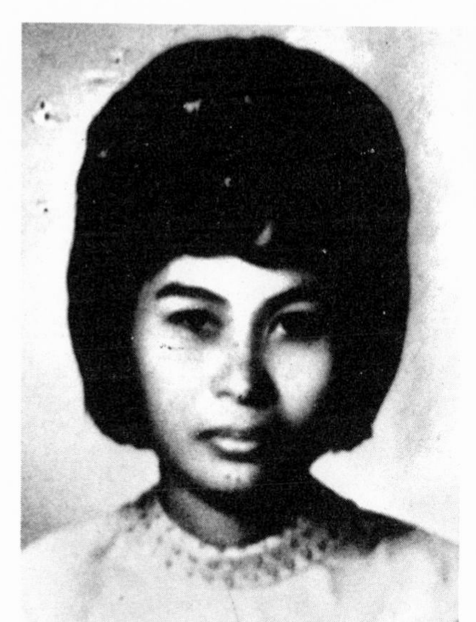

VALENTINA PASION

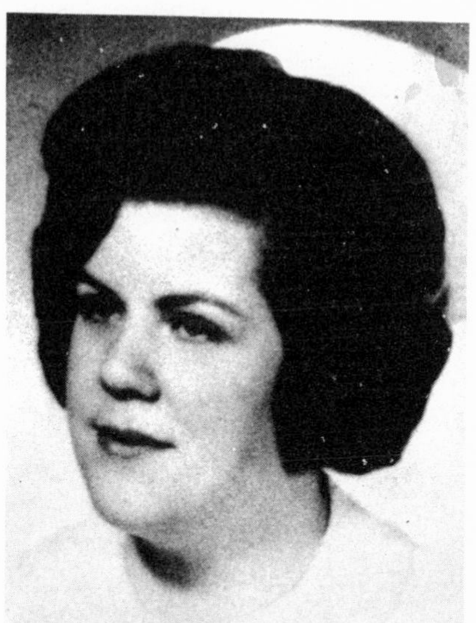

PAMELA WILKENING

PATRICIA MATUSEK

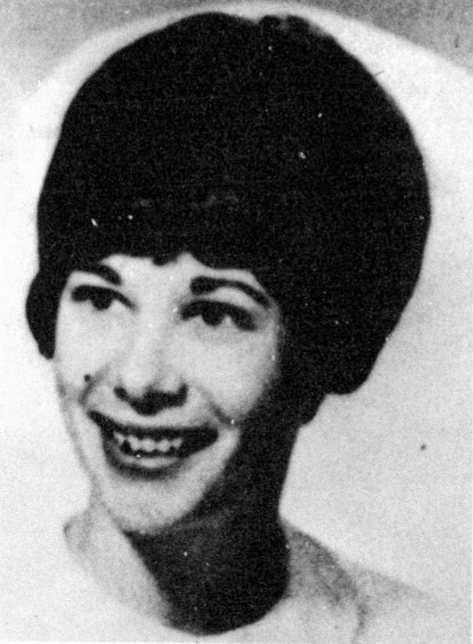

SUZANNE FARRIS

UPI Photos

The psychiatrist explained that he had to leave for another appointment. Speck nodded and said nothing more.

Despite Speck's depression, Ziporyn was optimistic about their progress. Speck was showing profound feelings of being rejected, isolated, a total outsider. As much as this depressed him, it drove him more and more to seek some kind of link outside himself. Ziporyn hoped to provide that link and felt the opportunity would not be long in coming.

The depression was by no means receding, but Speck was less inclined to resist Ziporyn's efforts to examine the roots of that depression. In fact, Speck was eager to take a look at his own personality. "I want to know everything you can tell me about myself," Speck told Ziporyn. "I want you to see my family. I want you to learn all you can and explain all this." Tears welled up in his eyes as he said once more: "If they don't pull the switch, I'll find a way to do it myself. I can't live with my conscience—could you?"

For a moment he brightened. "You know, Doc," he said, "I like you. Say, have a cup of coffee."

He called the guard over to the cell to get a cup for the psychiatrist. Carefully he poured out the instant coffee, using hot water from the tap in the cell, and handed it to Ziporyn, grinning through still moist eyes. Then he glanced quickly around him. He went over to the ledge to straighten out the growing piles of letters, cards and tracts—the latest, he showed Ziporyn, was a Jesuit publication called "Our Daily Bread." He spotted some cigarette ash on the floor and gingerly picked it up and deposited it in an ash tray improvised from a cardboard box. He patted the bed into tidy shape and then sat down again with a house-proud nod, finally satisfied that things were looking the way they should.

But his depression soon returned. He thumbed through "Our Daily Bread," shaking his head and repeating, with the tears returning, "This whole thing is like a nightmare for me."

Ziporyn noticed that Speck was squinting as he tried to read the text and asked him whether he needed glasses.

"Yeah," Speck replied, somewhat sheepishly. "I used to have a pair but I threw 'em away. I don't like wearing glasses."

This note of vanity, which was to become more and more pronounced as Ziporyn probed into Speck's behavior, struck the psychiatrist as entirely in keeping with the prisoner's fastidiousness in tending his grim cell. (In the hotel room where Speck had tried to commit suicide, police found among his toilet things a spray-can of Old Spice After Shave and Max Factor Eau de Cologne.) At the same time, Speck's poor sight offered a possible explanation of why he read so badly, since Ziporyn was beginning to suspect that he was considerably more alert than his reading skill would suggest.

On Thursday, August 18, Speck returned to court to hear his attorney, Gerald Getty, ask that eight mental experts be appointed to examine the accused man. "At this time," Getty told Judge Paschen, "there is a serious question as to the defendant's mental competence to stand trial." The panel of experts would be asked to report, first, on Speck's sanity at the time of the eight killings and, second, on whether he was now mentally fit to cooperate with his counsel and stand trial. Getty asked for two psychologists and six psychiatrists to be appointed. (It was not intended that the resident jail psychiatrist, Dr. Ziporyn, be included on the panel.)

Getty also asked for access to a list of the state's witnesses and all fingerprints pertinent to the case, as well as photographs, physical exhibits and scientific and technological data to be used by the state. Further action was deferred to September 1, when prosecuting counsel, Assistant State's Attorney William C. Martin, would answer Getty's petitions.

Back in his cell the next day, Speck sat and talked to Ziporyn as he had never talked before. He was depressed and pale, but quickly explained that this was because of his headaches. They had returned the previous night, throbbing from the back of his head over to his right ear, pounding with growing intensity through the night and all that day.

"Last night I thought my heart was in my head," he said. "It's really bad." Ziporyn suggested they turn out the harsh overhead light in the cell, and they sat in semidarkness.

Speck again offered Ziporyn some instant coffee. He insisted that the psychiatrist take a clean glass from the guard rather than use the paper cups in the cell.

About the previous day's court hearing, Speck said, "I didn't understand a thing that was happening." Ziporyn explained Getty's petitions, particularly with regard to the psychiatric panel. Speck said dryly, "I ain't gonna plead crazy." When the psychiatrist explained that a successful plea of insanity could save him from execution, Speck said: "I'll never see the chair."

Was Speck suddenly turning optimistic, discarding his usual acceptance—his bitter anticipation—of death? Ziporyn thought this was a possibility, given Speck's constantly switching moods. But then he noticed that Speck was pointing over his shoulder at the pipes running along the back wall of the cell. The prisoner made a gesture around his neck to indicate that he would hang himself before sentence could be carried out.

Ziporyn changed the subject to headaches and head injuries. They went over the childhood accidents again. Nothing of importance emerged except that Speck was no longer sure that his fall from the tree preceded the accident with the awning rod. Then he recalled when the headaches began.

"I was fighting this kid," he said. "It was in Dallas. I was sixteen. I had him on the ground, really giving it to him, and a cop came to break it up. He broke it up, okay—cracked my head with his club till he knocked me clean out. A year after that the headaches started. Man, those Dallas cops are brutal, real animals. They gave me a real hard time."

He paused a moment, as if waiting for a comment from Ziporyn, but when none came he continued: "I was always getting into fights. Hit my stepfather once, round about when I was eighteen. Man, did I hate him. Lindbergh, his name was. Mine too, till I got married and changed it back. One of his legs, the right one, was cut off halfway, after a car accident. So he had crutches. Thought I'd never hit him 'cause of those crutches. Just went on needling me. He was drunk. I was too, I think. Anyway, he came at me with one of those crutches and I hit him. Then he said he'd had enough and was gonna leave. I told him 'Fine,' and threw him out, and his clothes and things after him. I think my mother was glad to see him go. He came back a year later, but then left again, for good."

Ziporyn asked him whether he had ever struck his mother.

Speck looked shocked. "No, I would never hit her. I did hit my wife, Shirley, once. She was acting too friendly with some guy. Another time I got hold of a guy in a washroom, in Dallas. I thought he'd been hanging around with Shirley. I beat him up. I was mad."

He talked of his rages. "I got mad at just about anything. When I was a kid, just a teenager, in East Dallas, I was with some guys and we got some red-birds. Whew, they made me wild. We were watching a parade once and we had some blockbusters [white barbiturate pills with a yellow stripe]. I just passed out and they took me to a juvenile home. I don't remember exactly what happened after that, but I've been told that when my mother came to get me she says I was talking nice and polite, then suddenly I went wild. Started swinging and kicking at everybody. But I don't remember a thing about it myself.

"There was lots of times when I'd black out like that and not remember a thing. I get a glassy haze, like when you look into the sun. Remember once I was driving a souped-up '49 Ford, going maybe a hundred miles an hour or more, and I just passed out. Lucky my buddy Rod Kenney was with me. He grabbed the wheel just in time. Told me about it afterwards, but I wouldn't have known. I get those hazes all the time, had one when I was near my sister's home right here in Chicago a little while back. Get them all the time.

"Hey, would you go see my sister Martha for me? Write a note for me to her and I'll sign it so as she'll talk to you about me. And ask her for some clothes for me, maybe a jacket and a couple of shirts, a T-shirt, too."

Ziporyn agreed and then brought the conversation back to the subject of the murders. "Let's go over the murders again," the psychiatrist said, "and what Corazon Amurao said about it. You know, she's the one that survived."

Speck nodded and said in a soft voice, "I'm glad she did." He stared earnestly at Ziporyn.

"Now," Ziporyn continued, "she says you came in the back door, came up to her room and awoke her. Then she says you . . . or rather, let's say 'the killer'. . . ."

In the same soft voice, Speck interrupted the psychiatrist, "Let's just say it was me."

Ziporyn resumed the narrative of the evening's events. Speck listened but made no comment. There was a silence for a full minute and then suddenly Speck launched into a monologue that went on for twenty minutes, almost without a break. It was the first time Speck had ever given Ziporyn a detailed version of what he remembered of his activities around the time of the murders.

"I'd been on an ore boat and the hiring hall got me this job on a ship in Indiana. One of the sailors drove out there with me in a truck. I was on board maybe thirty minutes when they told me it was all a mix-up—somebody else had the job. So I came back to Chicago. I didn't have no room, didn't have enough money to get one either—just a few dollars. This was Tuesday. I asked a guy in a filling station if I could leave my bags there. Then I went to a beer joint about a block away and called my sister. I told her what happened, told her I was broke. She said she'd help.

"Near the bar there was an apartment house they were working on. It was raining hard, pouring. I went into the basement, wrapped something round my shoes for a pillow and went to sleep.

"Next morning I went to get my suitcase, but the gas station wasn't open yet, so I went across the street and had a Royal Crown. Back at the hiring hall they told me there was a job on an ocean boat. That sounded good and I told 'em I wanted it. You know, I love being a sailor. That's something makes me feel good. But they told me the job wasn't till the next Monday. I played a game of Hearts at one of the tables there, and my brother-in-law came in and gave me 25 dollars.

"I went off and got a room at the Shipyard Inn and started playing some pool. I'm a real good pool player. I won 10, 11 dollars. I had a big knife, really it was a dagger, like a bayonet. Anyway, I made another buck from that, sold it to some guy. I pepped myself up on a few red-birds, six of them and took a walk by one of the little lakes out there, then went back to the bar for a drink. I had some whisky and a pint of wine and got talking to these sailors, like I told you before. They took me to their room. It was dark. They had this disposable syringe and took this stuff from a bottle and started 'popping.' I tied a handkerchief around my left arm and stuck it in. All the way. Before I had the needle out I could feel, you know, feel—zzzoommm—a buzzing all over me, and I was feeling real, real good.

"The next thing I know I was back in my own room and it was morning. I had a gun and I don't know where I got it. I just sat there wondering where the hell I got that gun."

As he talked, Ziporyn asked him whether he had noticed any blood on his clothes that morning.

"No. I had on black Ivy Leagues and a new black shirt with white buttons. Everything was clean."

Speck stopped suddenly, stared at Ziporyn for a moment and then turned his face to the wall as he lay there on his bed. Softly he said: "I'm going to tell you something."

Not a sound in the cell for another minute. Speck slowly turned around to face the psychiatrist again and said: "There was blood on my right hand that morning. I didn't really see it or know what it was till I put my hand in the water and the water turned red. I thought I'd cut myself."

This observation was parenthetical in the narrative which he then calmly resumed. Speck did not seem to realize that he had just volunteered the most damning circumstantial evidence, which need never have been revealed to anyone. This revelation, more than anything else, dispelled any doubts Ziporyn might have had about Speck's story; it supported Speck's claims that he knew nothing of the events in the nurses' home. If these claims had been a carefully feigned "mental alibi," Speck could be expected to maintain a consistent front of noninvolvement. He would scarcely be prepared to offer unsolicited self-incrimination. This, on top of his readiness to accept at its face value his identification by police and press as the murderer, suggested to Ziporyn that Speck had neither the wish nor the guile to protect himself.

Speck continued: "I went back to the bar at the Shipyard Inn for some more wine. I still couldn't make out how I got that goddam gun. It bugged me. While I was there a detective came in and asked the bartender some questions. It didn't bother me. I didn't know why he was there. In the afternoon I heard them talking about the murders on the radio. I remember saying to the guy next to me at the bar, 'I hope they catch the son of a bitch.'

"I moved on to a few other bars in the neighborhood, and all day long the police were coming in and out, asking questions. I was wanted for a burglary in Dallas, and the cops were beginning to worry me. If they just decided to take everybody in they didn't like the look of, they might have found out I'd run away from Texas. So I beat it up to the North Side. . . . I played some more pool. I won a few more bucks. I checked into the Raleigh Hotel and went out again to pick up a prostitute. The papers say she was Puerto Rican, but she was darker than that, she was colored. She stripped to her panties and we just sat in my room drinking. We had a fight about money, and I went to sleep. She called the cops and they came and took the gun.

"The next day I saw the police picture of the killer in the papers. It didn't look nothing like me so I didn't know it was me, because of that flat top. My hair was never that short." (In fact, police artist Otis Rathel was widely praised for the likeness he had achieved in his drawing from Miss Amurao's description. "She had me soften the eyes," Rathel commented. "She told me he had a very gentle appearance.") Speck explained to Ziporyn, "I like my hair long. It looks better that way."

"It was Saturday afternoon when I first heard that it was me they were looking for. I couldn't believe it at first."

He broke off and rolled himself a cigarette from a packet of Buglers tobacco. As he did so, he nodded toward the guard sitting at a table outside the cell. "That night guard out there," he told Ziporyn, "he gets drunk. Last night he came right up to the bars and started cussing me. I told him if he didn't leave me alone I'd reach through those bars and beat the shit out of him." Speck grunted, looked at the psychiatrist for a moment and then leaned forward to say in a confidential whisper: "Don't say nothing, will you, Doc. He's an old man—he couldn't get another job if he was fired."

Ziporyn nodded agreement and returned to the subject of earlier events, before Speck's arrival in Chicago. "When you went back to Monmouth, what did you do there?" Ziporyn asked. "The police there are saying they'd like to talk to you about a rape case."

"I'm no rape-o," Speck said indignantly, adding with a sly smile, "I don't have to be. But I'd sure like to know what made me kill those girls. Why would I do a thing like that?"

"Well," Ziporyn began, hesitantly. "As a psychiatrist I might suggest you were working out some kind of hostility, anger, that you felt at your mother for marrying your stepfather."

"But I love my mother," said Speck.

"That's the whole point. You love her and maybe you're angry at her for betraying that love. At least, that's how you may feel unconsciously, without realizing it, I mean."

"That doesn't make sense," Speck replied. "Okay, I didn't like my stepfather and I didn't like the idea of my mother being married to him. But what's that got to do with those girls? Why should I kill them?"

Ziporyn explained how Speck's attitude toward his mother could work on his unconscious and be transferred to women in general. Speck nodded doubtfully. Ziporyn added that Speck was probably so heavily influenced by the drugs and alcohol he had taken earlier in the day that he could not be held responsible for the acts of that night.

"We could even say you didn't kill them, it was. . . ."

Speck cut him short. "It was me, all right."

Turning the Clock Back

ACTING ON SPECK'S REQUEST, ZIPORYN PAID A VISIT ON AUGUST 22 to his sister, Mrs. Martha Thornton, living in an apartment building on the North-West Side near the Kennedy Expressway. She would not let the psychiatrist in, keeping the door on the chain and talking to him through the three-inch opening. He explained that he worked at Cook County Jail and that her brother had asked him to visit her.

"Look," she said in a weary voice. "You may be right, but how are we to know for sure? We've been getting phone calls at five in the morning, visits from reporters, police, lawyers, ever since this whole thing started. My brother's lawyer said we weren't to see any more people."

Ziporyn explained that Speck had asked for some new clothes. She replied she might bring him something the next time she visited the jail, and closed the door.

"That doesn't sound like Martha," Speck muttered when Ziporyn told him, later that day, what had happened. "Man, I'm really nothing but trouble. All I've done is hurt my family, shame them. The best thing I could do for them is die. You wanna know something, Doc? That special lock they put on my cell, 'cause Clancy next door is an escape artist? Well, you couldn't chase me out of here. I wouldn't want to be outside—I'm afraid of myself."

"Dick, you're lucky you're not on your own jury," Ziporyn said with a smile. "You'd be too tough on yourself."

"Well, I deserve to die," he replied indignantly, "so what's the difference? After killing those girls? Are you kidding?"

His voice rose bitterly, and Ziporyn tried to calm him. Speck insisted over and over again that death was all he deserved. "There just ain't nothing else," he said.

"That's not quite true," the psychiatrist said. "There is a very useful thing you can do."

"Hang myself?" A half-smile flickered across Speck's face. The psychiatrist explained that there might be real value in Speck's trying to understand for himself what made him the way he was, how his attitude to his mother and to his wife triggered his responses to other women, how the effects of the head injuries interacted with the drugs and drink, what all this might mean in terms of his legal and moral responsibility for what had happened on July 14, 1966.

Speck listened attentively and then said: "But what good would it do?"

"Maybe if you had gone to a doctor about your headaches. . . ."

Speck glared fiercely and cut him short, "Doctors cost money." Then he added pensively: "But you know I've sure got a lot of head trouble. Last time I was in prison the barber gave me a scalp-cut, practically shaved it all off, like when they get a guy ready for the electric chair—and he said he'd never seen so many bumps on a guy's head."

The number of head injuries Speck had suffered over the years suggested he was almost compulsively prone to them, making his brain damage an agonizingly self-perpetuating process. Ziporyn nodded to Speck and said: "The bumps, beers and red-birds make a different person out of you. Without the alcohol or the drugs, you're Doctor Jekyll, the normal man. With them, you turn into Mr. Hyde, the monster." The psychiatrist hoped that these explanations would provide an antidote to Speck's depressive guilt feelings. It seemed to be working.

"You may be right," Speck said. "Not beer, though. Beer makes me feel good. Whisky makes me wild. When I'm on that I can do some terrible things. Like once I was aboard ship, on the *Randall*, there was this sailor—he was a good guy, but I just went after him, beat him up. I was drunk and threw some coffee in an officer's face, don't know why. I've attacked some of my best buddies and never knew anything about it. That's the funny thing, I don't know what happens till they tell me. Last year, I was in Dallas and I had a few drinks and some 'drivers,' you know—pep pills. Them and Wyman's glue make my headaches go away—wish I had some now. Anyway, I was talking to this guy, I think he was queer. Suddenly everything blacked out. Next thing I knew, the guy was on the ground, covered with blood, and I was battering at him with a tire handle. My buddy, Al Butts, pulled me off. He said I was a crazy man. I don't know why I did it."

He shook his head. His eyes were glistening. "Don't you think my mother," he went on, "begged, pleaded, cried, trying to get me not to drink. I only drank a little till I was fifteen, and then a little more, but later—man—when those headaches started, I really poured it in me. My mother didn't like it, didn't like it at all."

Ziporyn and Speck had been meeting regularly for over three weeks, but not till now, as Speck was reminiscing about his mother, did the psychiatrist resort to his stock-in-trade question: "What's your earliest memory, Dick?"

After a short silence, Speck replied: "Me and my sister were in our 'jamas. It was in Monmouth. I heard a sound like thunder. We ran to the window and looked out. There was a terrible car accident. A woman was screaming—she must have been badly hurt."

Here, Ziporyn could not help thinking, was an Adlerian's delight. Adler's theory holds that since a person remembers what is important to him, the very earliest memories are the most significant. They reveal a person's most fundamental learning—his basic conclusions on what life is all about—and they can show the pattern traced by his subsequent life. In Speck's case, it was obviously significant that his earliest memory was one of violence.

Speck's account of his childhood remained melancholy. He recalled that there had been some discrepancy in the newspapers about whether his mother had taken him from Monmouth to Dallas before or after his father's death. "I was still in Monmouth when Dad died," he insisted. "I remember seeing him in his coffin."

He thought again of Ziporyn's abortive attempt to visit his sister Martha. "Too bad you didn't get to visit with her. You'd have seen her little girls. One's thirteen, the other's fifteen. They're quite a pair, those two."

For a moment his gloom left him and a slow smile spread across his face. He spoke of his nieces with real warmth. "Quite a pair," he said again. With equal fondness he talked of their mother, observing how good she had been to him.

In the ensuing silence, Speck noticed that Ziporyn was looking at an overturned ash tray with its butts spilled on the floor in a corner of the cell. It was incongruous, and Speck guessed what the psychiatrist was thinking.

"The guard did that," he said, with an earnest look of apology. "I'll clear it up, soon as you go." Tidiness was as important as ever to him. He grimaced and rubbed the back of his head with a now familiar gesture. "Can you get me something for this headache?"

"Sure," Ziporyn replied. "Anything I can do to help."

"Don't want no help," Speck said petulantly. "I don't need no help."

As Ziporyn was leaving, Speck rose from the bed and said: "Can you get hold of Getty for me? Why doesn't he come see me? Did he give up on me? Some lawyer."

The psychiatrist shook his head and said he would inform Getty of Speck's wishes.

The ambivalence that pervaded Speck's nature was asserting itself now in his will to live. The fatalism was as strong as ever, but now it was competing with the desire to hang on. He wanted to die and to live, to reject help and yet retain some hope. By turns, he wanted to immerse himself in his isolation and reach out of it to the world outside him. He wanted the pills but did not want to think their acquisition involved help. At the same time, he did not want his lawyer or the world to "give up" on him.

Four days later, Ziporyn returned to find Speck cheerful, lighthearted, in the best spirits he had shown since the interviews had begun. The suicidal depression had lifted, however temporary the change might be. Ziporyn had learned not to expect his patient to sustain a mood for any great length of time. He recalled that Miss Amurao had said the intruder had been quite gentle at first. The obvious explanation had been that such an approach would be the best way of subduing the girls and keeping them in his power. If the intruder was Speck, however, it was by no means certain that this "approach" was a deliberate stratagem.

Speck seemed pleased when Ziporyn told him his attorney would be visiting him before the next court hearing, on Thursday, September 1. This hearing was to decide whether a panel of psychiatrists and psychologists would be appointed to examine Speck. Ziporyn asked him how he felt about the hearing.

Speck shrugged, totally unconcerned. "I don't care what happens," he said. "I'm prepared for the worst."

"If by 'the worst' you mean the electric chair," said Ziporyn, "you may be wrong. There's a guy called Heirens, William Heirens, who committed murders that shocked Chicago just as much as the nurses, and he didn't get the chair. He was jailed for life."

Speck showed interest in Heirens, and the psychiatrist explained how back in 1946 the seventeen-year-old boy had murdered and mutilated two women and a six-year-old girl. As Ziporyn told the story, Speck leaned forward, listening avidly. Several times he clicked his tongue in disbelief. When Ziporyn described how Heirens had treated the little girl, cutting up her body and hiding the parts in sewers around the city, Speck exclaimed with heated indignation: "The son of a bitch. How could anyone do a thing like that? A little girl, too. That's terrible. I mean, that's really terrible."

He paused, shaking his head incredulously, and then added: "Still, do you realize that I killed sixteen people?"

"How do you get sixteen?" Ziporyn asked.

"Well, those eight girls, my five sisters, my mother, my brother and my little girl. In a way, I killed them all. You know, I've been a bad lot. I've stabbed and hit people, but never when I'm sober. I never hit anyone when I was sober. The closest I came to it was when I slashed this guy in the washroom because he wouldn't stay away from my wife. Even then I had pills in me—red-birds and yellow-jackets. But murder is something else. I'd give anything to turn the clock back and bring those girls back to life."

Ziporyn recalled the incident of Speck's drunken fight with his stepfather and again asked him whether he had ever hit his mother while he was drunk.

Indignation seized him again as he replied: "I wouldn't lay a finger on my mother. I took good care of that. She'd yell at me if I was drinking. I knew how I got when I was drunk and I didn't want any trouble with her, so if I drank too much I stayed away from home. It was safer that way. I was always trouble at home, even when I was a little kid. Thinking about that gun they found on me after the murders, it reminded me of the first gun I ever had. I was six or seven and my brother Howie gave me a cap pistol. I shot it off at home and the whole place was filled with smoke. Boy, did I catch it for that."

The memory made him chuckle. "By the way," he said, "you didn't see this yet." He handed Ziporyn a letter, smirking with a certain smugness as the psychiatrist read it aloud. It was from a nineteen-year-old college girl called Susan. "Dear Richard," she wrote. "Ever since I read about you in the paper I've followed the day by day news. When I saw you were sick I nearly died. I want you to know there is someone who cares. . . ."

"Ain't that something?" Speck said. Ziporyn grinned appreciatively.

His headaches were still bothering him, he said, but they did not appear to be able to destroy his good mood that day. "I've got some headache pills now," he said. "They don't do much, just take the edge off. But you wanna know something funny? Last night I had the urge, sitting here, I wished I could find a way to shoot those pills in my arm. Can you imagine that? In the mess I'm in, and I wanna start popping again. I must be crazy."

Speck was still in good spirits at Ziporyn's next visit on August 29, three days before the court hearing on the psychiatric panel. Ziporyn explained that the panel, if approved, would test Speck's I.Q.

"I know all about I.Q.'s," said Speck with a grin. "I got a low one. They tested it twice when I was in prison, for jobs, and I couldn't pass. So they sent me out in the forest, cutting wood. I wasn't too bad in prison. Only got into one fight—over a game of dominoes. I guess there just wasn't enough whisky and pills around the prison to make me wanna fight more than that.

"While I was in prison I heard my wife was running around. When I got out I got me a sawed-off shotgun and went round to his house—I made Shirley give me the guy's name, told her I'd kill her if she didn't tell. I talked to his wife—he wasn't home. I waited out in my car. I watched three or four kids playing around the house. When he came, I shoved the gun in his face, but I couldn't do it, not with that family. Wonder what kind of guy he was.

"Once I thought I saw Shirley driving into a motel. Then another car drove in. I went and got a pistol, then came back and kicked the door down. There was nobody there. Last summer she left me for good. She said she had been seeing another guy. When she told me that, I went out and got drunk and smashed my car into a tree. Then I saw her in a tavern with a guy. I tried to get her to come home with me, but she wouldn't. I knocked 'em both down and left.

"You know," he added, suddenly weary. "The Bible says not to hate, but if there's anybody I hate in this world—besides that stepfather—it's Shirley, and that's the truth."

A Dead Ringer

BEFORE SPECK'S THIRD APPEARANCE IN COURT, ON SEPTEMBER 1, Judge Paschen's office received five anonymous telephone calls and a note, all threatening to kill the accused man. Precautions to protect Speck were as intensive as ever, and his tunnel walk with Collins and Adasiak was now led by Chief Deputy Bailiff Robert Craer, just to make doubly sure. On the seventh floor of the Criminal Courts Building, Speck, wearing a new blue suit, sat motionless but considerably more relaxed than on his previous appearances, to hear Paschen defer his decision on the psychiatric panel till September 9. But Getty's other requests, for access to the State's witness list and its documentary evidence, were granted.

The next day Speck was asleep when Ziporyn called on him in the afternoon. He lay on his bed in a T-shirt and shorts, his mouth open as he slept. When Ziporyn woke him, he grunted and stared sullenly in front of him without saying a word for five minutes. He was obviously disturbed, perhaps embarrassed at being caught in a state of undress.

"You seem quite depressed," the psychiatrist said hesitantly.

"Well, I just woke up, didn't I?" Speck was silent again for a few seconds and then went on: "Saw my sister yesterday. In the visiting room. Brought me these clothes." He pointed at the underwear he had on and, hanging from the pipes on the back wall of the cell, a pair of slacks and the dark-blue suit he had worn at the court hearing. "She wants to see you. She wants to talk to you."

"Why?" Ziporyn asked.

Speck shrugged. "Dunno. It was her idea. *She* wants to see you." He noticed Ziporyn was sniffling. The psychiatrist was suffering from hay fever. Speck produced a handkerchief and gave it to Ziporyn, insisting that he keep it.

They talked about the previous day's court hearing. Speck said he thought Getty was angry with him. "He must have been mad at me. Didn't say more than two words to me, and then just to ask me where I got the clothes," Speck said. Suddenly his irritable tone dissolved and he said earnestly, gripping Ziporyn's arm: "Did you see in the papers about them calls from people who want to kill me? Is Getty getting any threats, too? If he is, I want him to get off this case. I don't want him to get hurt."

Ziporyn mentioned that Getty was talking about having the trial moved out of Chicago.

"I don't see it'll make much difference," Speck said casually. "They'll sentence me to the chair wherever they hold the thing. But I'll tell you this—I won't go. Not the chair, man. I'll find some way to do it myself, anything but the chair." He pointed to the hot-water pipes and made a gesture around his neck to indicate he would hang himself. He thought for a moment and added: "You know, I'd prefer getting killed by a firing squad. Yeah, that'd be much better."

"Why is the chair so much worse?" Ziporyn asked. "Is it because of the pain?"

"Right."

"But they say it doesn't hurt."

"Oh yeah? Did you ever get an electric shock? I did. Once I burned myself with an electric wire. Hurt like hell."

The conversation was interrupted by raucous laughter from the cells on either side of Speck. In voices theatrically loud and aimed more at Speck than at each other, Louis "Gambino" Stamos and Mark Clancy were discussing the therapeutic advantages of a modern jail system.

"Hey, Clancy," Gambino yelled. "It's a great thing the way they give you psychiatrists in jail these days."

"That's okay," Clancy replied. "But it's no good having a male psychiatrist. I'd rather have a woman in here to talk to me."

Gambino snorted scornfully. "What would you be able to do with a woman psychiatrist? You've been in jail so long, your head and your balls have rotted away. You'd be no good with a woman psychiatrist."

They both roared with laughter and Gambino shouted: "Hey, Speck. How would you like a girl in there?"

Speck grinned sheepishly at Ziporyn and made no reply. Clancy called back to Gambino: "Speck can't answer you now. He's got a visitor."

"No kidding. Who?"

"The doctor."

"Ah, the immoral Dr. Ziporyn. What's he doing in there, Speck? Buggering you?" Gambino cackled with laughter and Speck blushed. He offered Ziporyn some coffee and they resumed their conversation. Speck was still obsessed with the idea that his isolation from the rest of the world left him with no reason to go on living. Ziporyn reminded him of the letters he was receiving as proof that some people did care what was happening to him. Speck nodded, not noticeably convinced, and brought over the latest batch of cards and letters. Not all of them bore out Ziporyn's contention, though there was the usual complement of tender notes.

One of them came from Cebu City in the Philippines. It was a hand-made card, like a Valentine. It had a cut-out red paper heart stuck on the middle, with a festoon of tiny red silk hearts pasted around it. It was addressed to "Dear Richard—From one who cares." Inside the card was a letter that said: "I do not think you are all bad. I am sixteen years old. I want you to know that the Virgin Mary's arms will always be open to you. You will find love everlasting there. If you ever feel sad and lonely then just say a prayer to the Virgin Mary. You will see how comforted you can be."

"You see," said Ziporyn, "not everyone hates you."

"Yeah," said Speck with a grimace, "one in 6,000," and handed Ziporyn two other cards, both with Chicago postmarks. Each had originally contained a dollar bill. Both had a weird air of mockery that did little to make Speck cheerful. Unexplained, the first was a blue birth announcement proclaiming "It's a boy," and the second said "Happy Birthday, You Nice Thing" beside a picture of a hairy monster.

"Well," said Speck, after a short silence. "Maybe not everyone hates me, but I sure hate my old lady."

Ziporyn was a little taken aback by the suddenness of this comment. There was no indication of what had stimulated it. "You mean your wife, Shirley?"

"Right. There's a guard here nights who reminds me of her. His name is Malone, like hers was. I hate that woman, I really do."

The next week Ziporyn paid his second visit to Speck's sister. This time he was allowed in, though not before he had shown an identification card through the chained door. The apartment was small and clean, with neatly arranged furniture. The colors in the living room were drab except for a few small religious pictures on the wall, one of them a version of the Last Supper. The windows overlooked the tracks of the Chicago Northwestern railroad.

Mrs. Martha Thornton was a small, dark-haired woman in her early forties. Her manner was calm, though she showed signs of wear in her drawn face. She asked the psychiatrist to take a seat at the dining table and sat opposite him with her hands clasped, waiting for him to begin. He asked her to tell him what she could of Speck's childhood.

"Richard was very close to Dad. He was the apple of his father's eye," she said. "He used to follow Dad around like a shadow." She did not see much of him after they moved to Dallas, but, she said, the member of the family he was closest to in Dallas was his sister Carolyn, two years younger than himself.

"He was always getting into fights with his stepfather," she added. "Richard couldn't bear that man, but then none of us liked him much. He was always getting drunk. He was supposed to be in the insurance business, but he had a mind like a three-year-old."

She confirmed Speck's long history of headaches. "He was always asking for aspirins when he was here. I think part of the reason for those headaches was because he wouldn't wear glasses. He's a bit of a dandy, a very neat and clean person, used to shower three or four times a day when he visited us this summer."

"Yes," said Ziporyn. "Dick does seem very conscious of his appearance."

"You mustn't call him Dick. He doesn't like that. He prefers

Richard," she said with a smile. She went on: "I think he enjoyed visiting us. He liked my two little daughters. He used to play cards with them, talk to them, tell them all sorts of things he would never tell anyone else. For instance, he told them about his bad drinking habits, and the effects it had on him, and the drugs he took. Always liked those kids. Of course, he adored his own child, too. When he was staying with us in July—just before it happened—he was walking around the neighborhood and saw a kid that reminded him of his own little girl. He tried to find her again but couldn't, and came home and told us about it. It was a strange coincidence because it was July 2, his daughter's birthday, so he went out into the garden and carved her initials on a tree—R. S.—Robbie Speck."

Mrs. Thornton smiled for a brief moment, but then added grimly: "At the same time, he was very depressed. He was fed up with not being able to get a job. There was always some other man would get in ahead of him, because of seniority or something. Anyway, it depressed him a lot. He kept on saying how the world wasn't worth anything and he'd be better off dead, and that was two weeks before the murders."

Ziporyn nodded. He was interested to see that Speck's suicidal thoughts had preceded the murders. "Yes, what about the murders. Any ideas?"

Mrs. Thornton thought for a moment and said: "Well, we've discussed this thing in the family, over and over. We've read all the reports. Carolyn—like I said, she was always the closest to Richard—she won't believe he did it. But she did notice something. We were looking at the pictures of the nurses and she said that one of them, Gloria Davy, looked just like Richard's wife, Shirley."

On September 9 Judge Paschen formally approved Getty's request for a panel to examine Speck's mental condition. State and county mental health experts would interview Speck and report back to the court so that a jury could decide on Speck's competence to stand trial.

Ziporyn visited Speck the same day to tell him of the conversation with his sister. They discussed her memories of him. Speck protested vehemently when the psychiatrist told him his sister had said his headaches probably came from his not wearing glasses.

"She's wrong," he said. "Sure I get eye headaches, but they come right here behind the eyes. The headaches that really bother me are the ones at the back of my head."

He was in full agreement, however, that his sister Carolyn, now living in Dallas, and he were very close as children. "Remember I told you how I fell out of a tree onto my head? Well, it was Carolyn who found me knocked out. She was the one who thought I was dead. She was hysterical about it."

Ziporyn let the conversation drift on a while and then stopped to take some papers from his briefcase. "I've got something to show you," he said. "Ever see this before?"

Speck leaned forward and saw that Ziporyn was holding up two pages from *Time* magazine. It was an account of the murder of the nurses. Speck studied a diagram of the house that showed the rooms where the murders were committed.

Nodding his head slowly, he said: "Looks like a new type of house. Look at that stairway, it's set right back from the door, the way they have it in modern places."

He turned the page over and looked at a picture of Corazon Amurao. "She sure is beautiful," he said. At the top of the page the eight photographs of the dead nurses had been cut out. "How come you cut something out here?" Speck asked.

"I'll show you," Ziporyn replied. He took the eight photographs, each cut out separately, from his briefcase and handed them, one by one, to Speck.

Speck had not seen all the press accounts immediately following the murders. This was the first time he had been confronted with pictures of the girls since he was brought to the jail. He stared at the first one, Mary Ann Jordan, for about half a minute, completely absorbed. He reached for the next, Suzanne Farris, shaking his head slowly, painfully slowly, from side to side and murmuring in a scarcely audible whisper: "They're so young, so pretty. Look at them, real pretty things, aren't they?"

Ziporyn slipped the third into his hand—Patricia Matusek. "Say, she's good-looking," Speck said with an appreciative nod. "Looks like Elizabeth Taylor."

The psychiatrist made no comment and held out the fourth to him—Gloria Davy. Speck reached for it and suddenly froze. He drew his hand back from the picture as if it might sting him. His eyes opened wide, his lips quivered slightly. He looked terrified. Ziporyn offered the picture to him again. He reached forward and gingerly took the tiny photograph with both hands. He placed it in the palm of one hand, like some poisonous insect, and as he stared at it, a rush of whistled air escaped through his lips.

"You know what?" he said, looking at Ziporyn with a stunned, distant gaze. "This is a dead ringer for Shirley."

He looked at Gloria Davy's photograph for another full minute without speaking and then took the other pictures. He shuffled through them all again and picked out that of Gloria Davy, placing it on top of the pile for another look.

"Why?" he said. "Why? It just doesn't make sense—them being dead, me being here."

The psychiatrist again chose not to comment, but turned back to *Time's* account and other reports of the murders and how the bodies were found. Speck listened attentively as Ziporyn read to him. Ziporyn was reading a report that the police had found Gloria Davy naked and strangled with a strip of clothing, her anus mutilated, when Speck stopped him. "What does 'mutilated' mean?" he asked. Ziporyn explained.

"That's disgusting," said Speck, twisting his face in a tight grimace. "I'd never do a thing like that. I tried it once when I was young, but it didn't work and I hated it anyway."

The psychiatrist pointed out that Gloria Davy was the only victim mutilated in this fashion, the only one found completely nude, and the only one the murderer had taken downstairs to kill.

"But what's so special about her?" Speck asked. "Why was she treated different than the rest?"

"You told me yourself what's so special about her," Ziporyn replied. "You told me she looks just like your wife. Well, it's possible—if it was you who did the murders—that the whole chain of violence was triggered off by your recognizing a resemblance between Gloria Davy and Shirley. Maybe when you first went into that house you were only intending to steal some money. You've told me how when you're on a lot of alcohol and drugs—and you say you were that day—you can get into a blind fury if something starts it off. It only needs to be something small, but in this case it may have been something big, as big as the hatred you say you feel for your wife. I don't know what happened between you and

Gloria Davy. We'll probably never know. But it's possible that her looking like your wife was enough to arouse your resentment. If she did anything in the slightest way to provoke you, it could be enough to spark off a whole blaze of fury in you. Even if she was not the first to be killed—you may have deliberately left her till later—her resemblance to your wife could have pinpointed the cause of your hostility toward all the girls. This is only a theory. No one can know for sure what actually happened—unless, of course, your blackout were to fade away—but these two things are certain: The treatment of Gloria Davy *was* different from that of the other girls, and her picture *does* remind you of your wife, whom you repeatedly say you hate."

Ziporyn paused, waiting for Speck to comment, but Speck remained silent. "Does any of this ring a bell for you?" the psychiatrist asked.

"Nope," said Speck.

However forcefully Speck had been struck by the resemblance between his wife and Gloria Davy, it seemed to mean little if anything now. He shrugged and turned back to *Time*'s picture of Corazon Amurao.

"She sure is pretty," he said.

The Dizzy Feeling

THE INTERVIEWS WITH THE PANEL OF PSYCHIATRISTS AND physicians had begun in earnest, and Speck was receiving them with mixed reactions. He was bewildered and at times exasperated by the persistence of their probing into the same areas of his behavior, his past, his activities on the day and night of the murders.

"It's not the same as the talks I have here with you. They keep asking me the same questions, over and over," he complained to Ziporyn. "Even if I wasn't crazy to begin with, this'd be enough to drive me crazy now."

His bitterest complaints were reserved for a psychiatrist whose Freudian orientation was more than Speck could bear. "That guy sure bugs me," said Speck. "All he talks to me about is dicks, dicks, dicks. He kept asking me whether I like sex books. That's all he could talk about, sex. I tell you, there's something wrong with him. He should be examined or something."

By contrast, Speck seemed to have enjoyed his interviews with Dr. William Norcross, the director of Bridewell Hospital. Norcross had been his attending physician from the time of his arrest at Cook County Hospital to his transfer twelve days later to the Cook County Jail. Speck made it seem that, compared with those of the psychiatrists, Norcross' interrogations were relaxed and easy-going. Even so, Speck's rapport with him was not so perfect that he could remember the physician's name correctly.

"I had a good talk with Dr. Zarkov Friday," Speck cheerily told Ziporyn at their session on Monday, September 19.

"Zarkov?" said Ziporyn blankly. "Who the heck's that? Don't you mean Norcross? Zarkov's the doctor in Flash Gordon."

"You're right, you're right," said Speck. "Knew I heard the name before. Anyway, he told me how I got that gun. Remember, I couldn't figure how I got hold of it? Well, Norcross says I got it from some whore. I remember her now. Met her the day I was with the sailors—you know, when I took those shots. Real ugly broad. I sure hope they don't bring her into court as a witness or something. I'd be ashamed for people to know I associated with something like that. I mean, she's real ugly—long hair all over her face."

He now remembered that the woman appeared after the sailors had left him on the Wednesday night preceding the murders, but that was as far as his memory of that night could now expand. The rest was still blackness.

Speck's mood remained ebullient, and the reference to the night of the murders did not dispel it. His experience with the psychiatrists might at times exasperate him, but not to the point of deep depression. His adverse reaction was rather one of playful mockery. He liked to call the doctors "my associates." Ziporyn commented on how much more confident and relaxed he seemed.

"Well, Doc, I've quit worrying about the chair. The way I figure, it'll be five minutes of being scared—five minutes it'll take from the cell to the chamber—then I won't be scared any more."

He said this without a note of mannered stoicism or, on the other hand, of the self-pitying melancholy that had often pervaded similar remarks in the past. He was straight-faced, matter-of-fact. But Ziporyn was not too sure how long this mood would endure if they dwelt on the subject. He returned to the interviews with the panel, but Speck was no longer interested.

"I don't bother to tell them much. What's the point?" he said. "But I'll tell you something I haven't told them. I have a split personality. My mother knows all about that. You see, when I'm sober, I'm . . . I'm . . . I'm, well, okay, but when I drink—I'll tell you. Once I smashed my hand through a wall rather than hit her."

Ziporyn noted that he was going over familiar ground. Speck pretended to introduce new material, but this was actually a pretext for repeating once more his insistence that he would never harm his mother. The psychiatrist noted how much Speck chose to stress this point—almost protesting too much.

As it turned out, Speck did not belabor the point this time. In referring to the incident with his mother he made an expansive gesture toward the wall opposite his bed. His eye caught something hanging there, and he broke into a smile.

"See my diploma?" he said. "I'm proud of that. That's the first thing I ever passed."

On the wall next to the bars was a diploma certifying that Richard Speck had passed the Emmaus Bible School Correspondence Course. As Ziporyn read the inscription, Speck went to a cubbyhole he had fashioned from a cardboard box and fetched his examination papers. With great pride he showed the psychiatrist his grades, which included a 70, several 80's and 90's and even one 100. He explained that he had obtained the question forms through the prison chaplain. As he showed his answers and checked the errors with Ziporyn, Speck muttered over and over again: "First thing I ever passed, first goddam thing I ever passed. Ain't that something? I tell you, I was dumb in school, but dumb. First thing I ever passed."

He scanned the questions and answers and stopped at one that asked the meaning of sin. "Yeah, sin," he murmured thoughtfully. "There's some terrible things done these days. Did you read about how that politician's daughter got killed, Percy's girl? Isn't that awful? She's such a pretty girl. I hope they catch whoever did it. It's terrible, the things people do."

For the moment, his own involvement in a deed of even greater dimension was forgotten. That involvement was what other people, the police, the press, told him about, not something he felt within his own consciousness. The murders of which he was accused, like the murder of Valerie Percy, daughter of Charles Percy, now Senator from Illinois, were something he had read about in the newspapers. His detachment could be total.

By the end of the same week Speck had scored a new success in the Emmaus Bible School Correspondence Course, winning another certificate with a grade of 77. As Speck raised his left arm to point out the second diploma, the psychiatrist noticed the famous tattoo just below the elbow—BORN TO RAISE HELL. The spidery blue-lettered words were spaced in three lines—BORN on the first, TO RAISE on the second, and HELL, barely visible, on the third. Ziporyn asked why the last word was so much less clear than the rest, almost obliterated, in fact.

"To tell you the truth, Doc," said Speck, after some hesitation, "I was trying to burn it out of my arm when I was in jail in Texas."

It seemed interesting, the psychiatrist thought, that Speck had only attacked the word HELL. Was it the Puritan in him?

"Why did you do that?" Ziporyn asked.

"I guess I was ashamed of it or something. I mean, it's not a nice thing to have on your arm, is it?"

Ziporyn smiled and said: "Given what's happened, I guess it is pretty ironic."

"Ironic? What's that mean?"

The psychiatrist explained, and Speck nodded solemnly. He understood what irony was, it seemed, but the irony of the situation did not appeal to him. Ziporyn asked him how he got the tattoo.

"I was maybe nineteen, and with this bunch of kids," Speck recalled. "We was in Dallas and we all went to this tattooer together. We all had something different—a skull, a heart, a girl's name—I couldn't think of nothing to have on my arm, so I asked the tattooer if he had any ideas. He suggested all kinds of things, slogans and stuff, and one of them was BORN TO RAISE HELL. That sounded kinda good, so I let him put that. Didn't mean anything special to me. I mean, what does something like that mean? Not much, does it? Never thought about it."

They talked for a while about other episodes of his Dallas years, escapades with the police, his head injuries. Ziporyn had discovered from casual conversation with the panel psychiatrists that Speck was not telling them about these incidents. Ziporyn pointed out to Speck how important this could be for his case, how direct an effect it could have on the sentence.

"Say," Speck interrupted him, "if they don't burn me, what will they do with me? Put me in some kind of nut house?"

Ziporyn explained that this was unlikely, unless it was part of the state's jail system, as at Menard, for instance.

"I'm not afraid of jails," Speck commented. "I've been in them. They don't scare me one bit. Like this one here, this is fine—you couldn't chase me out of here if you tried. Not like a Texas jail. All we did there was pick cotton. You know, one day I picked eighty pounds, eighty pounds. I thought I really was something. One thing here, there's no cotton up North."

There was a silence as they looked around the cell. Little by little, Speck's fussy sense of tidiness—he was forever bending down to pick up a scrap of paper or a crumb from the cake he and Ziporyn ate with the coffee—was asserting itself on the bleak cell. New "furniture," in the form of cardboard cubbyholes for his mail, extra underwear, toilet things, was arranged along the cell walls. His towel and face cloth were draped neatly across the bars. The cell could not yet be described as "cozy," but Speck was definitely leaving his mark. In one corner, at the end of the bed, Ziporyn noticed a small pile of paperback books, Westerns.

Speck caught his gaze and said: "My sister sent me those."

The psychiatrist recalled their first interview and Speck's difficulties with *Look* magazine. "Can you read them?"

"Yeah, pretty good, but there's lots of words I can't make out." Speck leafed through one, *The Virginian,* and said: "Like this one . . . Madam . . . Madamoy . . . what's that?" It was "Mademoiselle." Ziporyn pronounced it for him, and also another that puzzled him, "Monsieur," and explained what they meant. Speck nodded and asked: "What about this? It says something about a 'conversational ball.' Now what the hell is a conversational ball?" The sentence read, "They tossed the conversational ball back and forth." Ziporyn tried to explain, but the metaphor proved too confusing for Speck. The psychiatrist switched the subject to the psychiatric panel.

Speck said that as a result of talking it over with one of the psychiatrists, he now recalled in greater detail the afternoon he spent with the "ugly broad" before the night of the murders. "As I remember it now, I was with her before I teamed up with the sailors—anyway, before I had those injections—she was gone by then. She had this gun, and I made her give it to me. She was a whore and she was making me mad, the way she behaved. I can remember waving the gun in her face, and then she left."

The anger on Speck's face. his narrow eyes and his rising voice as he recalled the behavior of the "ugly broad" reminded Ziporyn of the prisoner's reaction to memories of his wife and stepfather. The psychiatrist sensed that there was a link. As Speck had already said, his stepfather and his wife were the two great hates of his life. They were both a manifestation of woman's betrayal: Shirley because he suspected she "ran around" with other men, and Lindbergh as the cause of his mother's betrayal of him, by replacing both his father and him in her affections. From this dual disillusionment Speck seemed to have developed an all-pervading suspicion of women, particularly in his sexual relations with them and when they displayed sexual looseness. It was Speck's experience that women gave their affections to men too easily and too freely. He reacted negatively even when he himself was the object of those affections.

Ziporyn picked up his briefcase and prepared to leave. As he stood in the doorway of the cell, Speck said: "Have you talked to the warden lately?" Ziporyn shook his head. "Well," Speck continued, "they'll probably tell you I tried to kill a guard the other night. He claims I threatened to choke him. He's crazy. How could I get at him from in here?"

"What was it all about?" Ziporyn asked.

"Claims I was being cruel to a cockroach. Tiring out the cockroach, he says. He's crazy. Did you ever see a tired cockroach? Anyway, they shouldn't have cockroaches in here in the first place. And if they do, what would I be doing, trying to tire one out? I tell you, that night guard, he's an old man. What can you expect?"

The psychiatrist left the cell. As the guard closed the cell door behind him, Ziporyn noticed a rolled newspaper emerging through the bars, hovering over the guard's desk and suddenly flicking the guard's cap to the floor. The newspaper disappeared back into the cell, and Speck's face appeared at the bars, grinning like an impudent schoolboy.

Four days later, Ziporyn was treated to a variation of this mime. When he arrived, Speck was fast asleep, so the psychiatrist went next door to chat through the bars to Gambino, who was always proudly ready with an inside story of Chicago's gangland. As Ziporyn stood outside Gambino's cell, a hand poked out through the bars of the middle cell, holding a glass of coffee towards Ziporyn. Not a word was said. Ziporyn took the coffee and thanked Speck for it. The hand slid back through the bars.

Ziporyn brought Speck some new Westerns to read. "Say, these are great," Speck said as he shuffled through them. He was evidently

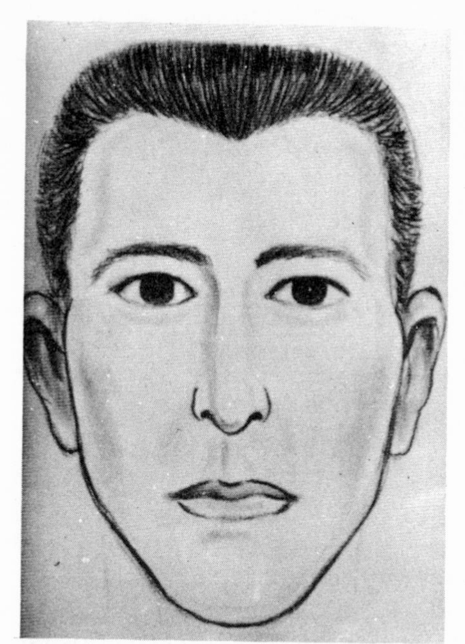

Police artist Otis Rathel's drawing of the slayer, based on Corazon Amurao's description. The photograph was obtained later from police files in Texas.

Wide World Photos

drawn to the books with the more violent-sounding titles. He put *Pirates of the Range* to one side, but lingered over *To Kill at Sundown*. Another title caught his eye, and he brandished the book at Ziporyn. It was called *Born for Trouble*. He looked at the psychiatrist quizzically, almost accusingly.

"No, Richard," Ziporyn said with a grin. "Just a coincidence, an accident. I didn't choose that deliberately."

Speck accepted the explanation without question. He was delighted with the books and beamed at Ziporyn.

"You know something? I'd go through hell for you. You've been swell."

Speck had shown many signs of friendship toward the doctor. This was the first time he had articulated it. Ziporyn was greatly encouraged by this show of trust, although he knew it was a fragile bond that needed to be cautiously nurtured. Speck was still in many ways a child.

Ziporyn explained to him with a laugh that it would not really be necessary to go through hell, but there was plenty Speck could do. "If you and I can put the pieces together here and learn what's behind crimes like the one you're accused of, so that people can understand these things and prevent them, you'll have done quite a bit."

"Yeah, that crime. You know, I can't pronounce what I feel about those girls."

"You mean 'explain'?"

"Yeah, I just can't explain what I feel. I don't know the words. It's in me, what I feel, but I don't have the words. Those people lost someone they love. They want to get even. I don't blame them. If it was my daughter, I'd want to get even, too."

"I understand how you feel," Ziporyn said. "It's quite natural, but it doesn't help, feeling like that. It's childish. Punishing you is not going to give those people back their lost daughters—it wouldn't help them."

Speck stared blankly at Ziporyn. The psychiatrist was not making much headway. He would have to reduce the argument to its simplest terms, with an easy analogy, however childish it might seem. Nothing else would get through.

"Richard," he began, "today is my birthday and. . . ."

"Happy birthday."

"Thank you. Yesterday my family gave me a little party. My kids. . . ."

"How many kids you got?"

"Three—a girl, she's eight, and two boys. . . ."

"How old are the boys?"

"The oldest is six, the baby is two. Anyway, my daughter. . . ."

"Nice family."

"Thanks. My daughter had her balloon busted by the baby and she went into a temper tantrum. She insisted that I should break the baby's balloon. I said to her that if I could get her balloon back by breaking his, I would do it, but since this would not happen, I didn't see any point in breaking one more balloon. Every balloon was important, so how did we benefit from having one less? Then she wanted the baby punished. I said that since he was only a baby, he didn't know what he was doing, he broke her balloon accidentally, with no intent, couldn't help the whole affair—it really wasn't his fault. She pouted, but she got the point—and she is only eight."

Speck said nothing, but his eyes were bright and he nodded his head slowly. He seemed to get the point, too. Ziporyn signaled to the guard that the session was over. As the cell door was opened, Speck stood up. Calmly he walked out behind the psychiatrist, pushing the sergeant into the cell.

"So long, Speck," he said to the grinning guard. "See you around."

He laughed loudly, turned around and walked back into the cell, pushing the guard back out again. "What a joke," Speck said. "Just try to make me leave."

"Did you watch TV last night?" Speck asked the psychiatrist, as he stepped into the cell on September 30. "I was on it."

"No, I didn't see you. Was this after your brain-wave test?" (Part of the psychiatric panel's tests was an electroencephalograph measurement of the electric activity of Speck's brain.)

"Yeah. When I came out, I had a coat over my head. Wasn't my idea—the officer did it. Whew, that brain test, I tell you. I was real scared at first. They didn't tell me nothing—just whisked me away from here. I thought I was being punished. Once I was there, though, I liked it fine. The lady there was real nice. She was kind of pretty. I shook her hand when I left." He broke into a grin. "You know, she gave me some pills. Made me high—felt good, real good,

I tell you, I was flying, man." As part of the standard procedure for electroencephalograms, to calm the patient before the test, Speck was given sodium seconal sedatives—"red-birds" to him. The doctors noted, however, that Speck's state of nervousness was increased by the pills.

Returning to the jail that night in a high state of tension, Speck assaulted a fellow prisoner. As Speck related the incident, "We were in the reception area and I noticed one of the guards had a gray hair on his shoulder. I kidded him about going around with old broads. The guard said old broads are sometimes still good, and I said, 'Yeah, nine to ninety, old ones, young ones, crippled ones.' Then this smart-ass next to me opened his big mouth and said, 'Dead ones?' So I swung at him, know what I mean?"

Speck waited for some kind of endorsement from the psychiatrist but did not seem perturbed when Ziporyn did not respond. The psychiatrist did observe, however, that Speck had once more reacted violently while under the influence of drugs. Speck continued: "You know, there's a guy in here was a buddy of mine at the Huntsville jail in Texas—Paul Thedford. Saw him over at the hospital the other day. I tell you, that guy is shit-scared. Man, he thinks he's a cert for the chair and he makes me feel all creepy when he talks about it. He's so scared, man. He told me he's on a murder charge and two counts of robbery. I asked him if he wanted to trade."

He paused, stared pensively at Ziporyn and added: "Look, Doc, will you do me a favor? Make sure they don't put Thedford in this tier with me. I mean, I'm scared stiff of the chair, too, but I can handle it right now. But if Thedford was around, babbling off about how terrible it was going to be and all, it could drive me crazy. I don't need that, Doc, know what I mean?"

Ziporyn agreed to do whatever he could. Then he told Speck there would be another brain-wave test soon, and this time he should try to relax. Speck nodded. "Now I know what it's like, I'll look forward to it. That feeling you get when they give you the pills, that's good. When I was still in the hospital at Bridewell, a girl came and stuck a needle in my arm. Some blood came out, then I began to feel real good and then dizzy. A little fat guy came with a pen and a pad of paper, and he started asking questions. About the murders."

The authorities at Cook County Jail had for some time been worried that Speck might have been given shots of Pentothal—thiopental sodium, popularly known as "truth serum"—while at Bridewell. Pentothal is a barbiturate administered intravenously, often used as an anesthetic in surgery but also given in lighter doses to make the patient sleepy to the point where he loses control of his conscious impulses. "Truth serum" is a misnomer, since the drug does not guarantee that the patient will tell the truth while under its influence, but it does greatly diminish a person's ability to manipulate facts to what he consciously feels is his advantage. By lowering a patient's inhibitions, Pentothal makes it more likely that he will tell the truth. With Speck professing total blackout for the period covering the murders, it was feared that some attempt might be made to use Pentothal, which the state of Illinois has deemed a highly irregular practice. The incident to which Speck was now referring had prompted rumors that Pentothal had been used, but there was no proof that that is what the injection contained.

"What did you tell this guy?" Ziporyn asked.

"I don't remember," Speck replied. "I just know I kept yelling, 'I don't care, I don't care.' But I sure liked that dizzy feeling. Maybe I'll get it again when they give me another brain test."

Ziporyn told Speck he was going next door to play chess with Gambino.

"Good luck," said Speck. "Beat the pants off him." He handed the psychiatrist a piece of banana cake to go with the good wishes. As Ziporyn went out, Speck shouted over his shoulder to Gambino: "You'll get yours now—you're playing with an educated man."

Ziporyn told Warden Johnson about Speck's experience at Bridewell, and the warden summoned Speck to his office. With Ziporyn present, he questioned Speck closely about Bridewell and about the incidents surrounding the murders. The warden showed particular interest in how much money Speck had had with him at the time. It seemed that on the Wednesday morning (July 13) he had had $25, won $11 playing pool, and then paid out $8 or $9 in rent. This would have left him with about $28. By Thursday morning, however, he had only $14 and some change. Johnson did not explain either then or later why he was so interested in the money, but Ziporyn surmised that it might have something to do with Miss

Amurao's statement that the nurses had given him money to "get him to New Orleans."

The warden was asking Speck whether he had had sexual intercourse with the woman he was with on the day before the murders. Speck shook his head. "I was too messed up," he said. "We was naked in bed and I tried, but I couldn't make it." The observation was made in a very straightforward manner, without any embarrassment, awkwardness or trace of bitterness.

Speck returned to his cell, and Ziporyn followed him for a short talk. As the psychiatrist approached the cell, the sergeant on duty looked up and said: "Your boy is getting mean. He threw hot water at me last night."

Ziporyn nodded but made no comment. These incidents were becoming more frequent. At that moment Speck was manifesting all the tensions that caused tantrums. "I'm sick of it, Doc," he almost shouted. "I've had it up to here, all this shit. I wish they'd kill me and get it over with. I'm sick of being a freak. Did you see today's paper? There's another story about me. Every fucking day they write about me. Doc, you know I've got a temper, well, I'm just about cracking, and you know what I'm like when I get these tempers. Once, I even kicked my mother in the head—of course, I was on pills, but still. . . ."

His voice tapered off into silence. Ziporyn stared at him, waiting. All this time Speck had reacted violently whenever it was suggested he might have attacked his mother in one of his tempers. Now, though it was not certain that he was telling the truth, with his defenses suddenly down, he was saying that he had struck her, and violently.

Ziporyn asked him: "Did you know what was happening at the time that you kicked your mother?"

"Nope," Speck replied. He was not interested in pursuing the subject. "Anyway," he went on, "now I'm going after everybody and the trouble is I know they're right and I'm wrong. I tell you, I'm cracking."

Ziporyn nodded and said he would get him some tranquilizers. As he left, Speck added: "'You know, I was going to ask you to get me a razor—they say it's all right for me to shave now—but I better not. The way I feel right now, I might do something, and I don't want to get you into a jam."

No Nightmares

A TRIP OUT OF TOWN PREVENTED ZIPORYN FROM SEEING SPECK for a week. When he returned, on October 10, Speck greeted him effusively, bustling about the cell to get the coffee ready. His stock of improvised furniture was growing. He had fashioned bookshelves for his Westerns out of cardboard, and had also made a footstool and more cubbyholes. On one piece of board he had pasted a suit of playing cards and hung it on the wall as a picture.

"You're a pretty handy guy," Ziporyn commented, pointing at the various knickknacks around the cell.

"Yeah, I was a carpenter once," said Speck, with a broad grin. "Liked it, too. I was a good carpenter—till I got fired. I was working as a carpenter in Dallas, and one of the guys I worked with was jailed for being drunk and disorderly. It's quite a custom. Anyway, his wife had to go out of town a ways to raise bail money for him. I went with her. On the road we had us a few beers and a few more beers and we finished up in this motel. She got me mad, the way she was behaving, it was disgusting, and I told her she was nothing but an old whore. First chance I got I lifted a hundred bucks from her."

The pattern of Speck's contempt for women, particularly when he himself was the object of their free and easy attentions, was now well established. Ziporyn pointed this out to him and suggested a parallel between his anger at his friend's wife and at his own wife.

"Yeah, I was ready to settle down when I got out of prison, but Shirley wasn't ready. Hope she's satisfied now. You know, I've been trying to wipe her out of my mind, but it's not easy. Like here, for instance. . . ." He rolled up his sleeve and pointed to a tattoo above his right elbow: RICHARD AND SHIRLEY. He had tried to burn it out—in the same way that he had attacked his BORN TO RAISE HELL mark—but without success. Both arms were a mass of tattoos. Etched at the top of his right arm was his daughter's name. Below that, less distinct, were the initials R. L., which he said stood for Richard Lindbergh, the name he took from his stepfather and which he kept until his marriage. This, too, he had tried to erase. Then came RICHARD AND SHIRLEY. Below the right elbow was a long dagger with a snake coiled around it.

On the last finger of his right hand was the solitary letter L. "I started to have LOVE and HATE on my knuckles," he explained, "but I stopped. See, at least I could hide the others under a long-sleeved shirt, but on the hands, it would show too much."

On the back of his left wrist was the initial R, for Richard. Above that was BORN TO RAISE HELL and, above the left elbow, the word EBB, topped by a grinning skull with a World War I aviator's helmet. Ziporyn asked about the word "ebb."

"It's slang," said Speck with a sly smile. "When I got it, the crowd I was with was saying 'ebb you' instead of 'fuck you,' know what I mean? There's one more tattoo you haven't seen yet." He rolled up his left trouser leg to reveal what he called "my dicky bird." It was an erect penis and testicles crudely drawn on his shin.

"Why did you have all these tattoos put on your arms and leg like this? What's it all for?" the psychiatrist asked.

"Aw, nothing special. All the guys was doing it, so I went along. Doesn't mean nothing to me. It was just the thing to do." Speck looked at the dagger on his right arm. "That knife reminds me—I was with some guys—I was about eighteen at the time—a guy called J. W. Milton and Jerry Cox, we were at Tennyson Park, that's a swimming place in Dallas. I'd had three or four yellow-jackets. A gang of about fifteen other guys came over the wall and started a fight with us. I had a barbecue knife I stole some place and went after them with it, just swinging away. They really ran. We laughed like crazy to see them run like that."

He sighed deeply and stared out through the cell bars. "I don't think it's so funny now, though. I don't blame them kids—guy coming at 'em with a knife, swinging wild—I'd run, too. I just don't know. When I got to be seventeen, I just went wild. I think a lot about it now. Look what's happened. Those girls—maybe if I'd known there was something wrong with me, all that wouldn't have happened."

Speck was growing maudlin again. Ziporyn cheered him up again with some new books. Besides a Zane Grey Western, he handed him a Vietnam novel about the Green Berets and a pocket Webster's Dictionary. It was the dictionary that interested Speck most. He thumbed through it with childlike fascination, murmuring to himself words like "corroborate," "hyperbolic," "pernicious" and "voluptuous."

They talked again of the murders, his moods, his angers, their possible interrelation. Speck was alert and curious about the implications. "Could this mean that if I can't control myself when I'm angry and go wild, that I don't know what I'm doing and that's what happened?" Ziporyn said this was possible and quoted Plato's observation that the wild beast is in all of us. He pointed out how this was apparent in many people driving automobiles when intoxicated.

Speck nodded enthusiastically. "Yeah, you're right. I'm a wild driver when I get drunk, but I tell you, when I'm sober and I'm driving and I see kids in the road, that's when I get scared all of a sudden. You see, I know then what the risks were when I was drunk."

For the first time Speck appeared to see the point of the possible causal relationship between his intoxication and his violent behavior.

Later that week, the jail was alive with gossip about a local murder in which it was rumored that a girl had been killed by her stepmother. Ziporyn mentioned it to Speck. "Bullshit," Speck replied. "She didn't do it. Her own daughter, or anyway her stepdaughter. She raised her, didn't she? She wouldn't kill her."

"Richard," said Ziporyn, straight-faced, "When it comes to murder, you're an amateur."

"What's an amateur?" Speck asked. Ziporyn explained the difference between an amateur and a professional. Speck thought for a moment and said: "Well, I don't want to get to be no pro."

He stood up from his bed and went over to the sink set in the wall to prepare some coffee, chattering over his shoulder like a gossipy housewife.

"Say, will you call my sister for me? You see, she's sending me $50 a month. That's way too much. After all, they got kids and all that. Tell her to take it easy."

He handed Ziporyn a glass of coffee and added apologetically: "I don't have no goodies today to go with it, but how about a piece of cake from my dinner? I won't eat it." Ziporyn shook his head, but when Speck began to look hurt, he accepted the cake from the dinner tray. Speck grunted approvingly. He brushed his trousers, straightened the tray and a few other things around the cell and sat down on the bed with a satisfied sigh.

"I been seeing my associates again," he said. "They showed me some cards with pictures and stuff."

"Oh, the psychologists," Ziporyn said. "How did you feel about it?"

"I liked it fine. What's it for?"

Ziporyn explained how the projective tests provided insights into how his mind worked, his attitudes, the pattern of his suggestivity. Speck nodded and said, not very convincingly, that he understood. "I liked the Draw-A-Person thing best," he said. Ziporyn asked him what kind of drawing he had done. In keeping with the fastidiousness of his personal habits, Speck had made two very detailed figures, paying careful attention to small points of clothing and other minutiae.

Ziporyn pointed to the novel about Vietnam, *Bloody Jungle,* lying on top of Speck's paperback library and asked him what he thought of it.

"That was great. Did you read it? It was real nice. I specially liked that part where they cut this guy's ear off. You know, I wish I was fighting over there. And I liked the book with all the words in it, the . . . dictionary, right? You know, reading can be fun." Suddenly he bent forward over the bed and a caricatured conspiratorial look spread across his face, his head hunched between his shoulders, his eyes narrowed to slits. He looked past Ziporyn to see if the guard was watching and then slowly lifted the corner of his mattress and brought out a dog-eared copy of a magazine called *For Men Only.*

Concealing it with his broad back to the door, Speck flicked through the magazine while Ziporyn leaned over his shoulder. "There's a cartoon in here that really cracks me up," Speck said in a hoarse stage whisper. "Look at that—isn't it the greatest?"

The cartoon depicted three characters—a businessman with briefcase, hat and overcoat, his wife sitting on a settee in a revealing housecoat with frilly lace underwear showing, and a man in pajamas, wearing a wig with a braid at the back. The man is squinting his eyes and holding a glass on a tray. The caption has the husband saying: "I don't care what you say—I don't believe that Chinese houseboy story."

Speck laughed as he showed it to Ziporyn. Ziporyn managed a chuckle, but was preoccupied with this new instance of Speck's involvement with the problem of wifely infidelity. The psychiatrist noted again that this theme was the one most likely to strike a responsive chord in Speck's unconscious. He regarded this as one more piece of evidence for his basic hypothesis that the murders might have been triggered by Speck's unconscious rage at his wife.

While they were still looking at the cartoon, Speck said: "You know you been talking about getting hit on the head. Well, there was another time I just remembered. I was high on yellow-jackets and went into this Humble Oil station near my house—Burnett's, I think it was called. and I tried to rob the guy. He caught me and hit me seven or eight times over the head with a tire tool. They say I just staggered away, but I only remember what they told me."

"What made you think of it now?"

"My head—it's really throbbing now. These aches are getting worse."

"Do they give you any pills?"

"Are you kidding? It's like asking the devil for a Bible."

Ziporyn promised to get him some medication. As the psychiatrist left, Speck called out to him through the bars: "Hey, ask the warden if I can have a radio in here, will you? I'd like to listen to some hillbilly music."

It was October 17, exactly three months since Speck's arrest. Ziporyn brought him a transistor radio. In seconds he had unwrapped the radio, stripped the back off, locked the batteries in place and found the country-and-western station, WJJD, playing the twanging strains of "Silver Dagger." Speck slumped into a blissful daze on his bed, then rose on one elbow and murmured: "Man, that's good for my soul. Gee, that's great of you, Doc, to bring me that."

He shouted out to the cells on either side of him: "Hey, Clancy, Gambino—listen—there's some real music."

"Switch the fucking thing off," they chorused.

Perhaps reminded by the music, Speck said: "How's my friend from Texas? Have you seen him?" He turned off the radio.

"You mean Thedford. Yes, I've seen him. He's okay, but still pretty nervous. He feels he's just as much in trouble as you are. He sweats a lot and he has nightmares about the murder." (Thedford was charged with killing a policeman.)

"Nightmares?" said Speck incredulously.

"Yes. Don't you have them?"

"Naw, I never dream. I just sleep. Funny, though, the other night I asked the guard to wake me in the morning. I didn't hear him shout at me, so he came in the cell and shook me. He says I jumped clear across the cell and stood there in the corner staring at him."

"I guess you were afraid," Ziporyn suggested.

"Maybe so, but I don't have no nightmares."

"Well," said Ziporyn, "Thedford is still going over the murder in his mind. He even hears the dead man talking to him."

"He does? Do you believe that?"

"It happens. For that matter," the psychiatrist said evenly, "a lot of people don't believe you when you say you don't remember the murders. They say you're lying to me, trying to cop a plea."

"Listen," said Speck in a low, solemn voice. "I didn't kill those girls for fun, I'll tell you that. I don't know why I killed them."

"Do you ever think about that night?"

"Naw, it's all gone. I only think about it when people ask me questions."

"Well, that's why Thedford has nightmares and you don't. He's still thinking about killing that cop."

Speck shrugged his shoulders. "Why should he? A man becomes a cop, he takes that risk—that's part of the job, he expects it. But those girls I killed, they didn't expect nothing, didn't harm nobody. That's really different—unless, maybe, the cop had a family."

Ziporyn interrupted because Speck was growing depressed and reversing an apparently positive trend. In the deepest sense, Ziporyn's assignment to anticipate the risks of Speck's suicidal tendencies was proving successful. Speck was evidently starting to repress his highly subjective feelings of horror and conscience-stricken self-disgust with regard to the murders. He was still bothered by reminders of his involvement, but the concern was no longer on the scale of an obsession that might make him dangerously depressive. His suicidal drives would diminish as he began to think more and more of the present and the future, instead of dwelling compulsively on the past. This would happen if he was able to come to terms objectively with the reality of the murders and possibly understand an unconscious motivation (if it was he who committed them). Reflecting on the innocence of the victims and the horror of their deaths accomplished nothing and could be emotionally destructive.

The psychiatrist began once more to examine the possible motivation for the murders, and Speck's response bore out his point. Ziporyn discussed Speck's rage over female infidelity, a rage related to his wife and set off, perhaps, by Gloria Davy's resemblance to her. Speck asked him why he thought this, and Ziporyn repeated the details of how Gloria Davy had been treated differently from the rest of the girls.

Speck listened for a moment and then stood up with a look of anguish on his face. "Stop," he said. "It makes me sick just hearing that."

Ziporyn stopped. He was satisfied that Speck was changing his stance and developing a more healthy attitude that did not seek to dwell on the morbid aspects of the murders. It was a useful point at which to end the session.

Speck's progress was real but by no means steady. By the time of the next interview, October 21, Speck had undergone more sessions with the panel of psychiatrists. One of the experts who examined him was Dr. Hervey M. Cleckley, professor of psychiatry at the Medical College of Georgia and co-author of the controversial psychiatric study *Three Faces of Eve*. Ziporyn learned from Cleckley that Speck had not even mentioned his head injuries or his history of intravenous drug injections.

"Why didn't you tell the doctor about your injuries and the injections?" Ziporyn asked. "You know how important it is."

"Well, he didn't ask me," Speck replied defensively.

"Didn't you feel like discussing the case with the doctor?"

"No, it's not that. I liked him. He talks my language—you know, Southern talk."

"Well, then, talk to the man. You can never tell what piece of information can save you."

"I don't know if I want to be saved. You know, Getty was here last week. I asked him what happens if I don't get the chair. The way he tells it, I can go to prison for 680 years or something like that."

"And if you do," said the psychiatrist, "you can get an education in prison, rehabilitate yourself, and if you prove yourself, you can eventually be paroled."

"What good would that do?" Speck said, pouting. "Twenty, thirty years in prison, I'd come out, no job, no family, what would I come out to?"

Ziporyn suggested that other men had been able to make successful adjustments after long prison terms, like Nathan Leopold.

"His rap partner got knifed, didn't he?" Speck interrupted.

"Loeb? Yes, that was for some homosexual affair."

Speck snorted with disgust. "I don't go in for that kind of junk."

Ziporyn wanted to persevere with the subject of a hopeful future, but he noticed that Speck remained unimpressed. Speck changed the subject for him. He went to his "coffee table" and picked up a magazine. "What do you think of this magazine someone sent me?" he asked. It was a copy of *U.S. News and World Report,* with the subscription stencil addressed to Richard Speck, Cook County Jail, Chicago, Illinois. "Who on earth sent you this?" the psychiatrist asked.

"I don't know. Somebody sent it to me, second one I've got. I don't read it though, don't like it. I guess it was some kook sent it to me, like the characters who send those crazy birthday cards and 'Get Well' things. You wanna know something, the world is full of kooks."

Ziporyn nodded in agreement.

They talked about Speck's next court appearance, set for October 24. Speck said he had complained to Getty about the bailiff who held his elbow when they walked into court. "Getty says it's for my protection, but I don't see why they have to hold me like that. I ain't gonna run away." Ziporyn told him he agreed with Getty, explaining that the court officials did not want Speck to be killed the way Oswald was in Dallas.

"You have to be kidding," Speck said with a scornful laugh. "Do you think that bailiff would protect me? I tell you, if he saw a guy come at me with a gun, he'd quit right on the spot and apply for a job as a janitor."

They both laughed. The mention of Dallas seemed to have set off a train of association in Speck's mind, and he began reminiscing about his teen-age days. "I used to know a girl in Dallas called Sally. She was from up North, so we called her 'Yankee.' I had a real sharp car then and I put her name—Yankee—in bright letters on the door. Every night the cops would wait for me. As soon as they saw that name 'Yankee' on the car, they knew who it was and, pow, they shipped me. Finally I got wise to 'em and covered the name with tape at night and took it off again in the daytime. Those cops are really something in Dallas. You have to watch out for them."

Speck walked over to his sink and grimaced into a "mirror" fashioned out of an old pie pan. "Doc," he said, as Ziporyn was leaving the cell. "Could you get me a toothbrush? My teeth are getting rotten, they're real yellow. Oh, and one more thing, can you get me anything like this *For Men Only* book? I like these war stories. I don't go so much for the girly stuff—that's okay and all—but I really like the war stories, know what I mean?"

A Razor Blade

THE PROTRACTED LEGAL PROCESS OF PREPARING RICHARD SPECK'S case for trial was taxing the ingenuity of the Chicago press and television to sustain the interest of the public. Speck's appearances in court had become routine, rendered unspectacular by the clockwork efficiency of Warden Johnson's well-disciplined guards and the impassive firmness of the sheriff's deputies assigned to protect the prisoner. The searching of the courtroom and "frisking" of spectators had lost its novelty and drama. The hearings themselves were totally lacking in any Perry Mason fireworks, consisting merely of technical sparrings in which the intentions of defense and prosecution counsel remained obscure. The less than spectacular court session on October 24 ended with Getty obtaining a continuance for the hearing of the psychiatric panel's reports.

As much to amuse themselves as to find something to interest their audience, the television cameramen and news photographers began trying to make Speck smile. By now he had made the once formidable trek to the Criminal Court Building so often that he was completely relaxed, even seeming to enjoy the trip. As a result, he was extremely cooperative, grinning in every direction. At one point he was asked to look at a photographer's bald head and this gave him fits of laughter, all duly captured for that night's newscasts.

"That guy's bald head," Speck later told Ziporyn, "I tell you, that really broke me up."

Ziporyn was not amused and rebuked Speck sharply. "You know

you shouldn't do things like that. Don't you see? It will prejudice people against you. They expect to see you serious and sorry, not clowning around. They'll think you're some kind of animal."

Speck pouted. "Well, I am an animal."

"Says who?"

"I do. I must be, to do what I did."

"But I've explained to you over and over that we all have murderous impulses in us. Mostly, we control them. In your case, the combination of head injury, liquor and drugs breaks your control. I don't believe you were responsible for your actions. Your impulses are no different from mine or anyone else's. That doesn't make you an animal."

Ziporyn shook his head in almost exaggerated disgust. He wanted Speck to see that he was angry. "Boy, if *you* can't be convinced, how do you expect a jury to get it?"

Speck was solemn, the funny bald head forgotten. "I don't expect them to. Like I say, Doc, I'm not afraid of that chair any more. I'm *in* it. All I'm doing is passing time. Every time Getty gets me a continuance, well, that's another week of life. It don't make no difference what I do—laugh or anything. That judge—he hates me. I saw him keep glaring at me today. I'm a dead man—so I just make the best of it I can."

Speck was on the defensive. He was constantly reminding himself of the horror of the crimes he was accused of committing, yet in public he appeared cool, even carefree. Ziporyn saw this as an unconscious effort to isolate his emotional reaction from his intellectual comprehension of the deed's enormity. This comprehension was expressed in his self-disgust when he spoke with Ziporyn, but in public it was carefully but unconsciously concealed by his blasé behavior.

This defense mechanism is very common in the type of obsessive-compulsive individual Ziporyn considered Speck to be, and its appearance now tended to confirm the psychiatrist's interpretation. It was in keeping with Speck's basically rigid and anal personality—a personality type characterized by elements of sadism and masochism. Speck felt hostile and punitive toward himself; both his aggressions and his depressions could be explained in terms of such a personality. His rigidity was classically illustrated by his compulsive neatness when tending his cell.

Assuming convincing evidence of such a personality, the murder of the eight nurses—if it was Speck who did it—could be explained as follows:

With the rigid and sadistic tendencies of an anal personality, Speck developed a hostility toward women which received nourishment when his mother gave herself to a stepfather and later when he feared that his wife was unfaithful to him. This hostility cannot be controlled when his inhibitions are low. Successive traumas have caused brain damage, which makes his emotional control difficult at any time. Under the influence of whisky and drugs—which he takes to relieve the headaches created by the brain damage—his tenuous control breaks completely and his hostility is left raw at the surface. This was his condition on the night of the murders. The hostility might still have been contained had there not been a trigger. This could have been provided by the resemblance between Gloria Davy and his wife.

In his present state of mind, Speck was unlikely to be responsive to even a simple outline of Ziporyn's ideas on his connection with the murders—though it was Ziporyn's constant intention, whenever possible, to acquaint Speck with these theories. At the moment, however, he preferred to change the subject. He took from his briefcase the toothbrush and the men's magazines Speck had asked for. Speck accepted both with thanks and eagerly flicked through the magazines.

He gave the nude pin-ups only a cursory glance, showing much more interest in the lurid illustrations of stories of concentration camps and battles. One of the pictures was of two dead Japanese soldiers.

"They committed suicide," Speck explained. "You can see, this one used his toe to pull the trigger—that one his hand."

This was not immediately apparent to Ziporyn from the picture, but a quick reference to the text of the story showed that Speck's observation was correct. The psychiatrist nodded and Speck grinned, almost triumphantly. He knew about such things. "I'm going to enjoy these," he said. "Thanks, Doc. I really like all this fighting and war stuff." He leafed through another copy and came across an article about the habits of divorced women and the "gay old time" they enjoyed. Speck's features tightened. There was no humor in his voice as he said, "Yeah, those divorcees—they really run around."

He began to complain of a severe headache. Ziporyn told him to take one of the pills and suggested he get some sleep.

On his next visit, Ziporyn stopped off at Mark Clancy's cell for a chat while the guard unlocked Speck's cell door. Clancy was a tough but by no means cold criminal, well adjusted to his role in and out of society and able to show considerable charm. He looked a little like the film star Tony Curtis, with baby-faced good looks and wavy black hair. He leaned casually against the bars, as if he were talking across a picket fence in his back yard. This jail had become his natural habitat. He talked of the endless maneuverings of his lawyer. They exchanged the trivia of jail gossip, how this or that inmate was getting on, and the chances of another man's getting out soon, and what ever happened to this or that son-of-a-bitch guard. Suddenly Clancy stopped and grinned, looking past Ziporyn's shoulder.

"Will you get this maniac out of here before we all go nuts?"

Speck had slipped out of his cell and was standing silently behind Ziporyn, expressionless, his eyes glazed, stock still like a dummy in a window display. The psychiatrist turned and Speck padded quietly away, moving lithely, with the grace of an athlete, his long arms hanging loosely at his sides.

"What a nut," said Clancy, with real warmth. He was evidently in some way fond of his fellow prisoner.

Ziporyn went on to Speck's cell and took off his jacket as he sat down on the bed. Speck admired the white ski sweater Ziporyn was wearing under his jacket. "I'm going to steal that sweater some day. It'd look real good on me." He handed the psychiatrist some coffee already prepared for his arrival. The "sessions" had by now taken on the character of a kaffeeklatsch, though the easygoing atmosphere often belied the tensions underneath.

Speck was pleased because his sister Martha had visited him that day and told him that he would probably be cleared of a couple of assault charges that the police chief in Monmouth had considered bringing against him. Speck had aroused suspicion in Monmouth by leaving in a hurry, not long after some assault cases had been reported. As he explained now, he had left because he was frightened that the authorities might discover he was still wanted in Texas.

"With my record in Texas, it would have meant twelve years. Way it turned out, I wish they would have got me. I'd give anything to be in a Texas jail now with only twelve years to go—instead of this. I'm tired of all this radio and TV business, for instance. My family's afraid to write to me. They're the ones who are suffering. If it was all over, people would leave them alone."

As he talked, he lit a cigarette, deftly bending a match double and striking it in one movement between the thumb and forefinger of his right hand. Once again, Ziporyn was struck by the size and grace of Speck's fingers.

"You have great hands," the psychiatrist said. "You could have been a fine craftsman."

Speck stared at Ziporyn, searching his face for signs of irony. "Are you kidding? Still, I guess I could have been a lot of things." He sounded bitter now. "I should have seen a doctor when I was eighteen, when I beat the hell out of my mother."

"When was that?"

"I told you about it—when they took me to that juvenile home, and my mother came to get me. They say I was just sitting there, talking nice and quietly, and then I went wild—beat my mother up. They had to flatten me out."

Speck had not previously made it clear that it was at the juvenile home that he had attacked his mother. He had lost his inhibitions about mentioning the incident, but not his self-disgust. His insistence that he would never do such a thing was now forgotten, his indignation at such a suggestion replaced by the same remorse that he felt every time he acted out his savage impulses. Ziporyn tried once more to explain that surrendering to impulse was not the same as taking deliberate action.

"Yeah—like those girls. I sure didn't do that for kicks. I don't know why I did it. I still don't remember anything about it, but I sure as hell wonder about it a lot, like *how* it happened. I mean, why didn't one of them yell or scream or something? Seems like one of them would."

A razor blade flashed between his fingers. Ziporyn had no idea how he had obtained it. Speck leaned toward Ziporyn, holding the blade just a few inches from the psychiatrist's throat, and said: "Look, if I'm such a killer, how come I don't kill you? I've got nothing to lose."

"That's easy to explain, Richard. You don't have whisky or pills in here."

Speck slipped the blade out of sight again. Ziporyn remained unperturbed. He was satisfied that Speck had progressed beyond the point where he would be dangerous with a blade. He learned later that Clancy had given it to Speck.

Speck sighed. "Yeah, that's the trouble. It's too damn easy to get pills. In Dallas I got them all the time. Like one time I was with some guys, drinking wine, and I had a couple of yellow-jackets. The guys left me—I remember that much. Next thing I knew I was sitting in my car in front of my home. I had nine sets of hubcaps with me. I took them, dunno why. Nine sets of hubcaps, can you believe that? I knew nothing about it. The screwdriver was on the seat next to me. I just threw them away."

"And you don't remember taking them?"

"Nope."

"And you don't remember killing the nurses?"

"Nope."

"Then how do you know it was you?"

The blandness with which he had told the story of the hubcaps was replaced with a look of taut rage. His tension brought him close to trembling.

"Why should that girl lie?" he shouted, so loudly that the dozing guard outside awoke with a start. "Why should she lie? Tell me that. She said it was me. The papers said it was me. The television, the radio, they all said it was me. Everybody said it was me. Of course it was me."

"You mean they've convinced you it was you who did it. How are you ever going to get a fair jury? If you've been convinced of your guilt by the press, how do you expect the jury not to be?"

"I don't care about that—I'm retired."

"You're what?"

His fury had subsided. "I'm retired—you know, given up."

"You mean 'resigned'?"

"Yeah, I guess that's it. Listen, Doc, I'm through. They'll never let me on the street again after what I've done."

"Don't you remember me telling you about Leopold? He got out."

"He only killed one person. I killed eight. Who would trust me out on the loose again?"

"Well, it's true a lot of people feel that way. Somebody asked me the other day if I'd trust you to baby-sit with my kids."

Speck looked indignant. "Why not? I like kids." He was proving as fitful as Ziporyn had ever known him, passing through moods of playfulness, bitter remorse, blandness, white-hot rage, and now tender warmth as he began to talk of children. "I really like kids," he repeated. "I know how to handle them. See, like maybe there's two of them on the floor, fighting over a toy or something. They scrap and fight and cry and everything. Then in two minutes, both of them don't want it any more, the toy. They're not so different than us. Me, at any rate. All the fights I've had—all for nothing. Don't remember most of them, even."

"Like you don't remember the murders?"

"Yeah, that's right. That's what was so weird when I heard them say 'Richard Speck' on the radio after the murders. I felt this funny feeling in the pit of my stomach. I couldn't think. At first I wanted to run. Then I thought that wouldn't work. Then I thought I should go to the cops, but that scared me. I didn't know what to do—so I tried to kill myself."

In the silence that followed, Gambino shouted: "Hey, Doc. How about seeing me before you leave?" Ziporyn agreed and prepared to go.

"Before you go, Doc, I have to tell you something." Speck was grinning impishly. "Yesterday, Gambino wanted a cigarette, so I rolled one for him from my tobacco. But I put a match inside. You should have heard him when it went off. Did he yell! 'Speck, you son of a bitch,' he said."

Ziporyn laughed. "You keep yourself amused."

"Got to in a jail, Doc. You know, jails are kooky places. See this tattoo, 'Born To Raise Hell'? Well, when I tried to burn it out while I was in prison, you know what they did? Gave me thirty days in solitary. They charged me with destroying state property."

However changeable Speck was proving in his moods, Ziporyn was now convinced that the risk of suicide had receded to the point where it would be quite safe for Speck to shave himself. The strict, round-the-clock reinforced guard was being maintained by the jail authorities as a sign of their continued concern for this most controversial of their inmates, but it was now a useful outward show more than a real necessity. As for the jail psychiatrist himself, his sessions with Speck had undergone a gradual transition from the specific assignment of anticipating the suicide risks to the more general routine of maintaining a surveillance of the mental and emotional state of a more than routine problem prisoner.

The Prosecution Makes a Move

EVERY DAY SPECK WAS SHOWING MORE SIGNS OF INTEREST IN THE world around him, an awareness that there was possibly a place for him in it, that there were things he could do. He was gradually realizing there was more to his life than passively waiting for trial and, as he continued to believe, execution. The maximum security block was provided with a television set, placed in front of each of the three cells in rotation. Speck had at first resisted watching it, both from his general lethargy and out of resentment at the networks' preoccupation with his case. After any one of his periodic court appearances he would angrily tell Ziporyn: "I'm sick to death of that thing. They must have shown me on it 400 times today. Can't they find some other animal?" But then the television newsmen began to lose interest, and Speck in turn found his interest in life returning. Lying face-down on his bed, he peered out through the bars of his cell to watch old movies. Best of all, he liked the Westerns, but he was particularly entranced one day by a science-fiction movie.

"This is great, Doc," he said, for once slow to rise for his talk with the psychiatrist. "It's called 'Beginning of the End.' It's about grasshoppers taking over Chicago. Isn't that something? Giant grasshoppers."

But there was more than television to hold his interest. He continued to construct "furniture" from cardboard boxes—that was what he used the razor blade for. Every item of his personal belongings—his clothes, toilet articles, books, magazines, letters—each had its own box, arranged in orderly fashion around the cell. He asked Ziporyn if he could bring him some airplane models to assemble. Ziporyn observed that Speck might be tempted, if he had not already thought of it, to find himself a makeshift stimulant by inhaling the glue. Speck scoffed at the idea. "I'm used to better highs than that," he said.

Instead—it was now October 31—Ziporyn brought Speck a 650-piece jigsaw puzzle depicting the Bangkok Floating Market, together with some more Westerns and men's magazines. Speck was delighted with the puzzle.

"How'd you know I like this kind of stuff? You know what I'll do? I'll get some glue from Clancy—don't worry, I won't do no sniffing—and when I've finished it, I'll stick it together as a picture."

He glanced through the Westerns and commented knowledgeably about the life and death of Billy the Kid. "Here's a picture of Garrett," he pointed out. "He's the guy who shot Billy, you know."

He added that he was looking forward to a movie on television about Billy the Kid later that week. He said he had been getting a lot of enjoyment out of television. That weekend he had seen Peter Ustinov's movie version of Herman Melville's *Billy Budd*.

"I liked that a lot," he said. "Only I didn't think they would hang him. When all those guys got talking at the end, I thought they'd let him go free."

Ziporyn was eager to learn of Speck's response to Melville's intricate discussion of justice in the court-martial of the young seaman accused of murder. He asked him what he thought of the arguments used in the trial scene.

Speck shook his head apologetically. "I couldn't follow it too well. Tell you the truth, I was sick that night—vomiting. I kept running to the bowl. My chest still hurts, it's still tender today when I press it here." He touched the upper part of his chest.

"Did you go on sick call?"

"I told the guards, but they said I was faking. Why would I do that? I'm comfortable here. I got my radio, the TV, the books—and I hate being sick. Well, after this, I can tell you, I'm not going to say nothing, even if I'm dying."

As he talked, he flicked through one of the men's magazines. He came across some pictures of girls in their underwear. He snorted: "Look at all these nude women. It's disgusting. I like the action stories." He turned back to the puzzle and looked at the pieces, planning how to begin it.

Ziporyn was determined to take advantage of Speck's growing curiosity about things outside himself. He wanted to stimulate any creative urge that might be glimmering in Speck as he emerged from weeks of deep psychological shock. The glimmer seemed to be there, but Speck himself appeared reluctant to recognize it.

"Richard," Ziporyn began. "Did you ever think of doing anything for somebody besides yourself?"

"Nope."

"Well, start thinking about it. You know, a baby is only concerned with himself. Then, as he gets older, he starts thinking about his family and his friends."

"What's that got to do with me?"

"You keep thinking you're all washed up, that if you go to prison for life, you might as well be dead. But that isn't necessarily true. There are ways you could still be a useful human being."

"Like what?"

"Like your skill with your hands. You like working with them, don't you? You like making things."

Speck grinned. "Yeah. I really would have liked being a carpenter. I like pounding nails."

This was not quite the emphasis Ziporyn was seeking, but he let it pass.

"Well, with those hand skills, you could do all kinds of things, things of beauty. You could be a painter or a sculptor."

"You mean like painting furniture?"

"No, I mean painting pictures."

"I'm not smart enough for that. Now Clancy, he could do it. But I don't think I could."

"You never know till you try. I know you have the mechanical skill. How would you like to try painting by numbers, for a start? Did you ever try that?"

"Yeah. I did once. I liked it. I did some in Dallas. I was doing it one night while I was baby-sitting with Robbie. Shirley was out, you see. I heard a car pull up and heard the door close. I looked out and some guy was letting Shirley out of his car down the street a bit. I ripped up that painting. Next week I was in the penitentiary. See, I started to drink again. I just didn't care."

Ziporyn's efforts to divert Speck from his central predicament were being channeled inexorably back to his patient's abiding, deep-seated obsession, but this time the psychiatrist was determined to keep clear of the subject. He talked again of painting and told Speck he would bring him some pictures at their next session, in four days' time. This would be the day of Speck's next court appearance. Speck talked lightheartedly of what a circus these affairs were becoming. "Everybody acts silly—those guards, they're all grinning at the cameras and trying to get into the picture."

The psychiatrist suggested that it was only natural for them to want publicity. "Didn't you—before all this?"

Speck nodded and recalled how proud he had been when the newspapers reported the rescue operation to take him to the hospital in Michigan when he got appendicitis aboard ship. He looked for the clipping, but could not find it. He found a postcard, instead, which he showed Ziporyn.

"This is from that Lois. Remember that girl who wrote to me when I first got here? I still don't know who she is, but I wrote to her because she put her name and address here."

"What did you say?"

He looked a little sheepish and remained noncommittal. "Just thanked her for writing."

"Why did you write?"

"Dunno." He grinned, but would say nothing more. They had once before talked of the Cleveland doctor, Samuel Sheppard, who had corresponded from prison with a woman he later married. Speck had been impressed with this at the time and Ziporyn wondered whether he was not entertaining similar thoughts for himself. Whatever the truth was, Speck was undoubtedly finding new preoccupations beyond the murders and the forthcoming trial.

The reports of the psychiatric panel were completed by the end of October. Despite an admonition from Judge Paschen not to reveal or discuss the contents of the reports, one of the psychiatrists on the panel let it be known a few days before the November 4 court hearing that the panel felt Richard Speck was mentally competent to stand trial. Gerald Getty stated that he would ask for the trial to be taken out of Chicago because press coverage had been prejudicial to the selection of an impartial jury. On November 2, Assistant

State's Attorney William Martin asked to see Dr. Ziporyn at the State's Attorney's office in the Criminal Court Building.

Seated at a long table in his conference room, Martin wasted no time with formalities. "Mr. Getty," he said, "is not going to press the issue of competency Friday, but we want to have the record show the psychiatric situation. As you no doubt know, the panel has found Speck to be competent."

"Yes, they left no doubt about that."

"Well, what I want to know from you is what *you* think of Speck's mental condition."

"I think he understands the nature of the charge, and he is capable of cooperating with counsel."

"Then you agree that he is competent to stand trial?"

"No question. Also, I think he knows the difference between right and wrong. However, I don't think he was capable of making the distinction at the time of the crime."

"So you think that he was insane at the time of the crime."

"Yes, I do."

"Your testimony would be, then, that he could not adhere to the right because of mental defect?"

"From my point of view, that's correct. However, I will concede that the term 'mental defect' is subject to semantic argument. For example, is a man who is rendered out of his mind by self-administered drugs to be described as the victim of a mental defect? It's a matter of interpretation."

Martin nodded. Referring to reports Ziporyn had made for the jail on his interviews with Speck—reports subsequently subpoenaed by both prosecution and defense—Martin said: "In your first report, you diagnosed Speck as having a brain syndrome due to head trauma. Do you still feel that way?"

Ziporyn said he did. Martin asked him whether he had discussed his views on Speck with defense counsel Getty.

"I had one talk with him," said Ziporyn. "I told him nothing beyond the fact that I considered myself neither for the prosecution nor for the defense. My records and opinions are available to both sides. If I am to testify I want to be a court's witness, subject to adverse examination by both sides."

"Fair enough." Martin paused, stared at the ceiling, seeming to calculate his next step. "There's a recent court decision holding that the prosecution must advise the defense of helpful testimony. Of course, it's in Getty's interest to know you feel that Speck was insane at the time of the crime. I'll notify him.

"Now, you do feel that Speck is competent to stand trial?"

"Yes, I do."

"Would you sign a statement to that effect?"

"I don't object—but why?"

"I have to consider possibilities. If Speck is adjudicated competent, the point might be raised on appeal that the psychiatrist who saw him the most was never asked for an opinion. The men on the panel saw Speck at most twice. Dr. Haines saw him three times. But you see Speck twice a week."

"That's true. And there's a good deal he tells me that he doesn't tell the others. He's a funny guy—do you know him?"

"Never talked to him. I see him in court, of course."

"Well, for example, I know he never told Cleckley about his head injuries. I'd be surprised if the panel could agree. What do *they* think is wrong with him?"

"Mostly, they feel he's a sociopath."

In response to Ziporyn's questions about the panel's reports, Martin admitted that the electroencephalogram and psychological tests on Speck were negative, that is, did not show evidence of organic or functional disorders indicating insanity. Ziporyn pointed out that while positive test results would have indicated the possible existence of mental disorder, negative results did not conclusively rule it out. It was generally agreed, Ziporyn said, that present EEG and psychological testing methods were not sensitive enough to account for all pathological conditions.

"Speck is no sociopath," Ziporyn stated flatly.

"Why do you say that?" asked Martin.

"Because a sociopath by definition is unlike Speck. First of all, the sociopath is self-seeking and looks for a way out of every tight spot. Now look at Speck. What's your prime case? Corazon Amurao and the fingerprints. There have been rumors that Speck dated one of the girls. He denies it vigorously. Would a sociopath deny it? Of course not. He would say: 'Of course, I dated one of those girls. Of course, I was in that house.' That would immediately weaken the fingerprint case. Why shouldn't a man's fingerprints be in a house he's visited? But Speck says he never was in that house before. If he was a sociopath, he'd grab at that point. The girl he's rumored to have dated can't deny his story—she's dead. He could even say Corazon Amurao was jealous or didn't like him—anything."

Martin nodded thoughtfully but made no comment.

Ziporyn continued. "I've also told Speck repeatedly that I feel his head injuries are significant, and I've explained their significance to him. Yet he doesn't bother to tell that to Cleckley. A sociopath would make a whole production out of this. And there are other things he's told me, things that are self-incriminating."

Ziporyn was thinking about the blood that Speck told him he had washed off his hands the morning after the murders were committed. Martin did not ask Ziporyn what he was referring to. The psychiatrist thought it better, therefore, to leave it until it was possibly brought up at the trial. (Ziporyn learned later that Martin already knew of Speck's having washed the blood from his hands.) "Another thing about sociopaths—they have few feelings of anxiety, guilt or remorse, yet Speck has all of these. And they don't have loyalties to other people. But Speck is very loyal to his family. I believe he sincerely loves them. But these are things I have learned in many talks with him. Nobody could learn this in one or two interviews."

Martin again nodded and said: "I'll have to think about it. It's a strong argument. Now, what about that statement?"

Ziporyn said he would sign one then and there. Martin had an assistant draw up a statement that Dr. Ziporyn considered Richard Speck competent to stand trial. Ziporyn signed it and Martin shook his hand amicably as he left.

Crimes and Peccadillos

ANOTHER DAY IN COURT, NOVEMBER 4, 1966. PUBLIC DEFENDER Getty was granted a continuance to November 16 to hear his motions for the furnishing of Chicago press and television film stories pertaining to Speck which might have a prejudicial influence on a jury. Getty was also asking for a change of venue because of the prejudicial atmosphere in Chicago. In preparation for the trial proper, the Federal Bureau of Investigation delivered to the court elaborate wooden models of the inside and outside of the house where the murders were committed. It was noted by the FBI that the models, measuring 5 feet wide, 3 feet high and 3 feet deep, had cost $5,609 to build.

After the court hearing, Ziporyn visited the maximum security block, where his first glimpse of Speck was a pair of stockinged feet poking through the bars. The psychiatrist was surprised to find his patient lolling on a chair, comfortably padded with blankets, his feet up on a horizontal bar, looking more like a cowboy recovering from a night in jail on a "drunk and disorderly" in Dodge City, Kansas, than a man in his sixteenth week of custody on a capital charge in Chicago, Illinois. Chairs are not customary cell furniture. Ziporyn had been conducting his interviews with both of them sitting on the bed. The chair in Speck's cell was as unusual as cell bars would be in a living room.

"Okay. Where did you get it?"

Speck grinned. "Warden gave it to me."

"Don't hand me that. Where did you get it?"

"I don't know why you don't believe me. The assistant warden does."

"Makowski?"

"Yeah. He was here yesterday. He asked me where I got it. I told him the warden gave it to me."

"Well, I just saw the warden. I told him you had stomach trouble and couldn't eat the food. He's going to be down here tomorrow to see you. What are you going to tell him?"

"Him? Tell him the assistant warden gave it to me."

They both laughed.

Formal prison regulations were strict. The attitude of prison officials to their observance was flexible and geared to any threat that a deviation might represent. In theory, Speck's possession of a razor blade was a horrendous thing that the public and its Chicago newspaper watchdogs would have been outraged to discover. In practice, given Speck's improved psychological condition and the positive use to which he put the blade in constructing his makeshift furniture, there was no harm done and the psychiatrist felt it was best to leave things as they were. Worse things, apparently worse, such as a drop of alcohol, might be sneaked in from time to time in other parts of the jail, but discipline did not suffer. The reality was more important than the theory. As for the chair—it was a luxury the jail officials would benignly let pass unnoticed.

Ziporyn noticed that the jigsaw of the Bangkok Floating Market was completed and lying on the floor on a spread-out magazine cover. "Did that give you any trouble?" he asked.

"Yeah. Almost pitched it out through the bars a couple of times."

"But you did a nice job. In a way, getting the pieces to fit right, that shows the carpenter in you."

Speck smiled appreciatively. He liked compliments. Over the many years of violence he had known, his ego had come close to total disintegration. If Speck was to acquire the ability to come to grips with his present situation, his self-awareness needed to be carefully restored. Empty flattery, like patting a child on the head, would have only aroused his old hostilities, but genuine approval of actual achievements, however slight, was of real value to him.

"Talking of carpenters," Ziporyn said, taking a newspaper from

UPI Photos

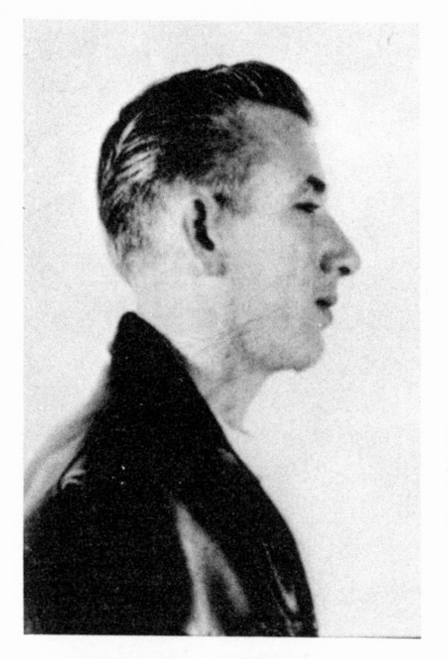

Police shots of Richard Speck, from the Dallas County Sheriff's Department. The pictures date from 1965 (*upper shots*) and 1961 (*lower*).

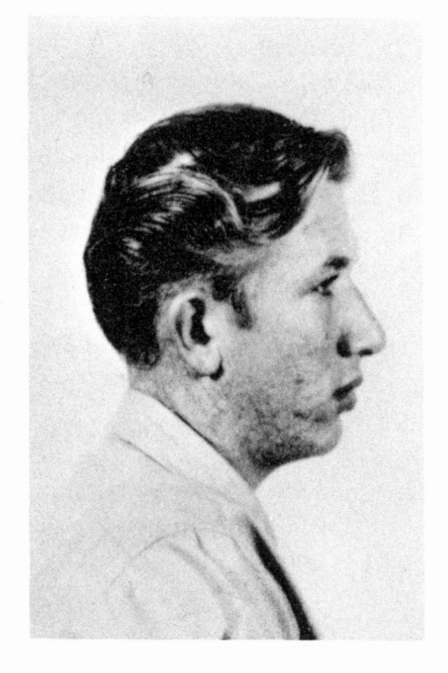

his brief case, "did you see this?" He showed Speck a picture of the wooden model of the nurses' house and told him how much it cost.

"Boy, they sure love me," said Speck.

Ziporyn went on to tell him he had had a meeting with the Assistant State's Attorney. "He wanted to know if I thought you could stand trial. I told him I feel you can."

"Okay." Speck did not seem to care one way or the other.

"The panel thinks you can, too. They think you're in great shape. They also think you're a sociopath."

"What's that?"

Once more, it was important to define words in the simplest terms. "Well, they think you killed those girls for kicks."

"Hell, they're crazier than I am."

Ziporyn reminded him that it was partly his own fault, since they did not all know about his head injuries. "Didn't you tell them?"

"Only if they asked me." Speck pouted. He was sulking again. "Some did, some didn't."

"And if they didn't ask you, you didn't tell them?"

"Yeah, that's about it."

"That's a big help. I know you figure it's hopeless, but it doesn't have to be."

"I want it to be. I want it over with. I'm ready for the chair."

"Don't give me that. You want to live as much as I do. You're just talking, to talk yourself into not being afraid."

"Nope. I'm tired of it. They drag me to court, take pictures, look at me like a freak. I'm tired of people telling me what to do. Yesterday I was out in the corridor and this guard stuck his key in my back and shoved me in the cell. I want out. If everybody didn't know my face I'd try to get out of here with Clancy." (Clancy's escape artistry was much respected and his success taken for granted.) "But where could I go?"

Speck was growing more surly and irritable. It was a familiar pattern of behavior following his days in court or his interviews with members of the psychiatric panel. He fiddled with his transistor radio. It would only play very softly. Ziporyn offered to get him some new batteries. Speck accepted the offer without any great show of enthusiasm.

Ziporyn tried to penetrate this fitfulness.

"You say you want out, but I thought you told me once before we couldn't chase you out of here."

"Well, I changed my mind." Speck's eyes darted around the cell and looked, almost furtively, at a card stuck to the wall. It was from one of his girl correspondents, Lois.

"I see," said Ziporyn. "Lois?"

Speck nodded. "I wrote to her."

His interests were certainly expanding beyond the confines of his past deeds and present imprisonment. "Did you remember who she is?" Ziporyn asked.

"Yeah, she's a friend of my niece."

Ziporyn accepted the answer skeptically, and Speck quickly changed the subject. He apologized for forgetting the customary cup of coffee. He explained that he had a bad headache and that the jail hospital would not give him any more pills for it. Ziporyn told the guard to telephone for the headache pills to be sent down, but the nurse on duty refused because "they're not ordered."

Ziporyn left the cell and went angrily to Warden Johnson's office to break down the bureaucratic barriers. With the warden's help, he obtained two Darvon capsules and returned to the maximum security block, handing them to Speck without a word.

Clancy commented from the next cell: "Lost your illusions about the world, Doc? I'll tell you why it happened: it's just vindictiveness. He's a bad boy, so the nurses don't want anything good for him. Let him suffer. That's why that guard stuck a key in him. Everybody wants a personal chance to play God."

Further comment was silenced by the sound of the television set, which Gambino had turned on full blast for the evening newscast about Speck's latest court hearing. The announcer was saying that the judge had agreed to Getty's request for newspaper, television and radio files on the Speck case, but they were to be furnished at the defendant's expense.

Speck roared with disgust: "At my expense!" He did not choose to distinguish between his own nonexistent resources and the funds being provided by the Public Defender's office. Once again, he became angry and impatient at the television treatment of his case. "Ain't there no other crimes they can talk about?" he shouted.

When the newscast was finished, Ziporyn stayed with Gambino to hear him reminisce about the "good old days"—the days when, as

Gambino recalled, Frankie Belcastro tried one holdup too many, making the mistake of confronting Dead-eye Dick, the peerless Chinese marksman. After talking with Gambino for about fifteen minutes, Ziporyn turned to leave the isolation tier. He had decided that it was futile to say anything more to Speck in his present state of irritability and walked past his cell without a word. Speck had been childish; there was no point in spoiling him. But as he was leaving, Speck stopped him.

"Say, Doc, I wanted to tell you something. You can read my brain like a book. That business about the chair. You were right. I am scared."

Speck was evidently reacting to Ziporyn's coldness. He was eager to win back his attention.

"I'm glad you understand," Ziporyn said. "And I think I understand, if it was you, why you did the murders."

"Why did I?"

If Speck was being more receptive now, it was worth Ziporyn's while briefly to reiterate his theory. He might be more ready to understand it.

"I think Gloria Davy reminded you of Shirley."

"But why did I kill the rest of them, then? I don't hate nobody—except Shirley."

"That's my point. And that's why you apparently treated Gloria differently."

"What do you mean, differently?"

"Well, you did things to her you didn't do to the others, or at least that's what it seems from the reports."

Speck reached through the bars and his powerful hands gripped Ziporyn by the shoulders. He stared wildly into the psychiatrist's eyes. All memory of their previous discussion of this issue had gone.

"What did I do to her? Tell me the truth. You've got to tell me the truth."

"Look, I won't lie to you. You see, she wasn't there at first. She came in later. You took her to the bedroom with the others. I don't know what happened. The police said they found some alcohol in her blood. Maybe she said something, maybe it was just that she looked like Shirley. Anyway, you took her downstairs, stripped her. . . ."

Ziporyn stopped. Speck's head slumped forward between his

shoulders. When he raised it again, his eyes were glistening with tears.

"Doc, I'd die eight times over if I could bring them back. I should have been shot the first time I hit my mother. And I choked Shirley once. I'm just no good."

He was close to breaking down completely. Ziporyn tried to reassure him. "Look, Richard, you didn't ask for any of the things in your life that made you do the things you've done. It's no more your fault than a cripple's limp is his fault."

Speck nodded and said nothing. Ziporyn patted him on the shoulder and turned to go. "Say, Doc," Speck added. "Take some money out of my account, will you, and buy me some of those paint things we was talking about."

The psychiatrist said he would bring him the paints at their next meeting. As he went out through the maximum security block's main door, he heard Speck calling: "Good-by, Doc, good-by." Again his moods had described a full circle, beginning with the playfulness over the stolen chair and ending with a cheerful parting. In between, he had been hostile and then deeply grateful when the psychiatrist had satisfied his need for dependency by obtaining the pills for him. The gratitude turned into a passive, clinging friendship when he found Ziporyn cold and aloof, paying more attention to Clancy and Gambino than to Speck. Speck remained a child, reacting only to the need of the moment, the only consistent thread being his sense of alienation.

A Question of Manhood

FINDING A PAINTING-BY-NUMBERS SET FOR SPECK WAS NOT THE straightforward task Ziporyn had expected. The psychiatrist walked into a downtown Chicago toy store and asked the saleswoman where the painting sets were located. Instead of merely directing him to where they were so that he could look for himself, she insisted on accompanying Ziporyn to the painting display to offer her help.

"How old is the child?" she asked cheerfully.

"Well, er, well—not too young," the psychiatrist stammered.

"Here's a lovely picture. How about this?" She pointed to a rustic scene of a cow.

"No, I don't think so. Do you have something more complicated? He's very good with his hands."

"I see." She looked pensive for a moment and then brightened. "I think I've got just the thing, then. What about this?" She took down one of the largest of the sets. It was a deep-pink study of a nude woman.

Ziporyn coughed and turned almost as pink. "No. I don't think that's quite appropriate. Perhaps you have something, um, non-personal?"

Finally, he settled for some bland seascapes.

Speck was enthusiastic about the painting set, particularly because the pictures came with a frame. He examined the painting equipment and asked some questions about paint thinners. He was eager to start. He promised that the first painting would be a gift for the psychiatrist.

"I'm sure glad you brought me these paints. I was running out of things to do. Even that puzzle's finished now."

Speck pointed to the jigsaw puzzle, which was now glued and mounted on the wall. Somehow Speck had managed to obtain the glue, probably from Clancy, but Ziporyn thought it better not to ask at this stage. He was satisfied that Speck's present frame of mind made it unlikely that he would use the glue for anything but sticking jigsaw puzzles together. The psychiatrist noted that, when the subject did crop up, Speck no longer recalled his "high" days on drugs with quite the same relish that he had once shown. They seemed to have lost their appeal.

Ziporyn asked whether he still bothered to read the Westerns, many of which lay apparently untouched in a corner. Speck admitted he had lost interest in them. "I'd still like some of those male magazines, though. Can you get me some more?"

This reminded the psychiatrist of something he had picked up in the drugstore on his way to the jail that day. He drew out of his briefcase a copy of *Detective Cases*—"All Stories True." The cover was a color version of the newspaper picture taken of Speck lying in a prison bed after his suicide attempt in July. Beside his expressionless face were pictures of the eight dead nurses surrounding a picture of the survivor, Corazon Amurao. The cover headline read: CHICAGO ATROCITY: THE NINE LIVES OF RICHARD SPECK. The magazine also promised stories on "Who Set Fire to Lucy?", "The Secret of the Strangled Nude" and "Sex-Slasher and the Texas Teens."

Speck took the magazine in both hands and stared at the pictures of the nine girls. "They sure were pretty," he muttered. Slowly he read aloud the headline of his story, stumbling over the word "atrocity" and adding a bitter emphasis to the "nine lives of Richard Speck." The endless television, radio, newspaper and magazine treatments of his case never ceased to provoke resentment at a new twist to the tired words describing him.

"What's 'atrocity'?" he asked. The psychiatrist provided a definition and Speck nodded, turning to the article on the inside pages. There were more pictures of the girls. He pointed to the picture of Gloria Davy. "There's the one that looks like Shirley." This was just another fact to him now, something to be taken for granted like his own name. He read through the account of the murders and his capture, taking issue with various points as he went along. He objected particularly strongly to suggestions by the Municipal Court psychiatrist, Dr. Edward Kelleher, that the murders were the work of a "sexual psychopath." "I ain't no sex-killer," said Speck, almost sulkily. For Speck now, guilt was not an issue; his guilt could be taken for granted, but his motivation was important to him. Kelleher was also quoted as saying the killer had evidently done a certain amount of planning for the crime. Again Speck was indignant. "I never knew anything about the place."

He came across a reference to one of his earlier encounters with the law, when he had been fined for throwing a brick through the window at a woman who had ordered him off her porch. "That! Want to know about that? That woman was a lezzie—know what I mean? Lesbian. And there was a queer living with her. I was with a bunch of other guys, and I wasn't the guy who threw the brick, anyway."

This was the second time Speck had talked of violence directed against homosexuals. He had attacked a homosexual in one of his many fights. Ziporyn suspected that, like many similar cases, particularly with his repeated signs of sexual insecurity in relation to his wife, Speck was reacting against a doubt about his own virility.

His other quibbles were trivial but no less heated in their expression. He was especially and inexplicably annoyed by the phrase "sentenced to three years in jail."

"It wasn't jail," he said. "It was prison."

When he finished the article, he turned back to the cover and stared at his picture. "You know something," he said, looking up at Ziporyn with almost a smile on his face. "The only thing I like about that picture is my eyes. They sure come out a nice blue." Vanity was his most resilient quality. It always seemed able to show up, with almost girlish naïveté, in the midst of his deepest irritations. He handed the magazine back to Ziporyn and added: "I used to read these things all the time. I sure never thought I'd be in one."

But Speck did not have a monopoly on the mass-murder headlines. In the second week of November, 1966, an eighteen-year-old high school senior, Robert Benjamin Smith, made five women, a three-year-old girl and a baby lie on the floor of a beauty parlor in

Mesa, Arizona, and proceeded to shoot all of them. Only the baby and one of the women survived. As usual with the murder cases he read about in the newspapers, Speck was incensed, but in this case the reasons became more personal. He did not get a chance to talk to Ziporyn about it for a few days after the report of the murders, because Ziporyn had taken a week off to visit relatives. When Ziporyn returned, Speck was eager to discuss the murders.

"Did you read about this guy in Arizona while you were away? What a guy! Said he wanted to be famous. Said he was inspired by the Chicago case. Boy, I'd like to take care of him. If I could have a last wish, it would be to kill him. That's all—just kill him and I'll die happy."

"Easy, there," said Ziporyn. "Don't you feel sorry for him?"

"Sorry for him? After what he did? Made those women lie in a circle and shot them? And there was little kids there, too. And he said if his parents came in, he'd kill them too. He deserves to die. He'll be famous, all right. There are lots of famous people in the cemetery."

"Yes. But Richard, don't you think that a person must have something wrong with him to do all that? Don't you think he must be sick?"

Speck stared at Ziporyn, wide-eyed with incredulous amazement. "Are you sure you read about this in Detroit? Listen." He spoke slowly, deliberately, as if the psychiatrist were a child who needed to have some simple facts drummed into his head. "He . . . made . . . them . . . lie . . . in . . . a . . . circle . . . and . . . he . . . shot . . . them." Speck punctuated his anger with a typical non sequitur: "He said he did it to be famous. Well, George Washington is famous—he's dead, too."

Ziporyn's experience as a psychiatrist made him familiar with the frustrating reality that a patient could appear to understand and even agree with a line of reasoning painstakingly explained, but would not necessarily understand the same reasoning at a later time. Once more Ziporyn explained that Speck could expect many, many more murder cases like his own and that the important thing was not to concentrate so much on the horror of what happened as on why it happened.

"That's why we're talking—to learn as much as we can about what makes you tick—maybe it will prevent a killing some day."

"Yeah—except that now it's the other way around—now I've got thirteen deaths on my conscience." Speck had once accused himself of taking sixteen lives—the nurses plus the members of his family, "killed" by shame and worry. Now he combined the eight nurses with the five persons murdered in Arizona to augment his guilt this time to thirteen deaths.

"Nonsense," said Ziporyn. "You can't blame yourself for every murder in the country."

"If he hadn't read about me. . . ."

"He'd still be a sick kid, so forget about him."

Speck sighed deeply, suddenly tired. His anger was an exertion. "Yeah, I've got my own problems. I go back to court this week, don't I? I wish it was over. It's all hopeless. If I don't get the chair, I'll get 480 years or whatever it is."

"Doesn't mean a thing, how many hundreds. In Illinois you automatically come up for parole after twenty years."

"That's a big help. In twenty years my mother and half my sisters will be dead. I won't have anybody."

"You'll have your daughter."

"I won't; that's all over. Out of prison at forty-five—an old man!"

"Don't be so flip about that. I'm nearly forty-five and I don't think it's all over."

Speck grinned and shook his head. He could never accept a comparison between himself and the psychiatrist. Ziporyn, Speck always insisted, was an educated man; his life meant something. But he, Speck, was no good. No good at twenty-five, and another twenty years were not going to improve things. Ziporyn tried to persuade him of the possibilities of a life at forty-five. He showed him a photograph of his two-year-old son. Speck was enthusiastic and asked to see more. The psychiatrist took out other pictures of his family—his wife, his other son and daughter. Speck showed a great interest in each photograph. The whole idea of family life brought forth in him a warmth and fondness that was quite unlike any of his reactions to other subjects. Ziporyn doubted if this side of Speck had been revealed to any of the psychiatrists on the court panel who chose to characterize him as a sociopath. The pictures reminded Speck of his own family.

"I saw my sister Friday. She says my mom is sick—had a stroke after all this happened. See, I'm just no good—ruined my whole family."

Again Ziporyn fought his patient's backward-looking preoccupations. "You can't brood about the past. You've got to live and plan for the future. You *might* get out in twenty or twenty-five years. You *might* remarry. You *might* have more children."

"No, I won't."

"How do you know?"

"I won't."

"Why not?"

"Because I can't."

Speck seemed to have no perspective on the relative importance of the things he chose to tell Ziporyn. His sudden revelation, true or false, that he could not have children was made as nonchalantly as a comment about last night's television program. However many times Ziporyn had told him of the importance of telling the panel psychiatrists about his head injuries, Speck had gone his own casual way and talked or remained silent as the mood took him. Such naiveté was too consistent and too often self-damaging to be the result of guile and calculation.

"Who says you can't have children?" Ziporyn asked.

"The doctor told me. I had an infection."

"Clap?"

"Worse."

"Syphilis?"

"Soft chancre syph. I let it go about a month—couldn't afford a doctor. But it got to really hurting. I told my mom. She gave the money to me. I remember—it was $12 a shot. And local treatments, they hurt like hell."

"But what makes you think you can't have kids?"

"The doctor said it, and I believe him. After all, long as I was with Shirley we never had any kids."

Speck explained that he was twenty when it happened, about four and a half years ago. Ziporyn was puzzled.

"But what about your daughter, Robbie—isn't she four?"

"Yeah, well, you see Shirley was carrying her then."

The psychiatrist still did not understand how Speck's post-syphilitic sterility fitted in with the birth of Robbie. He asked Speck to explain further. Speck said nothing for perhaps ten seconds, just stared at the floor between his legs, then shrugged his shoulders and said with a sigh: "Well, you might as well know it—Robbie isn't mine. I just married Shirley to give the baby a name."

Ziporyn did not accept the entire story at its face value.* Speck was apparently denying his fatherhood in a desperate effort to protect Robbie, to save her from the shame of connection with him.

"Have you had any sperm studies since that time—to find out if you really are sterile?"

"No. I'm finished. I know that much. That girl really fixed me."

"Do you know the girl with whom it happened?"

"Never forget her. Sure would like to get back at her. She was Chinese or Japanese—some kind of Oriental, know what I mean?"

Extending the hypothesis of what might have happened on the night of the nurses' murders, it was possible in the turbulence of Richard Speck's mind that the presence of the Filipino girls reminded him of a previous encounter with an "Oriental." This could have fanned the flames of a rage already kindled by the sight of a girl resembling his wife. Speck's suggestibility in his calmest moments was a marked characteristic. At a time of extreme disturbance it could be impossible to resist.

* Speck's story seemed to be fabrication. His wife later said that the child was indeed Speck's daughter.

"Nothing Like a Dame"

DEFENSE COUNCIL GETTY WAS EAGER TO KEEP OUT OF COURT THE psychiatric discussion of Speck's mental competency to stand trial once it was known that the court panel had reached a positive decision. Evidently, he did not want the arguments surrounding his client's mental condition to be aired before the trial, since they might prejudice potential jurors against any insanity plea he might choose to make. However, at the hearing held on November 16, Judge Paschen overruled Getty's objection to the court's fixing November 28 as the date for the hearing on the question of competency. "I would be remiss in my duty," said the judge, "if I did not make the competency issue a part of the court record in this case."

Getty introduced two other petitions on the basis of alleged prejudices created by press reports of the case. He asked that the murder indictments against Speck be considered legally unsound because the twenty-three grand jurors who voted the indictments were prejudiced against Speck and that the trial be moved out of Cook County because it was impossible there to obtain an impartial jury. With newspaper clippings, radio transcripts and television film clips as his evidence, Getty said: "No person could be devoid of malice and hatred and ill will against this defendant after reading or hearing this material. We would have no way of knowing that the prejudicial, biased, hearsay data had been washed or discarded from the minds of prospective jurors. I submit that the press has disclosed everything in this case the Warren Commission deplored in news reports on the assassination of John F. Kennedy."

Judge Paschen denied the petition against the indictments, but deferred a decision on the petition for a change of venue until the hearing set for the competency question.

Two days later, Ziporyn found Speck in a cheerful mood. Any irritating effects from the latest court appearance had by now worn off. He was particularly pleased with the turpentine the psychiatrist had brought him. Speck had complained the last time that his paint brushes were clogging up. Now, he said, he could make more progress.

With a typical switch in subjects he suddenly asked: "Have you seen Getty lately? He asked me about you when I was in court. He wanted to know what you thought about me."

"What did you tell him?"

"I said you thought I was drunk when this all happened."

" 'Drunk' is only part of it. But I wonder why Getty doesn't ask me these questions himself."

Speck asked Ziporyn to tell Getty not to press his petition for a change of venue.

"Tell him I don't want to go nowhere else."

The newspapers always described Speck as a "drifter," a "loner," "shiftless." Unable to peg him to a particular place or job, they made the point that he had never found it possible to stay put. It was obvious to Ziporyn that Speck did not find this mobility especially appealing. His wistful affection for family life, like the house-proud care with which he looked after his cell, bespoke a desire for stability, something denied him since his earliest childhood at the death of his father and the subsequent move from Illinois to Texas. His cell offered him reassuring familiarity, and a change would disrupt the small amount of tranquility he had been able to find there. Ziporyn preferred for the time being to emphasize the legal advantages of a change of venue.

"Getty wants to protect your rights, Richard. He feels you can't get a fair trial in this county, so he wants you somewhere else. It's a good legal move."

"I don't care about that—and I'm not worried about the trial—I'm ready to take my medicine."

Speck's changes of attitude—bravado or fear—to his possible punishment had by now become mere tokens to reinforce the particular line of argument he happened to be following at the time.

"Are you still so sure you're guilty?" Ziporyn asked.

Speck exploded with a shout, "Hell!" Ziporyn quieted him down with a gesture of the hand and said: "I know, Richard, I know. We've been through all that before—but there is one thing that bothers me. I can't understand how you could stab all those girls and not be covered with blood."

"I wasn't. I went down to the bar the next day in my same clothes—there wasn't any blood."

"That's what I mean. Did you ever see anyone get stabbed?" Ziporyn saw immediately that this was a superfluous question, an impression Speck quickly confirmed. "Yeah. Got stabbed myself." He pulled up his shirt to show a scar on the upper left side of his chest. "I was with a bunch of the boys in a joint in Texas, and there was some talk, know what I mean? This guy jumped me—stuck me right there. I was bloody all over."

"Okay. So how come you weren't bloody all over on the morning after the murders?"

"I don't know."

They were interrupted by the sound of the television in Gambino's cell. The news announcer was saying that the issue in a possible retrial for Jack Ruby was whether he had killed Lee Harvey Oswald "without malice." Ziporyn asked Speck whether he understood what this meant. Speck shook his head, and the psychiatrist explained the basic importance of premeditation in the legal view of murder.

"I sure didn't plan it, I'll tell you that. You know, I sit here sometimes and I still can't believe that I'm a murderer. Me! I just can't believe it. I mean, I've never really been in trouble. In court, they said thirty-six arrests, but most of that was just drunk and disorderly or juvenile stuff. I've only been in jail three times."

Speck sighed and Ziporyn suppressed a smile at the thought of how the Chicago public would have received the statement that Speck had "never really been in trouble."

"You know what I wish?" Speck continued. "I wish I had gone back to Texas and told the police about that other case I was mixed up in, told them: 'It was my car that the stolen goods were in. Lock me up.' Then I wouldn't be in this mess. Now I'm a 'mass-murderer.' I didn't even know what 'mass' meant until I looked it up in that dictionary you gave me."

"Do you know now?"

"Yeah, it means a lot of people—like massacre, I guess. And I'm a mass-killer, but I still can't believe it. Of course, I've been violent when I was drunk. Once I saw Shirley in a car with a guy. I was drinking but I still knew what I was doing. I ran around that car with a knife, trying to get that guy, but I couldn't. A couple of days later I saw him again and I just walked up to him and said, 'Do me a favor—don't mess around with my wife.' But I would have killed him when I was drinking."

Ziporyn suggested that Shirley might have been equally to blame in the failure of their marriage. Speck agreed and nodded vigorously.

"Yeah, that's true. That's what my mother said. She told me to get rid of her."

The temptation for the psychiatrist to use the time-honored admonition: "You should have listened to your mother" was great, but he managed to resist it. Instead, he returned to a matter that had been bothering him, the question of Speck's fatherhood. "That stuff you told me about Robbie the other day," said Ziporyn. "Were you pulling my leg? I thought maybe you were trying to protect her."

Speck stared unflinchingly into Ziporyn's eyes for a full minute and then slowly answered: "May God strike me off this chair if I'm lying."

"Okay. But I have a feeling that you can be very protective."

It was not clear that Speck saw the relation of this to what he had said about not being Robbie's father, but it did start off a train of thought.

"Well," he said, "I do stick with my buddies. I remember one time about five years ago, me and some guys got into a disorderly charge in McKinney, Texas. The judge fined us $25, but he let the McKinney guys we were fighting with go. I was so mad, I told the judge right there in court what I thought of him. He added $100 to my fine. They took us to jail to work it out. I had the money; I could have paid my fine—but I didn't want to leave the boys."

Ziporyn saw this as a useful opportunity to bolster up Speck's still fragile self-confidence. "What you've told me is very interesting," the psychiatrist said. "Everybody thinks you're some kind of monster, but look at all your good points. You're loyal to your friends, you're generous. You're devoted to your family. You're skillful with your hands, you have a sense of humor—you've got a lot of things going for you. Considering all the bad things you've done in your life, you are in many ways a very likeable guy."

While Ziporyn was speaking, Speck had bowed his head. When he raised it again, his eyes were filled with tears. Ziporyn saw in that moment that Speck had perhaps never before been confronted with his good qualities.

Almost in a whisper, he said: "Thanks, Doc. You don't know how I feel. I was in court and I heard somebody say: 'Here comes that murderer.' I felt that small." He held his forefinger and thumb an inch apart.

Ziporyn patted his shoulder and rose to leave. He noticed that an "Exit" sign that Speck had mockingly tacked up over the door was now covered by a pin-up girl in bra and panties. Underneath, the prisoner had written the caption "Miss Death Row, U.S.A."

Speck grinned as he saw Ziporyn looking at the picture and said, "Brightens up the place."

"Nothing like a dame," Ziporyn agreed.

"You know," said Speck. "That Dr. Haines, he really makes me mad."

Ziporyn wondered what could have suddenly reminded him of his interview with the panel of psychiatrists. "Why?"

"Questions he asked me. Like, did I ever mess with boys? Hell, I'm not that way at all."

Speck was still eager to insist on his masculinity. The discussion of the pin-up on the wall—an outward symbol of manliness for him—evidently reminded Speck of Dr. Haines' suggestion that he might be something less than masculine.

Ziporyn was aware that Speck had been showing many signs of latent homosexuality—positively, in his vanity and his fussiness around the cell, and negatively, in his hostility toward women, his strong reaction against "queers" and his resentment at the questions of Dr. Haines. In his response to these questions he was showing what is psychiatrically known as reaction-formation: suspecting a dangerous element in his personality (homosexuality, for Speck), a person goes to the opposite extreme in his behavior to prove that the suspicion is false. Ziporyn knew that many of his colleagues would consider this aspect of his patient of primary importance. Ziporyn, however, saw these manifestations of homosexuality as a definite component of Speck's hostility toward women, but by no means the basic problem. The roots of this latent homosexuality could only be guessed at, since so little had been revealed about Speck's earliest years. Of his relationship with his father, it was known only that it had been very close. His father died when Richard was six, and there is no indication of how strong a figure he had been. But it was also apparent that Speck had been extremely close to his sister Carolyn and his mother. Whatever contributed to his latent homosexuality in his early, Oedipal years may have been intensified with the arrival of his hated stepfather, leaving Speck without a strong male figure to identify with in his adolescence.

As if to give comic emphasis to Speck's current preoccupation with things masculine, Clancy stopped Ziporyn on the way out and said: "You know that Speck, he was after me the other day. You know what he said?" Clancy launched into a perfect imitation of Speck's broad Texan drawl. " 'Clancy,' he told me, 'Ah'll bet you're a helluva lady's man when you're out of here—take 'em to football games and thuh opeera, really show 'em a big ole tahm.' "

Sitting on his bed, Speck was doubling up with uncontrollable laughter.

A Broken Toy

IN SPITE OF THE PILLS HE WAS GETTING REGULARLY, SPECK'S HEADaches were growing worse and more frequent and he was sleeping more to overcome them, but in vain. The cell was in darkness and Speck was sleeping when Ziporyn visited him in the afternoon of November 21. A large piece of cardboard on his chair instructed: "Wake me when you come, Docter [sic]." As Ziporyn pushed the door open, Speck sat up and swung his legs off the bed. He walked silently across the cell to prepare the coffee. The psychiatrist handed him a sandwich he had brought. Speck accepted it without a word. The prisoner went over to the sink and dampened his hair to slick it back neatly with his long fingers before turning on the cell light. Ziporyn asked him how he felt, and after a couple of noncommittal answers they lapsed into silence again.

After five minutes, Speck turned to Ziporyn and said: "I'm sorry I'm not talking. I woke up with a terrible headache."

Ziporyn nodded but said nothing. At least Speck had improved to the point of recognizing the connection between his headaches and sullen moods.

"Boy," he went on. "I have them all the time now, but I haven't had one like this since I had sunstroke in prison."

"Since you had what?"

"Sunstroke. I got it at the prison farm in Texas, when I was waiting to be released."

"Richard, I've changed my mind about you. You're nuttier than a fruitcake. Frequently I've told you that anything related to your physical health, and particularly your head, is important. Here you've a major condition affecting your head and you've never bothered to mention it. Why didn't you tell me?"

"Well, you never. . . ."

"I know, I know. I never asked you. That's what I mean. What a kook!"

Speck was grinning bashfully. He saw the point—not that he was going to do anything positive about it. Ziporyn walked around the cell, which was beginning to look like a miniature art studio. On the radiator three paintings were drying. One, of a swan, was almost completed and two seascapes were still in their early stages. The paints had given Speck renewed incentive for his love of signs and slogans. The latest, on the big lock of the cell door, was: RICHARD SPECK, BORN: DEC. 6, 1941, DIED: ?

Ziporyn thought it best to drop the subject of the sunstroke. Speck understood the issue, but he seemed no more willing to start helping himself now than he had been in the beginning. They discussed his painting progress and Speck explained that he was giving it all his time now. He no longer bothered with the Westerns.

One of Speck's regular guards, Sergeant Campbell, walked into the cell. He was an earnest but amiable type, always eager to start a discussion. He looked around the cell, showing great interest in the paintings but making no comment. Suddenly he turned to Ziporyn and said: "Say, what do you think about the Bavarian elections—all those neo-Nazis doing so well?"

Before Ziporyn could reply, Speck intervened indignantly. "Hey! What's the big idea? The Doc didn't come here to talk politics." Speck had become very possessive, often showing resentment if Ziporyn seemed to spend too much time with Gambino or Clancy. The rapport that the psychiatrist had sought to establish and maintain had grown strong roots.

The sergeant took the hint. He smiled and left the cell. Waiting till the door had clanged shut behind the guard, Speck said in a confidential tone: "I heard from that Lois—she wasn't my sister's friend, like I thought." (He had originally said, unconvincingly, that she was a friend of his sister's daughter, but the distinction was not worth pursuing. He seemed to like the air of mystery surrounding her.)

"Who is she, then?"

"I don't know—but she sent a picture." Speck shouted over to Gambino's cell. "Hey, Tony, let's have your girl friend's picture." He winked at Ziporyn. "I gave the photo to Tony." The vicarious attachments that prison inmates form, often with girls they have never met, are cherished but easily transferred. Speck's gift to Gambino was at once a gesture of simple generosity and also a means of distancing himself from even the flimsiest involvement with a woman. Lois's picture was passed through the bars to Speck, who handed it with a sheepish grin to Ziporyn. The grin burst into a roar of laughter as Speck saw the less than appreciative expression on the psychiatrist's face.

"Hey, Tony, you ought to see the Doc's face. I don't think he likes your girl too much."

Lois was firmly Gambino's property now, and Speck was happy to add scorn to his own disengagement. The gaiety was short-lived as new headache pangs made him wrinkle up his face in pain.

Ziporyn said he had intended to visit Speck's mother in Dallas, as Speck had once asked him, but decided not to because of her illness. Speck nodded.

"Yeah, they say she had a stroke or a nervous breakdown." But he looked disappointed that Ziporyn had decided against the visit.

"Do you still want me to see her?" the psychiatrist asked.

"I do. She must think I just butchered a bunch of people. You know how she must feel. You should go and talk to her."

Ziporyn said he would discuss it with Speck's sister, Mrs. Martha Thornton. Speck tried a smile of thanks, but a headache pain cut it short like a slap.

Speck's whimsy expressed itself in constant experiments with his cell. On November 25, three days before his competency hearing, the cell was bathed in a weird, red glow. It was scarcely possible to make out the prisoner lying on his back on the bed. As Ziporyn walked toward the cell, Clancy called out: "You better have a long talk with Speck today—he's confused about his sexual identity."

Speck swung himself off the bed as the psychiatrist entered the cell. Nodding toward the ceiling, where he had painted the light bulb red, Speck said: "Looks like a whore's place, doesn't it?"

"A real red light," Ziporyn commented.

"It's more a titty pink," said Speck, as he reached up to unscrew the bulb and replace it with an ordinary light. "Oh, and there's a new note from Lois." He gave it to Ziporyn to read. She told Speck she wanted to visit him and would do so if he agreed.

"When's she coming?" Ziporyn asked.

"You have to be joking. I wouldn't have her here. You saw her picture, didn't you? I wouldn't want to be associated with anyone that homely. If I'm drunk that's different—but not sober."

His vanity persisted. Reputation remained something intimately personal for him, totally divorced from the wider notoriety he had gained from the murders. He had been worried once before about the possible impact in court of "that ugly broad" testifying that she had been in his company before the murders took place, and now, within the confines of the maximum security block of Cook County Jail, he was concerned that his reputation as a man of discriminating tastes should not suffer from his association with the less than glamorous Lois.

Together with the ritual cup of coffee, Speck proudly presented Ziporyn with one of his three paintings, a swan floating serenely on a river, meticulously executed, with a neat monogram painted in white in one corner, "R.S. 66." Speck was pleased with the compliment Ziporyn paid him, and then, almost as if seeking some kind of reward, said with a pout: "Say, you know that radio? I broke it. I had it hanging on the bars here and I reached out to poke the guard while he was watching TV—and I hit it and it fell on the ground. I was sick. Do you suppose you could get me another one?"

The account of the accident and the request were delivered in a breathless, childlike rush of words, which he resumed after Ziporyn agreed to get a new radio. "See, I was thinking, if you could get me another one, I'd tape it to the wall over there. Then I'd run the wire and speaker from this one here to my bed. That way, I wouldn't knock it down again. Okay?" He searched Ziporyn's eyes for some sign that he had justified the new purchase. Ziporyn nodded. "Thanks, Doc." And then, for good measure, "Really made me sick, losing that. I really miss it."

They were interrupted by Gambino, who shouted: "Hey, Spike, here's your magazine." Speck grinned as he reached out through the bars to take back one of his men's magazines from Gambino's outstretched hand. "See, Doc, that's what the boys call me—Spike." He obviously liked his new nickname, another token of acceptance and affection, from the source that mattered most to him—his peers.

He harked back to the radio once more. "Doc, you don't have to work tomorrow, do you? You don't think by any chance you could bring it tomorrow? I really was sick when I broke it."

Ziporyn decided to draw a firm line and told him he would have to wait till after the weekend. Seeking affection was one thing; exploiting it would be bad for the progress of their talks.

Sergeant Campbell came into the cell and asked if he could join them for coffee. Speck, master of his domain, consented but insisted that the guard use a glass other than the one he reserved for Ziporyn. "This glass is the Doc's. I'd put his name on it, except I can't spell it." While Campbell was preparing his coffee, Speck and Ziporyn looked through a magazine article about the need for stricter gun laws. The article even mentioned Speck and the fact that he had been found at one point after the murders waving a gun around in a hotel room. They talked about guns and violence in general, and the particular role of alcohol in Speck's life.

"Tell me," Ziporyn asked. "You've been involved in burglaries. Do you think you have the guts to stick up a place cold sober?"

"You know something, I'd be too chicken. I asked Clancy about it once. He said: 'Hell, if they get in my way I'd blast them.' But once I needed some money and I had a .22. I knew a liquor store I thought I'd try and rob. I had a six-pack of beer in the car and drank three cans, but I was sober. Beer doesn't bother me. I was nowhere near drunk. Anyway, I took the gun, got out and I was halfway to the door—stone cold sober, like you said—and I suddenly got the funniest feeling—shot right through my body."

"Butterflies?" suggested Campbell, who was listening intently.

"No, it was like knife pains through my chest. I was shaking. I went to my mother, borrowed $20 and I was still shaking. That's when I got drunk."

The endless anecdotes of Speck's past crimes always showed him activated by the intoxication of alcohol or drugs. This was the first indication of the converse, that even when his mind was made up to commit a crime, he might be immobilized by the fact that he was not drunk.

"How much does it take to get you drunk?" Campbell asked.

"Like I say, beer doesn't bother me, but half a pint of whisky and I'm out."

"What about red-dogs?" Campbell continued.

"You mean red-birds," said Speck with the slightly scornful tone of an expert dealing with the uninitiated.

"Yes, red-birds. How about them?"

"Two makes me high."

"Did you ever mix them—red-birds and whisky?" Campbell asked.

Speck nodded and a grim smile flickered in his eyes. Campbell, solemn as ever, persisted in his interrogation. "What happened?"

"Eight murders and the electric chair."

Speck delivered the line deadpan and gave Ziporyn a quick, wry look. They understood, he seemed to say, but what could one expect of an outsider like this guard? The prisoner turned on the guard in mild exasperation.

"Listen, Sergeant. Who's the psychiatrist around here—you or him? Get out of here. Can't you see we're busy?"

Ziporyn was pleased to see that Speck was now understanding without difficulty the role that alcohol played in his actions. The psychiatrist emphasized the point again, saying that intoxication made Speck readily capable of irresponsible and often violent action. Speck agreed and contributed as evidence another from his endless fund of brawling incidents.

"Yeah. Once I pounded hell out of a real good friend. He had false teeth. I knocked them out. Then, when I came to—I'd been really smashed at the time—I took him home and washed the blood off of him. I should have quit drinking when I hit my mother."

Clancy passed by the cell on his way to fetch his supper and glanced in at Ziporyn and Speck talking together. "Doc, are you still sitting with that lunatic? You got guts, Doc, real heart."

"I'm not afraid of Richard," Ziporyn replied, rising to leave. "He's sober now."

Speck laughed appreciatively. But something else was uppermost in his mind as Ziporyn went out.

"Don't forget the radio," he said.

The Panel Delivers a Judgment

THE COURT HEARING ON RICHARD SPECK'S COMPETENCY TO STAND trial began on Monday, November 28, with the selection of a jury and was continued the next day to hear the psychiatrists' testimony. Speck had not yet returned from Monday's court session when Ziporyn arrived in the maximum security block. The psychiatrist took the opportunity to discuss Speck with Clancy, a man who Ziporyn felt was unusually perceptive about the prison staff and his fellow inmates; someone, moreover, who spent twenty-four hours a day in close contact with Speck (week by week Speck had drawn closer to Clancy as Gambino remained remote, often aggressive). It was Clancy who launched the conversation.

"You'd better have a talk with your boy. He's getting real hostile."

"Must be tension about the hearing. What did he do?"

"Nothing to us, but he really goes after the guards. You know," said Clancy in his most knowing and confidential manner, "I'm not a psychiatrist, but in my opinion, he's not all there. He's in a world of his own. I can't quite put my finger on it. He knows what's going on, and I think in some ways he's more intelligent than quite a lot of people, but he's just odd. I can't explain it in words, but he just doesn't always react right."

"That's the brain damage," Ziporyn explained. "He's in contact, he's coherent, he's oriented, he knows reality and he can reason correctly—but he can't always fully control himself. When he's sober he hangs on pretty well, but every now and then, he does something bizarre—an impulse from his unconscious rather than from his reason—and that's what has been striking you. A monster from the id appears. But when he's sober, he shoves the monster back into the cage without too much trouble, which is why here in jail the incidents are only short-lived, but enough to be noticed. On the other hand, when he drinks, the control is gone—the wild beast is loose."

"Some beast," said Clancy.

"We all have it. But we're not brain-damaged, so we can control it. The defect in the cases of brain damage is in the brake mechanism."

In discussing the case with Clancy, Ziporyn was confident that he would appreciate more of the intricacies of the psychiatric process than would his patient, Richard Speck. Clancy was a thoughtful, literate man. He preferred the translated works of French poet François Villon to Westerns and men's magazines.

Speck arrived back from court and Ziporyn followed him into his cell. Speck was overjoyed when the psychiatrist handed him the new radio he had asked for. He turned it on and off, checked the tone and examined the inside. He beamed with delight at the sounds of his favorite country-and-western music. Then he switched it off and turned to Ziporyn.

"Gee, thanks, Doc. It's like Christmas. Man, this is a beauty. Did your wife like the picture I gave you?"

"Yes, she did."

"Did she know I did it? What did she say?"

"She says you have talent, but she thinks you ought to try freehand work."

Speck's eyes gleamed briefly and then closed tight for a second as his headache returned. He asked the sergeant to get him some pills. "I had terrible headaches all weekend," he told Ziporyn. "Couldn't get any pills on Sunday and I wound up fighting with the guards." The pattern was obvious by now and needed no comment from Ziporyn. Speck himself was making the connection.

Speck handed Ziporyn a piece of apple pie he had bought especially for him—"Figured you'd be hungry"—and went on to talk about the day he had spent with his attorney, Gerald Getty.

"I told Getty about the pictures. He said you'll make an artist out of me before you're through. Then he asked me who has seen me the most and I told him you had. He wanted to know why I couldn't be crazy. I said I was sorry, but I'm not. Then he wanted to know why I'm always joking and laughing. I told him that was just the outside. If I was to act the way I feel inside, I'd go crazy. I'm all cracked up inside."

Ziporyn was interested to see Speck examining his motivations and emotions. "Did you tell Getty all this?" the psychiatrist asked.

"Yeah. He said that I acted different at Bridewell. Hell, I was all weak from loss of blood then, scared of everybody. I pulled myself together here. But if I didn't kid around, I'd explode."

Ziporyn said he would explain all this to Getty at the meeting he had planned with him.

Speck continued: "Getty asked me if I'd settle for fifteen to twenty-five years. I told him I could do that on my head. But he must have been joking—I'll never see the street again. I'll tell you this. I hope I can go to a nut house."

"Why?"

"I'd never make it in prison, Doc. Those guys would ride me, call me a woman-killer and I couldn't take it. I'd fight back. They'd get me."

This is a common fear of prisoners involved in crimes like the one Speck was charged with. There are some crimes that even the most hardened criminal will not countenance. For Speck, violence was the rule of life, not the exception. He had no reason to expect anything else. In his fear of being hurt by the other prisoners there was no trace of resentment. Fatalistically, he saw it as his inevitable deserts. It was not likely to impress Speck, as it did Ziporyn, that a man like Clancy, who was revolted by the horror of the murders of which Speck was accused, could still develop a real affection and concern for him.

Speck added: "Getty said he'd never had a client go to the chair. I told him I was sorry to spoil his record."

This kind of remark, once fraught with agonizing despair, was now just an easy quip. Speck turned eagerly back to his new radio. Opening the back, he noted that it took flashlight batteries rather than the 9-volt batteries he had saved from the old radio. He offered them to Ziporyn. "Take these for your kids. They're still good." Ziporyn accepted them with thanks and left Speck listening seraphically to an accordion version of "Tennessee Waltz."

The competency hearings which continued November 29 and 30 had a foregone conclusion. Gerald Getty assumed that his client would be found competent to stand trial. He therefore concentrated on a change of venue for the trial (which he obtained), and sought to avoid detailed examination of the competency issue. But William Martin, Assistant State's Attorney, with Judge Herbert Paschen's support, insisted on having members of the psychiatric panel heard in open court and their conclusions read into the court record. The report stated:

> The panel is in unanimous agreement that Richard Speck is competent to stand trial at this time. Directed to attempt to ascertain the mental status of Richard Speck on July 13 and 14, 1966, the panel is of the further opinion that Richard Speck was responsible for his behavior as of July 13 and 14, 1966.
>
> The diagnosis established by the panel in accordance with the American Psychiatric Association nosological classification [systematic classification of disease] is sociopathic personality, anti-social behavior, with alcoholism. These opinions are in accordance with legislative standards established by Illinois statutes.

The signatures to the report—Roy R. Grinker, director of the Institute for Psychosomatic and Psychiatric Research at Chicago's Michael Reese Hospital; Groves B. Smith, psychiatric consultant for the Illinois State Penitentiary at Menard; Edward J. Kelleher, Chicago Municipal Court psychiatrist; Hervey M. Cleckley, Professor of Psychiatry at the Medical College of Georgia; William J. Norcross, Speck's attending physician at Cook County Hospital; and Vladimir G. Urse, superintendent of the Cook County Hospital mental health clinic—represented an impressive professional line-up against Dr. Marvin Ziporyn's contention that Speck was not a sociopath. Ziporyn knew the panel had the backing of two other leading Chicago psychiatrists—Dr. William H. Haines of Cook County Hospital and Dr. Roland P. Mackay, neurologist at the Wesley Memorial Hospital—and other neurological experts consulted in the course of the examinations.

Ziporyn considered Speck fully competent to stand trial. As to his mental status at the time of the murders, to describe Speck as "responsible for his behavior" suggested that he was aware of his acts. Ziporyn had no reason to believe this until it could be demonstrated that Speck's "blackout" was, as many of the panel psychiatrists believed, a feigned amnesia. In four months of intensive questioning since their first meeting, on July 29, Speck had given Ziporyn no sign that his inability to remember the events in the nurses' home was feigned, nor had he shown the guile of a man successfully concealing his responsibility for his part in those events.

However, these were legal points relevant to the trial of Richard Speck, in answer to the court's mandate. What concerned the psychiatrist more directly was the panel's diagnosis of Speck's mental status: "sociopathic personality, anti-social behavior, with alcoholism." Ziporyn turned for his text to *Modern Clinical Psychiatry* by Noyes and Kalb. On the subject of Anti-Social Personality, it states: "Individuals without the capacity to form significant attachments or loyalties to others, to groups, to codes of living. They are callous, convince themselves that their actions are reasonable and warranted. They have no critical awareness of their own behavior. They show few feelings of anxiety, guilt or remorse. They are cynical, devoid of a sense of honor or shame. They feel pride in their unlawful accomplishments and consider punishment as an expression of injustice."

From their limited access to Speck, scarcely more than ten interviews in all, none of the panel members had the opportunity to gain more than a fleeting, shallow impression of Speck's innermost thoughts. As Speck later told Ziporyn, he had been selective in his choice of what to reveal or conceal in his conversations with the panel psychiatrists. He even concealed information which might have helped; for example, withholding pertintent facts about his head injuries from some members of the panel. From this it probably followed that he was not consistently willing to confide his deepest feelings to them. Thus Ziporyn understood why the panel had not been able to come to any firm conclusions about Speck's attachments and loyalties—bonds that Speck had made apparent to Ziporyn time and time again in their conversations over the past sixteen weeks. Speck's concern for his sisters, his mother and his daughter, and his solidarity with the gang he knew in Texas, refusing, when he could have made bail, to desert his companions in trouble in the McKinney jail—all this bespoke real loyalties, even the semblance of a code of living. Time and time again, he had expressed deep anxiety about the future, a life he saw without hope; guilt about the crimes he was accused of, even though he could not recall committing them; and the most self-mortifying remorse for the "pretty girls," the pain of their families and indeed of his own family. Anxiety, guilt and remorse are not emotions to be found in an anti-social personality. Yet the panel found Speck to be anti-social.

A. Arthur Hartman, an expert in psychological testing, had been called in during the panel's examinations of Speck to carry out tests with the prisoner. In apparent support of Ziporyn's thesis, Hartman found in Speck "underlying depressiveness and suicidal thoughts associated with feelings of guilt, anxiety and despair." But Dr. Hervey Cleckley, who emphatically endorsed the diagnosis of his fellow panel members that Speck was anti-social, makes the point in an article on sociopathy in the *American Handbook of Psychiatry:* "Though the sociopath gives the impression of reliability, insight, affection, remorse, despair, sincerity, feeling, suicidal conceptions, etc., in reality he does not feel these things." In the end, then, it becomes a question of whether the emotions Speck revealed to his interviewers were real or false.

Whether Speck was truly remorseful, anxious, guilty, affectionate, or only feigning these emotions, is finally for the judgment, experience and interpretative bias of his interviewers to decide. Ziporyn had the highest respect for the judgment and experience of the panel psychiatrists. He was also aware of the possible interpretative bias of some of the psychiatrists who had frequently shown a tendency to diagnose sociopathy in the criminals they examined. But with regard to the specific question of the genuineness of Speck's emotions, Ziporyn felt confident that his conversations with Speck over four months, in an environment where Speck was comfortable and not in an office where many of the panel's interviews had taken place, had given him a rapport with Speck which none of the others had had time to develop to anything like the same degree. This rapport, all the psychiatrists would agree, offered Ziporyn much greater opportunity for accurate diagnosis than they had had. They were answering the needs of a court order to judge Speck's competency to stand trial and had a deadline to meet.

It was significant that only Dr. Roy Grinker had attempted what he called a psychodynamic speculation—a psychiatric interpretation of Speck's role in the acts of violence of which he was accused. Grinker suggested that Speck had a deep hostility toward women, probably connected with ambivalence toward his mother and hatred for his wife. His affable nature when sober invited sympathetic treatment by women, which he found unbearable because it seemed to sap his masculinity. Grinker felt that Speck did not deliberately plan the crimes of which he was accused, nor was sex his motive. He speculated that Speck's violence was triggered by a show of friendship by the nurses when they were touched by his gentle manner—something Corazon Amurao emphasized in her statement to police. This friendliness was another assault on his masculinity and moved him to violence.

Ziporyn considered this a shrewd hypothesis, but believed that Grinker's diagnosis of Speck as a sociopath was an opinion based on insufficient evidence.

Evidently none of Grinker's colleagues had felt that the available material, given the short time at their disposal, was sufficient to attempt his kind of speculation. Ziporyn was convinced that their unanimous diagnosis should have been given similar circumspection. Grinker, Ziporyn was informed, had reached his diagnosis of a sociopathic personality because he felt he had no alternative: the electroencephalographs had not shown any organic disorder or other indication of psychosis. Urse, Cleckley, Kelleher and Smith also considered the EEG results a key element in their diagnosis.

But the EEG is a highly fallible guide to the existence of significant brain damage. In EEG tests about 10 per cent of the readings of normal people show abnormalities similar to those seen in brain damage. Conversely, 15 per cent of people with a history of serious disorders such as epilepsy show normal readings on an EEG test. This happens because some seizure discharges caused by brain injury are so deep in the brain that they do not appear on the EEG recordings. The equipment is just not sensitive enough to locate those discharges. In fact, EEG technology is not advanced enough to be of any value in more than 60 per cent of cases. The fact that EEG findings are suspect 40 per cent of the time was enough to convince Ziporyn that the possibility of brain damage as a significant factor in Speck's personality could not be dismissed just because the EEG revealed no important organic disorder.

Cleckley wrote in his book on sociopathy, *The Mask of Sanity:* "In the writer's frank opinion, many of the patients listed in the post-traumata group [of a veterans' hospital] are really psychopaths. Men who have sustained skull injuries and have records of concussion . . . are nearly always given advantage of the possibility that their maladjustment results from cerebral trauma. Everyone knows that while personality changes follow such injuries, they do not always do so. . . . No doubt, it is better to let a hundred guilty men go unpunished than to hang one who is innocent. And so this policy in regard to diagnosis may be justifiable."

But the panel psychiatrists decided to rely on the EEG tests. Thus Speck's brain damage was excluded from their conclusions.

On the subject of "Conduct Disorders with Organic Brain Disease," Cleckley wrote in his book: "Without attempting to treat this subject fully, it may be said that a clinical picture in many respects similar to that of the psychopath is sometimes found after cerebral injuries. . . . In the writer's experience [such cases] are relatively rare, but there is no doubt that they exist."

It was Ziporyn's feeling that Richard Speck might present one of those cases. At any rate, it was not a possibility that was automatically to be excluded by the EEG tests. His own experience with Speck, under all emotional conditions of tension, depression, cheerfulness, even gaiety, had convinced Ziporyn that Speck was not a sociopath. He had been able to sense when Speck was trying to manipulate him and he had also seen Speck with his guard down, totally unprotective of himself. On the other hand there were both causes and symptoms in his history to suggest a pattern of brain damage which could create, in Cleckley's words, "a clinical picture in many respects similar to that of the psychopath." Ziporyn's hypothesis was of a man mentally ill and unable, under certain conditions created by alcohol and drugs, to control his violent instincts, rather than a sociopath, a man generally, but by conscious choice, hostile to his social environment.

UPI Photo

Richard Speck, flanked by his attorneys, Public Defender Gerald Getty (*left*) and Jerome Wexler, assistant public defender.

Madonnas and Prostitutes

Ziporyn's next visit to Cook County Jail was on December 2, two days after the hearing. He went to the warden's office, where a secretary told him Speck would be arriving shortly for an interview with Warden Johnson. On the secretary's desk was Speck's completed jigsaw puzzle of the Bangkok Floating Market.

"He's giving this as a present to the warden," she told Ziporyn. "How come he isn't giving it to you?"

Before Ziporyn had a chance to answer, Speck arrived with a guard. He gave Ziporyn a perfunctory nod and stood silently at the warden's door, waiting to be admitted. The psychiatrist watched Speck for a moment, then walked over and said quietly, out of hearing of the others: "What are you pouting about? Are you mad because your trial has been transferred?"

"Yeah, I'm getting rid of all my stuff," said Speck, gesturing toward the jigsaw puzzle. Ziporyn could not help being amused at the thought that while he had been wrestling with the psychiatric issues raised by the panel's report, Speck's attention was focused on the fact that he would be moved out of his cozy cell on the maximum security block. The preoccupation did not betoken any sociopathic urge for self-preservation, since his chances of a successful insanity defense had been dealt a serious blow by the panel's findings.

Speck spent twenty minutes with Johnson and then returned to his cell. Johnson told Ziporyn of a visit he had made to Speck that morning.

"I came down there," said Johnson, "and Speck was looking out of the cell door, needling the guard. He said: 'The paper says I got the I.Q. of a ten-year-old. I always told you you were nothing but a baby sitter for an idiot,' and he started to laugh. Then he saw me and said: 'Here's Big Daddy now.' I'll Big Daddy him." The warden chuckled, his big frame rocking with merriment at the thought, evidently relishing the nickname. He went on: "He wanted to talk to me alone, so I sent for him here. He said he wants to burn here with all his friends around him. He's upset at getting moved. I explained the procedure to him."

When Ziporyn arrived at his cell Speck was lying in the dark, the usual sign that he had a headache. Speck confirmed this by squinting painfully as he switched on the light. The psychiatrist asked whether Speck had been getting his medicine.

"Yeah, but this time it didn't help." The court hearings had taken their toll.

"You've been through a lot this week—a bit rough for you."

Speck nodded. "Those guys lied about me—all of them. Like this one guy said I couldn't subtract 7 from 86."

Ziporyn laughed. "Well, you can't. You know you can't."

"Yes, I can."

"Okay, go ahead. How much is 7 from 86?"

Speck went through the elaborate motions of thinking, stroking his chin with one hand, staring up at the ceiling.

"78?"

"There, you see. It's 79."

Speck grinned. "Well, I only missed by one. But anyway, they kept telling stuff that wasn't true. One of them said I'm a psychopath —no, that's not it . . . a socio . . . socio. . . ."

"Sociopath?"

"Yeah. What's a sociopath?"

Ziporyn explained and Speck shook his head vigorously.

"That ain't me. That guy—like I told you, all he talks about is dicks, dicks, dicks. And he kept asking me if you was going to testify. I told him you was an educated man and had lots of degrees and things, so you knew about me, not me about you."

Ziporyn took up the question of the correctness of the panel's testimony at the hearing. "They may have been wrong about a detail here or there," said the psychiatrist, "but all they said was that you understand the nature of the charge and you can cooperate with counsel. In other words, you can stand trial. There's no argument there, is there?"

"No, I'm not crazy. All the same, I don't like them telling stuff that ain't true."

"Well, there's one thing that I noticed. Dr. Grinker said that the shot of drugs you had on the day leading up to the murders was out of an inhaler. That isn't right, is it?"

"No, it was out of a bottle, like when you get penicillin. I've had inhaler juice before, though. See, I stick it in here—these veins on the back of my hand—and boy, I feel the buzz. But it makes me wild. Once I ripped the dress right off of my wife. I didn't know what I was doing. Anyway, wish I had some now. And another thing—they call me pill-head and drifter, but I can tell you I could have had any one of those jobs back, even after I was fired."

The claim seemed about as convincing as his ability to subtract 7 from 86, but Ziporyn let it pass. Speck was in a reminiscing mood and his talk of jobs brought back a memory that made him smile.

"You know that job I had in Dallas driving a 7-Up truck? I used to deliver to Jack Ruby's place. Once, I cheated Jack Ruby out of $36. You know, charging him for stuff I didn't really give him. We put it down, collected the money and then carted it off with the empties."

The psychiatrist stared at Speck in disbelief. It seemed like a completely invented story. Speck misinterpreted Ziporyn's look and took it for disapproval.

"I was only making $45 a week and I had a wife and baby to take care of." His need for self-justification made it more likely that the story was true.

Speck's thoughts went back to the court hearing. Angrily, he paced the cell and said: "And Getty—he just wants publicity. Why did he ask for that change of venue? What does it mean?"

Ziporyn explained about moving the trial out of Chicago, and Speck looked miserable. Once more he became a lost little boy. "Can I come back here after the trial?" They discussed the various prisons he might be sent to if he received a prison sentence. He objected to Joliet because he had heard from Gambino that the beds were just steel rods, and also to Stateville, for no particular reason. Then the conversation turned to the trial, another forbidding prospect —"more people saying lies about me."

"They're not lies," said Ziporyn, trying to be patient with Speck's irritability which was obviously due to his headache. "People just get details confused sometimes. And you know, I might testify too. You're going to be mad at me too, when I testify."

"No, you can say whatever you like."

"Well, remember, it's not a popularity contest. The idea is not to say you're an angel. If I testify, I'll tell the truth as I see it—that you have had severe head injury, that you drank to stop the pain. . . ." And again Ziporyn outlined his theory. Speck listened carefully, almost as if it were entirely new to him.

"Getty said I left quite a trail that night. He said they found I was in and out of bars, wild drunk. They say I waved a gun in a boy's face. I told Getty I wasn't hiding anything, so that's why it was easy to trace me. I didn't know anything had happened that should make me hide."

And again. "You don't remember any of this?"

"Nothing."

"Nor the killings?"

"No."

"You're sure you killed them?"

"It's hard to believe, even now. I'm no killer. Guess I am though."

"It's hard to argue with the fingerprints."

"Yeah, but there's one thing I can't understand. What was I doing over there—it's so far away. The nurses' house is about a mile from the Shipyard Inn, where I was staying that night. At least, that's what Getty says. Over a mile."

"That's an easy walk."

"Not if you're against walking, like me. I don't walk nowhere."

Their discussions of the events surrounding the murder had by now become as casual as a conversation about a detective story they had both read. The emotional content, which had so often triggered deep depression in Speck in the past, now had little effect.

After sitting silently for a few minutes Speck suddenly asked, "You going to see my mother?"

"If your sister gives me her address. She's not too keen on the idea."

"Listen, it's me who's going to be executed, not her."

Ziporyn suggested that Speck write a note to his sister Martha Thornton. With some help in spelling from the psychiatrist, he composed the following letter:

Dear Martha,

I would like very much for you give Mr. Ziporyn mom address. He wonts to talk to her about me and tell her just what happened. it well make me happier for her to know so please give it to him.

Love Richard.

Ziporyn left with the letter and Speck called him back to say: "You give me hope, Doc, every time I see you."

December 5, the day before Speck's twenty-fifth birthday, found him in a suitably festive mood. A parcel had arrived from a woman well-wisher in Montreal. It contained candy, drawing pads and charcoal, and a black turtleneck sweater, which Speck was wearing proudly when Ziporyn arrived for their regular session. The psychiatrist expressed his admiration, and Clancy, who had overheard from next door, shouted: "That's a gift from the Maritime Union."

Speck laughed and handed Ziporyn a glass of coffee. He beamed happily as Ziporyn wished him a happy birthday, and pointed to the cell wall where he had stacked three birthday cards, from his mother and his sisters Carolyn and Martha. The psychiatrist gave him some birthday presents—another jigsaw puzzle, a new paint set, a model airplane and a magazine entitled *Adventure*. The magazine had a headline offering "$200 for your story."

"Maybe I should send mine in," said Speck.

"Not a bad idea. I'm sure they'll be happy to send you the $200."

"Yeah. Well, I've had enough publicity. Why don't they write about that guy in Arizona instead of about me?"

"You've captured the public imagination. For one thing, you're the original."

"Yeah, killer of the century."

"Besides, the Arizona guy just shot them. Now in our society shooting doesn't bother people as much as sex. Sex is bad. You can make a movie about shooting, hurting, killing as many people as you like, but show one with two people making love and you go to jail. So, in your case, the thing is that nobody knows what happened in the nurses' house. Half the people think you raped those girls."

"What?" Speck's voice rose incredulously.

"Sure. They think you're the stud of the century."

Speck laughed in a disbelieving manner, but he gave the distinct impression that the notion pleased him.

"That's impossible. I couldn't rape no eight girls."

"You know that and I know that, but the general public doesn't. They think you are some kind of sex symbol. Why do you think those women keep writing to you?"

Speck's laughter grew louder, his pleasure at the fantasy growing with it. "I couldn't rape two girls, let alone eight. No man could do that. Truth is, I was probably too messed up to rape anybody. You can't do it when you're on drugs. I'm no rape-o. I never raped a girl in my life—well, maybe one, in Dallas, but it really wasn't rape. She was just shy so I held her arms while my buddy did her. Then I did. But we all laughed about it afterward. But you don't have to rape women. There's always whores and lots of girls. You buy them one drink and they're yours. We used to call them nymphos in Dallas."

The suggestion that he might be considered "the stud of the century" had made a direct if unintentional appeal to the masculinity he was always so anxious to fortify. Now he was eager to embellish the legend with the boasts of past exploits.

"My sister Carolyn," he continued, "had a girl friend. I laid her the first time I took her out. The next night I took her out with three of my friends. We all laid her—me first, though. I'm funny that way. I won't take sloppy seconds."

He was so carried away with his bravado that he forgot the sequence of events in his previous rape story. He merely knew it was the proper, masculine thing to reject "sloppy seconds." His friends had probably talked like that, so why shouldn't he? Consistency is not important in legend-making. What was important to him was the proof of his point about the easy availability of women, not just to boost his own image as a Don Juan, but to show what worthless creatures such loose-living girls are. He was full of scorn for the girl he claimed to have "laid" with his friends and said he had warned his sister Carolyn to stay away from her.

"I've had lots of pleasure from women. I like them." His expansive tone suddenly froze to a cold snarl. "All except one. I've got hate, jealous hate for her. Shirley. She's the only woman I've ever hit sober. Oh, yeah, and her mother. That woman—I wonder what she's thinking of me now. She was always low-rating me. Once I came round to her house, pulled out a Luger and fired four shots. Then, I hit her at a New Year's party. Oh yeah, and one more time when I was sober. That old whore in Dallas. That's what I got sent back to prison for. I hit her because she owed me money. I was sending her tricks [customers] and she didn't pay me."

"What about the time you hit your mother?"

"No, I was stoned then. I wouldn't hurt my mother. She's the only girl that knows me. But I could have killed her that time. That's when I should have given up drugs. Wish I had. But outside of Shirley and her mother, I like women. But I'm no sex fiend. Now Tony Gambino, he's a sex fiend. He loves these magazines." Speck thumbed through the men's magazines, snorting in disgust at the pictures of girls in bras and panties, one showing half-naked girls cavorting at a party.

"Who would get excited about those? I've been to parties like this. Maybe that doctor that's always talking about dicks. You know, I told him I like motorcycling. He asked me did I ever get an erection while riding my motorcycle. Imagine that! He's a dirty old man."

He talked about his exploits with motorcycles, adding: "I like to drive. I had a car—I called it 'Hell on Wheels.' This cop chased me for speeding one night, took my license. The next night, I had this nympho with me. He saw me in the parking lot. I didn't drive more than ten feet and he stopped me for driving without a license. I told this girl to give him her pussy or I'd have to go to jail. He took her. Never gave me any trouble after that.

"I'll show you how dumb those Dallas cops are, though. One night, my friend was driving and a police squad started chasing us, for speeding. He outran them. Another police squad joined in. We outran them, too. Pretty soon there was half a dozen police squads after us. Finally, they shot the tires out. We jumped and ran. They caught us and, you know, they fined us $10. All that for a lousy $10 fine."

Speck paused. He was in good spirits and these memories of the escapades of his youth made life exciting again for him. It was as if he were already an old man. The emptiness of his future made the past all the more vivid. He sighed and added as a comment to his boisterous career: "I had a lot of fun and a lot of women. But they're so easy to get—why would I want to rape any?" He strode to the cell wall and he took down the birthday card from his mother. He grinned and puffed out his chest as he opened the card and slowly re-read "Happy Birthday" with his mother's scrawled addition, "and lots of love."

For Ziporyn, Speck's anecdotes had revealed more of the nature of his ambivalence toward women. His personality, which the psychiatrist had marked as obsessive-compulsive, was typified by his rigid, moralistic, even puritanical attitude toward sex as demonstrated by his disgust with doctors' inquiries into his sex life and his scorn for the pin-up girls in the magazines. It was an attitude that enabled him to have sex only with "loose" women, almost as an act of contempt, since sex for Speck was a dirty thing and the women got what they deserved. The other side of his ambivalence was the love and respect he retained for his mother, "the only girl who ever knew me," and perhaps his sisters Carolyn and Martha. This kind of ambivalence, typical of the obsessive-compulsive, is known as the Madonna-Prostitute complex because it assigns every woman to one category or the other. Thus, his mother and sisters were in Speck's eyes Madonnas; a simple birthday card from one of them could turn his irritability into exhilaration. But in his mind his former wife, Carolyn's friend, the friend's wife who had tried to seduce him in a motel, the "nympho" with him in the Dallas parking lot—valued as nothing more than cheap bait to avoid a spell in jail—were all regarded as Prostitutes. In the rigidity of Speck's mind, there was no woman in between those two categories. No woman was an individual with good and bad qualities; she must be categorized, either worshiped or despised, adored or subjected to any abuse.

If the nurses had tried to win Speck around by being friendly, they would have succeeded only in becoming identified with the "Prostitute" pole of his complex, inviting his contempt, hatred and, ultimately, violence.

A Meeting with Getty

AT THEIR NEXT MEETING, A WEEK LATER, ZIPORYN MADE A POINT of explaining to Speck how his attitudes toward women operated as a Madonna-Prostitute complex. He began by recapitulating the split in Speck's behavior between the Jekyll of his sober hours and the Hyde of his periods under alcohol or drugs. "As a matter of fact," Ziporyn went on, "that's the whole pattern of your personality—split in two —what we call ambivalence. Like love and hate. Understand me?"

Speck shook his head but stared hard at the psychiatrist, obviously trying desperately to comprehend.

"Here's an example," said Ziporyn. "You told me you like women. Well, you do, and on the other hand, you don't. You like respectable women, but if you think that a woman's involved with sex, you dislike her very much."

"That's true," said Speck, nodding solemnly. "I was at a dance one time and I was talking to a girl. She was married and she started to proposition me. I picked up a glass of whisky and threw it in her face.

"Exactly," said Ziporyn, and recalled the incident with Speck's friend's wife at the motel when he stole $100 from her. Speck laughed at the memory.

"Yeah, she deserved it."

"See what I mean? Women are treated well as long as they behave. But when you think they're cheating, you really get to hate them. Now, the point is, as long as you're sober, you can handle these feelings. But when you drink and take drugs, then your anger and resentment get out of control and you become a wild man."

"That's true," Speck said again. "I never wanted to tell you this, but the boys in Dallas used to call me 'the butcher.' Remember I told you about that butcher's knife I had when I went after that gang once? That's how I got the name."

They turned to some drawings Speck had made with the charcoal and pad that the woman from Montreal had sent him. One was a page of vultures, well copied from one of his magazines, with his own personal caption: "Born to die in Hell." Others were caricatures of President Johnson, also copied from magazines. For what it was worth to the President's next electoral campaign, Speck did not think too highly of his fellow Texan. Ziporyn suggested that Speck write and thank the Montreal woman for her gift. Speck could not make out the name and address and was surprised when Ziporyn told him she was married.

"I'll be darned. I'll write to her, but I got lots to do here. I want to get all these paintings finished before they move me."

"They won't move you so soon," the psychiatrist said. "Not before the trial and that won't be for a couple of months."

"That trial really scares me. Sitting there, all those people looking at me. You know they're thinking 'Killer, killer.' Tell you one thing. I'm not going to the witness stand. I can't talk in front of strangers. You know how long it took me to talk to you."

Speck was generally showing a much greater self-awareness and was probably voicing a sound reason against taking the witness stand that even his defense lawyer had not considered.

Whatever defense Getty was considering for his client, he kept all his options open when talking to Ziporyn on December 12 at his office in the Criminal Court Building. (This was the second conference between the two men. In the summer, Getty and his assistant, Jerry Wexler, arranged a meeting in Warden Johnson's office with the warden present. At that time Ziporyn was reluctant to give detailed findings to one side without giving identical information to the other. He did, however, indicate in a guarded manner that in his opinion Richard Speck had mental problems.)

Wexler and another aide, James Gramenos, were present when Getty opened the discussion. Affable and direct in manner, Getty came straight to the point. His first remark was simply: "What do you think of Mr. Speck?"

Ziporyn outlined his theory of Speck's obsessive-compulsive personality, with the Madonna-Prostitute complex underlying his hostility toward women, his poor control of that hostility because of the combination of brain damage, drugs and alcohol, and the possibility that violence was triggered by Gloria Davy's resemblance to his former wife.

Getty did not seem encouraged. "That panel," he said, "they all said he was competent, and I understand you think so, too."

"That's right, I do."

"But Speck says he doesn't remember what happened that night —unless he's lying."

"I don't think he's lying."

"Why not?"

"Because if he was a sociopath, as they claim he is, and he lied, then he'd lie consistently. I know I would. The strongest evidence against him is the fingerprints and Miss Amurao's identification. Now, a lying sociopath would say perhaps that he dated one of the girls and, maybe, helped move furniture or something, had a fight with Miss Amurao, et cetera. That would explain the physical evidence. But he denies all of it. A lying sociopath wouldn't tell us about the blood on his hands when he's accused of killing eight people. . . ."

"He told me about that, too," interjected Getty.

"You see? And certainly a lying sociopath would harangue every member of the panel about all his head injuries. But half the time, he didn't bother to mention them. So when he says he doesn't remember, I believe him."

Getty was showing more interest. "Okay. So if my client doesn't recall the murders and can't tell me about them, how can he cooperate with me?"

Ziporyn agreed that this was an interesting legal point, but added: "He does, however, know what he's charged with and he cooperates as best he can."

Getty went on: "The panel finds no brain damage." He showed Ziporyn the electroencephalogram report, which noted "irregularities" but "no epileptiform discharges," that is no discharges were recorded by the EEG that would indicate brain damage. But even though the EEG test did not make a positive reading on brain damage, Ziporyn thought it was wrong to conclude, as many of the panel psychiatrists apparently had done, that these EEG findings were normal. The "irregularities" were there and undeniable. Dr. Roland Mackay, interpreting the EEG, suggested in his report that the irregularities were consistent with the normal in someone aged twelve or thirteen. The fact remained, said Ziporyn, that the findings for Speck, aged twenty-five, were not normal.

Ziporyn explained to Getty that negative readings on EEG tests did not provide conclusive proof of the absence of brain damage, owing to the insufficient sensitivity of the instruments, which made 40 per cent of their readings unreliable. Getty asked whether this could be documented, and the psychiatrist referred him to the standard textbook by Noyes and Kalb, *Modern Clinical Psychiatry*.

Psychological testing—such as Thematic Apperception Tests, Rorschach identification of ink blot shapes and Wechsler-Bellevue intelligence tests—was, said Ziporyn, just as fallible as EEG. "There are in fact no reliable measurements of impairment of brain function due to brain-tissue damage. So there's nothing in black and white to rule out brain damage."

Getty wanted to know what the symptoms were.

"In brain damage," said Ziporyn, "the problem is conduct disorder. Patients express deep remorse and retain the capacity for criticism of their own behavior, a self-criticism that seems to have a compulsive quality. There is often a big discrepancy between intellectual grasp and primitive behavior. As the psychoanalyst Dr. A. A. Brill said, these people are 'masters of what they say, but slaves of what they do.' They are impulsive and aggressive on occasion, even though they make good emotional contact and can discuss things clearly. Like Speck. And they have headaches, dizziness, impairment of memory, a narrowing of interests, and irascibility. They are irritable, quarrelsome, impulsive and subject to outbursts of rage and aggression. They are petulant, resentful, self-centered and willful. Like Speck. And most important—they have a reduced tolerance for alcohol and drugs. These things make them explode. Like Speck."

He paused for comment from Getty, but none was forthcoming. Ziporyn acknowledged that the same symptoms could be found in someone who had not suffered brain damage. "So with identical symptoms and no clear objective findings, the diagnosis is a matter of the examiner's expertise and bias. For myself, when I am faced with a set of symptoms that could have two possible explanations, one obvious and simple and the other vague and complex, I choose the simpler in the absence of more convincing evidence. In this case, for instance, head injury causes all the symptoms we have noted in Speck. I prefer that explanation to the one that these symptoms are due to an ill-defined personality structure, with an ill-defined, dubious cause. That's where my disagreement with the panel lies."

Getty nodded.

"And of course," said Ziporyn, "I know Speck well, at least better than the panel. I know his headaches are real—and that's a characteristic symptom of brain damage from head injury."

Getty suddenly grew excited. "Right," he said. "You know, I've added up the time that the panel spent—eight hours total—whereas you really know the man." (The figure Getty used evidently did not include the time spent in electroencephalogram and psychological testing, but this did not invalidate his point.)

They talked about the trial and its likely date. Getty explained that he wanted Speck to stay in Chicago as long as possible so that he could continue to confer with him. Ziporyn observed how upset Speck had been at the prospect of moving.

"I know," said Getty. "Isn't that the darnedest thing? He says he's happy here. He gets upset about the most peculiar things—like being called someone with the I.Q. of a ten-year-old."

"You see," Ziporyn said, "these peculiarities are minor, but they are typical of the picture of the brain-damaged individual. Similarly, if you can show evidence that he has blacked out before and been violent, it will help the case. Speck says he has, but you need confirmation." He then told Getty about friends of Speck's who had been with him when he said he blacked out in an automobile and others who could possibly testify about Speck's behavior under the influence of alcohol and drugs. He also told Getty he wanted to visit Speck's mother in Dallas and showed him Speck's note for his sister Martha.

"What's the good of it?" asked Getty.

Ziporyn explained that he wanted to get the mother's view on incidents that Speck had related and to verify his information about the prisoner. Getty agreed to help arrange the visit.

A Parakeet with Clipped Wings

WHILE GETTY WAS HEARING FROM ZIPORYN ABOUT THE SIGNIFICANCE of his client's frequent blackouts and the rages that often accompanied them, Speck himself was growing more and more furious, muttering curses and swinging around his cell in disgust. The focus of his anger was nothing more than another jigsaw puzzle, this time an Alpine scene, laid out on the cell floor.

"That damn puzzle," he told Ziporyn, a few hours after the psychiatrist had left Getty, "I started it, did it wrong, tore it apart. Now I'm doing it again. I'm gonna pitch it out of the door, it's giving me a headache."

By way of consolation, Ziporyn offered Speck a bottle of Jade East after-shave lotion he had asked for. With his usual precision, Speck carefully unwrapped the package and took the bottle out. He took a deep, appreciative sniff of its contents and commented, with what was by now a typical association: "Once when I was in jail in Dallas, Shirley brought me some Old Spice. I drank it. Man, was I sick! Stomach cramps, really doubled me up."

"I hope you don't intend to drink this."

"Not me, I get too sick. I was thinking of trying that turpentine you brought me for the paint set, but Clancy said it could kill me."

Ziporyn agreed. Speck was evidently no less prone than any other prison habitué to think of sampling alcohol in whatever form it might come.

"Well, I won't drink this stuff. I'm comfortable now—making the best of things."

He glanced around the cell, pointing out the various amenities he had acquired—the paintings, new clothes, his growing library of books and magazines. In the background his radio was playing softly—country and western, as usual.

"Batteries holding out?" Ziporyn asked.

"Yeah, but you know, the guy that comes in to clean the cell, when he opens this door tomorrow, I'm not going to say a word—I'm just going to pop him in the mouth."

"Why?"

"He stole one of my batteries."

"Remember what I was talking about the other day? You're a real Puritan at heart."

Speck looked at Ziporyn blankly. "What's that?"

"I mean, you have a strong sense of what's right and what's wrong, and you believe in rewarding good and punishing evil."

"My sisters are like that. You're right. I'm like that, too."

"And your mother?"

"She's really strong on that," Speck said emphatically. "She's real religious. And so am I now, look here."

He was wearing a new blue and gray sport shirt his mother had sent him. He opened it at the neck to reveal a silver crucifix. He explained that the prison chaplain had given it to him. Ziporyn nodded. He was thinking how Speck's rigid concepts of good and evil might strike a jury asked to consider whether Speck had been able to distinguish between right and wrong at the time of the murders. If Speck's claimed blackout was false or otherwise unacceptable to the jury, his frame of mind as he was currently revealing it would leave him defenseless.

"Yeah," Speck continued. "My mom always knew what was good and what was bad. She was the one always told me whisky and drugs would be my downfall. The time I burned the couch—did I ever tell you about that? I came in all pilled-up, fell asleep. Next thing I knew, my mom's brand new couch was on fire. I just staggered up and went into the bedroom. Next morning, my mom told me—she told me it'd be my downfall. And here I am. She was right."

The thought of his mother pleased him, kept him calm when the memory of this violent incident might have made him angry again.

He was particularly pleased when Ziporyn told him Getty was arranging for the psychiatrist to visit his mother in Dallas.

Speck's threats to "pop" anyone who made him mad were not limited to those who outraged his sense of right and wrong. Friday, December 16, was a particularly bad day for Speck, and this was made apparent to Ziporyn before he even reached his patient's cell. The guards outside the isolation tier eyed the psychiatrist balefully as he made his way down the "boulevard." The guard who admitted Ziporyn to the maximum security block said: "Are you going to see Speck?"

"Yes."

"You're not going to defend him, are you?"

"I may."

The guard said nothing more. He gave the psychiatrist a withering look and walked away. Ziporyn did not have to wait long to find out why the guards were showing hostility. Speck proceeded immediately to explain what a poor day it had been for him.

"I got to go to court Monday," he said. (Monday was set for the judge's decision on where the trial would be held.) "The barber wouldn't give me a haircut. I got so mad I threw a can of Sprite at him. Then the guards got after me. I was like a wild man—I swung and hit one of them."

"You hit a guard?"

"Yeah, I was mad. So then that Sergeant Trudeau came in here. He told me that if I didn't watch my step, he'd take me outside. I told him 'Any time.' "

This kind of purposeless aggression, motivated by little more than an affront to his vanity, was not the act of a sociopath. A sociopath had some notion of what he might gain by an act of aggression. He certainly would not lose sight of his self-centered preoccupation to the point of senselessly jeopardizing his position as Speck had done with the guards. Speck's aggression was typical of the impulsive, futile outbursts of the brain-damaged personality. Such outbursts need only the slightest trigger, in this case the prospect of not looking as neat as he might for his next court appearance. With violence so close to the surface even when drugs and alcohol were beyond his reach, it became all the more clear how he might react when they were available to him in limitless quantities in perhaps the most provocative of circumstances.

Ziporyn tried to explain the pointlessness of Speck's actions. "Listen, Richard, you're being silly. You're in enough trouble as it is. What good can it do you? And anyway, these guards aren't picking on you—they're just trying to get along."

Speck looked as guilty as a child caught with his finger in the jello. "Yeah, I know. It's me, not them. I just can't help myself."

The psychiatrist tried to comfort him by saying he understood that Speck wanted to make himself presentable for Monday's court hearing.

"Yeah, that's when I find out where I'm going. Hope I get back here. Say, Doc, can I ask you something? Do you suppose I could have a parakeet when, if, I get back here?"

"I don't know why not."

"See, they make good company for a guy all locked up."

"Of course. I'll talk to the warden."

"Course, I'd need one with his wings clipped, so he'd stay in the cell. But I'd really like one."

Ziporyn recalled a phrase of one of the more perceptive psychiatrists who had examined Speck, referring to Speck's "little-boy attitude." He exerted a disarming charm, which would explain why nine nurses might have felt that he posed no real threat, despite his gun and knife, and striking enough for Corazon Amurao to have recalled through her hysteria how "gentle" he was. The man who blindly lashed out at his prison guards was asking for a parakeet, with clipped wings.

The psychiatrist asked whether he was growing tired of his books and puzzles.

"Well, I don't read too much any more, but I'm still working on that puzzle. It's almost finished. This was a real hard one. The mountains were easy, but there's lots of different blues in the rest of it."

When Ziporyn suggested he give up jigsaw puzzles because they might be giving him headaches, Speck protested. "No, I like them. You bring me one you want framed. I'll do it for you."

He was as eager as ever to be able to offer the doctor something, something that might elicit gratitude, win him acceptance. Ziporyn walked around the cell. Everywhere he turned, there were pictures, puzzles, model planes, the accumulation of dogged, mind-filling activity, balm for a mind that was forever slipping back to agonizing thoughts of a horror as incredible to the accused man as it was to the world awaiting judgment on him. For the moment, however, such thoughts were distant. Speck moved ahead of Ziporyn and took the bottle of after-shave lotion from one of the shelves. It was half empty.

"I wanted to show you this before you saw it yourself. I didn't drink it. I gave half to Clancy."

"Okay," said Ziporyn. But Speck was not sure that the psychiatrist believed him.

"No, really. He liked the smell, so I gave him half."

"I believe you."

Speck still was uncertain. "I'll prove it to you. Hey, Clancy," he shouted. "Didn't I give you half a bottle of after-shave lotion?"

"Half a bottle of what?"

"Tell the Doc about the after-shave lotion."

"I don't know what the hell you're talking about."

"Aw, I should have known better than to ask," said Speck with a chuckle. He put the bottle back and sat down again with the psychiatrist. His efforts to prove that he had not misbehaved with the after-shave lotion were entirely in character with the person who wanted a parakeet, who wanted to do a jigsaw puzzle for the doctor—the little boy who needed gratification of his whims, compliments for his efforts, approval of his good behavior, the little boy who had lost his father before he had had the chance to develop under the guidance and example of a strong male figure of authority.

But his boyish interlude was over and thoughts of his stunted adulthood returned.

"Did you see TV last night?" he asked Ziporyn. "They had a Steve McQueen movie on—it was called 'Baby, the Rain Must Fall.' "

"Did you like it?"

"It was the story of my life . . . about this guy, he had a hot temper and was always messing things up. And he went to prison. And while he was in prison, his wife ran around on him. That picture really got to me. They've had some good stuff on TV this week. Did you see 'The Sniper'?"

"No, but isn't it about a guy with a rifle who kills people for nothing? What do you think should be done with a guy like that, Richard?"

"I guess he belongs in a nut house. I guess I do, too. I must . . . the crazy things I do. Did I ever tell you about the time I hit a guy with a tricycle? It belonged to my girl friend Sally's kid brother. This guy kept trying to go out with her. I warned him. One day, I caught him over there. I just picked up the tricycle and hit him. Lucky he wasn't hurt bad."

Such anecdotes seemed endless. Ziporyn was aware that many of them must be apocryphal. But true or false, they revealed important facets of Speck's personality. The boasts of imaginary exploits attested to his unrelenting urge for bravado, the need to assert his masculinity. The genuine accounts were further testimony to the pervasive violence embedded in his psyche. It had become evident to Ziporyn that one of the ironies of "the Speck case" was that the prosecution might be preparing a dossier of just such episodes to present the argument that Richard Speck was capable of acts of violence, including the murder of eight nurses. The psychiatrist was inclined to use precisely the same material to show that the Richard Speck accused of the murder of eight nurses was the man who had so often in the past proved himself to be the sick victim of a damaged brain.

Ziporyn told Speck he was going to see his lawyer again. "Is there anything you want me to tell Getty?"

"Just say I was here when you got here, and still here when you left."

The imp was back.

Christmas Cards

GERALD GETTY WAS ACCOMPANIED BY JERRY WEXLER, HIS CHIEF assistant, at his next meeting with Ziporyn. They again went over the EEG reports on Speck and the autopsies of the eight nurses. Wexler brought up the fact that the police, during examination of Gloria Davy, had found evidence that her rectum had been mutilated. The autospy report, however, said that there had been no remarkable findings in any of the girls' body cavities. Wexler shrugged his shoulders and said: "There are still a lot of mysteries in this case."

Judge Paschen had not yet informed Getty where the trial would be held. The Illinois towns of Rockford, Quincy, Rock Island and Peoria were all under consideration. Getty cut short the discussion of the trial's venue and asked Ziporyn:

"What do you think Speck's condition was at the time of the murders?"

"I don't think he was able to control his actions at the time."

"Because he was drunk?" Wexler put in.

"That's part of it."

"Let me play the devil's advocate," said Wexler. "You know, just being intoxicated is no defense."

Ziporyn nodded. Getty showed the psychiatrist the relevant section in the chapter on Criminal Law in the Illinois Revised Statutes. Article 6, dealing with responsibility, says in its paragraph on "Intoxicated or Drugged Condition":

A person who is in an intoxicated or drugged condition is criminally responsible for conduct unless such conduct either:

(a) Negatives the existence of a mental state which is an element of the offense; or

(b) Is involuntarily produced and deprives him of substantial capacity either to appreciate the criminality of his conduct or to conform his conduct to the requirements of the law.

Ziporyn read the section twice. He nodded thoughtfully and then said: "But there's one point I want to stress."

"What's that?" said Getty.

"This was not straight alcoholism. This was a tandem thing—drugs on a damaged brain, a brain by definition hyperreactive to alcohol."

"All right," said Wexler. "But look at it this way—would it have happened without the drugs?"

"No."

"Ah, you see!"

"But on the other hand, the drugs, without the brain damage, wouldn't have done it either. It's a combination. Speck's personality, the brain damage, his bad experiences with his wife and the resultant hostility, the drugs, and the trigger of the chance resemblance of one of the girls to his wife—they're all vital components. Leave one out, any one of them, and you'd have had no crime. It's like determining what makes an automobile go—the electrical system, the engine, the driver, the gasoline. Try leaving any one of them out and see how far you get. The problem is complex. There's no 'one and one equals two.' "

Getty smiled grimly. "Do you think you could get that across to a jury?"

"Are you kidding?" Ziporyn replied. "No disrespect, but I'll give you odds you don't stand a chance."

Three days later, Ziporyn had to leave for New York on some private business and his schedule at the jail left him only about fifteen minutes for his regular Monday meeting with Speck. He was tempted to forego the meeting, but he also realized that his patient had come to depend on their conversations. Speck had developed, whatever the panel psychiatrists had said about his sociopathic lack of loyalties, a real attachment to the doctor. Besides, Monday had been a court day for Speck—the judge had named Peoria as the site of the trial—and he would probably be feeling the usual strain. There was a good chance that he would be considerably upset if the psychiatrist did not see him for the routine session.

The psychiatrist went to Speck's cell as usual and found that his guess had been right: Speck was waiting for Ziporyn with particular eagerness, sitting on the edge of his bed as the doctor came through the entrance to the maximum security block and then leaping up when the cell door was opened. Speck thrust an envelope into Ziporyn's hand. Inside was a Christmas card with the words: "Merry Christmas Dr. Ziporyn, wife and kids. And a Happy New Year. Best wishes Richard Speck." While Ziporyn read it, Speck bustled about the cell, preparing coffee, getting the glasses ready, chattering all the time—once more the busy housewife.

"You know that girl?"

Ziporyn thought quickly. "Lois?"

"Yeah, she came to see Tony on Saturday. She's crazy. She told him that she went out with me. I never saw her in my life. And she says I made her go down on me. And she told him that I knocked all her teeth out. She's crazy. I never knew her."

"Well, all kinds of people are going to have wild ideas about you. I told you people think you're a stud."

Speck laughed heartily. "She's been in this place three times. She wanted to know if Tony was a big shot in the Mafia. She must be a nut. She told all that stuff to Getty. She's lying, though. I never saw her in my life."

He was repetitively indignant on the point, but there was no way of telling whether he was protesting too much; nor was there any clear reason for him to lie one way or the other. He brought the coffee over to the bed, and Ziporyn told him about the latest meeting with Getty.

"Do you remember my telling you about the girl whose rectum was mutilated?" Ziporyn asked.

"Her what?"

"Her rear end."

Speck shook his head. "It wasn't me. I only did that to a girl once, and I didn't like it. If you're not going to do it to a girl the right way, might as well not do it."

They talked about the psychiatric panel's reports. Speck recalled their previous discussion of the panel's diagnosis of him as a sociopath and that the psychiatrists thought he was "a guy who does it for fun." Ziporyn went over with him the incidents in which Speck had revealed a strong moral code, as in his throwing a glass of whisky in a girl's face at a dance when she had tried to betray her husband by making advances at Speck. The psychiatrist also reminded Speck of the loyalty he had shown when refusing to desert his friends in jail when he had the bail money in his pocket.

Speck grinned shyly. "You know how it is, I couldn't leave the boys, could I?" Ziporyn pointed out that his view of Speck's loyalty and other qualities belying a diagnosis of sociopath was not shared by the impressive group of psychiatrists on the court's panel. Ziporyn stood practically alone.

"It won't do any good," said Speck. "It's like these movies. A whole posse wants to lynch somebody and one guy tries to stop them. You know what happens, don't you? The hanging party goes on, right on schedule."

"But I guess I'm not all that alone. You've got Getty on your side, and he. . . ."

"Getty!" Speck's voice was filled with scorn. "He only comes around when they take the pictures. Like today in court. He made me pose for those photographers and there he was—right in the picture."

His pique was by no means caused by an unwillingness to share the limelight with his defense lawyer. His natural vanity did not include a lust for notoriety in the Chicago press. At all times Speck had shown a profound dislike for the perpetual publicity the court appearances were bringing him. He seemed contemptuous of anyone who would consider such publicity worth chasing.

It was time for Ziporyn to leave. He thanked Speck for the Christmas card.

"Okay," said Speck. "You know, I was thinking of sending one to Martin."

"The prosecutor?"

"Yeah, I like him. He looks like my pal, Rod Kenney."

Ziporyn smiled at the prospect of the Assistant State's Attorney receiving a Christmas card from the man for whom he was seeking the death sentence. "That would really get him," said Ziporyn.

"Wouldn't it? He'd fall over dead. Maybe I will—when I send one to Getty."

"Haven't you sent Getty a card?"

"No, I'm saving him for last."

Ziporyn nodded. In typically boyish manner, Speck was working out his anger at Getty in a way that would only be recognizable to Speck himself. The psychiatrist left the cell with Speck's blessings for a good trip. The contrast between his ostentatious hostility toward the lawyer and his affable manner toward the psychiatrist could not have been more pronounced, and was evidently an effort to throw his present loyalties into stronger relief.

Two days before Christmas, Speck was ready for Ziporyn with a new way of brewing coffee—"prison-style," as he called it—which filled the cell and indeed the whole of the maximum security block with a thick odor that was not exactly coffee-like. He was brewing the coffee in a tin can of indistinct origin, which may have accounted for the indefinable smell. Proud of his new technique and oblivious to its odorous effect, Speck grinned cheerfully at Ziporyn as he came into the cell. He explained that Gambino had taught him the new method. Ziporyn accepted his coffee gratefully without commenting on the odor. At the same time, the psychiatrist handed Speck a package.

"Here's a little gift for you. Merry Christmas."

As ever, Speck took great care in unwrapping the package, removing the Scotch tape without tearing the paper, folding and placing the wrappings neatly to one side as he reached the gift itself—a small set of oil paints, which came with four canvas boards, a sketch pad and a set of pastels. Fascinated, he studied the color-mixing chart, handled each of the brushes, stroking the hairs like the fur of a pet, examined the palette and mixing cups, sniffed the turpentine and the linseed oil. He unscrewed the cap of each of the twelve tubes of oil paint and squeezed them gently till a little of each pigment appeared at the top. Not one detail of the whole kit was left uninvestigated. Earnest concentration showed in every line of his face, his usually slack lips were pursed tight, his eyes narrowed. He had given his whole being up to this little set of oil paints. Suddenly, his face flushed with excitement, his eyes glowed as he smiled at the doctor. He picked up the paint set, eased himself past Ziporyn and then rushed through the cell door, which had been left unlocked after the psychiatrist's arrival. He went straight to Clancy's cell, followed closely by Ziporyn.

"Hey, Mark," Speck yelled. "Look at this."

Clancy was himself an accomplished amateur painter, specializing in portraits, one of which—depicting Jacqueline Kennedy—he later presented to Speck. He looked the set over with an ostentatiously expert eye, relishing the deferential attention he was receiving from the young novice next door. He began explaining how to use and care for the new equipment in a knowing, professional tone.

Speck was delighted. "I'm gonna paint a Mona Lisa," he announced.

"I'll give you all the help I can," said Clancy, his air of condescension lightened only by the affectionate smile that played around his mouth. "But one thing I want to warn you about—don't wake me up at four in the morning. Get that? No lessons between 4:00 and 6:00 A.M."

Speck turned to Ziporyn and said: "I *will* try and make a picture. Try! Hell, I'll do it!"

He went back to his cell, bathed in a euphoria that went much deeper than the thought of his Christmas gift. The cause, as he quickly made clear to Ziporyn, was two Christmas cards, from his mother and his sister Carolyn. Proudly he showed them to the psychiatrist.

"Pretty great, aren't they?" said Speck. "And Martha and her husband Gene came to see me, too. You know what? For the first time, we really talked. Before, we just sat around and looked at the wall. There was never anything to say, know what I mean? This time they seemed to feel there was some hope. We really had a talk. And I saw Getty's guy, Jerry Wexler. He told me lots of people were on my side—said you were on my side."

"What else did he say?'

"He said I'd die of old age. But I dunno. I don't want to die behind bars."

"One thing at a time. First you have the trial to worry about."

But Speck was not worrying. His mood continued cheerful. Even in discussing the grim prospects of his future, he remained unperturbed. Nothing could have been more matter-of-fact than the way he put his next question.

"Say, Doc. If I get the chair, how long will it be before the appeal is settled?"

Ziporyn explained to him how these things could stretch for months and even years. Speck discussed the subject as if they had been talking about the lease on a house. The spectre of the electric chair, at least for the time being, seemed to have lost its horror for him. Ziporyn assured him that Getty would know how to handle the appeals if they became necessary.

"Yeah," said Speck, with a smirk. "Unless he gets mad at me. Did I tell you he blew up at me, last time in court? See, he wanted me to pose for pictures with him. And I said that he only came around when they took pictures. I said that if he wanted to get famous, he should get famous off somebody else. So, he blew up. He said he knew I gave you permission to write a book and how come I gave it to you instead of him? He said I should let him have first crack. I said that you were the only one that really knew me. That's why I was willing for you to write the book. How could Getty write a book? He's hardly seen me."

"Yes, but he knows the legal side. He could write a book about that."

"I guess. But anyway, they gave me a form and told me to sign it. So I did."

"A release for a book?"

"Yeah."

Speck's voice was full of scorn. Once again, he was eager to distance himself from his lawyer in order to win the psychiatrist's approval. Authorizing books afforded him a convenient way of distinguishing his loyalties by distributing favors, as with the Christmas cards, delaying the one for Getty till last. The very pettiness of his methods exposed his complete lack of guile.

"It's funny," said Speck. "My mom always said that she could write a book about me. Once I was high and shot off a .22 in the house. That's when she started talking about what a nut I was and should be in a book or something. I thought it was funny—a book about me. Now I suppose it makes sense. I don't want anybody to write anything that will hurt my family. But as for me, I don't care what they say."

"Yes, you do. You're a sensitive guy. Look how upset you were when they said you had the I.Q. of a ten-year-old."

"Well, how would you like somebody saying you had the mind of a ten-year-old?"

"But you yourself once told me that when you were in prison once before, they said you had a low I.Q. That didn't seem to bother you when you told me, but when they said the same thing in court or in the papers. . . ."

"In prison they said I was stupid. Stupid is one thing—a ten-year-old mind is another."

Speck made the pronouncement impatiently, as if the psychiatrist should have already been aware of this bit of wisdom.

"Talking of prisons," Speck continued, "I got a letter from an old prison buddy. He wanted me to go to Portland when we got out. He said he wished I had gone with him. I wish I had, too."

He sighed. There was no bitter irony in him now. To an outsider, the horror of the murders was perpetual and reinforced whenever the subject arose. It probably would have been inconceivable to an outsider that Speck, the man who had to live closest to this horror, might adjust to the situation and see the horror recede. Yet the adjustment was necessary to Speck's mental survival, the major goal of Ziporyn's assignment. The progress made so far was by no means permanent. Deep, gnawing remorse was constantly re-emerging, but Speck was better able to handle this emotion now. For the moment, the idea of sharing his friend's safer lot moved him to nothing more than a wistful thought of a missed opportunity.

"I wish I had gone with him. But I didn't. I went back to Dallas. I worked, got a check for $130 take-home—for two weeks—and the same night I had $15 left. Spent it all on whisky, pills, gave it to women. I was always generous with my money—just threw it away."

Ziporyn was interested to see Speck recognize this quality of generosity in himself without any self-congratulatory note. Even the self-rebuke was made in a flat, unemotional manner. Speck was in a balanced, philosophical mood. He was as well as Ziporyn had ever known him.

"Nobody Deserves to Die"

On his last visit to the jail—on December 26—before the trip to Dallas to see Speck's mother and sister, Ziporyn brought his patient some elementary instruction books on oil painting. He found that Speck had made his own good progress without any aids. His first original creation was prominently displayed on the radiator when Ziporyn walked into the cell. The psychiatrist admired, sincerely and without flattery, the technical achievements of good perspective and proportions, especially good for a first attempt. The painting provided ample proof of Ziporyn's impression of Speck's manual gifts. The painting's emotional content was no less revealing. A tree stood in the center foreground, leafless, skeletal, on a grassless plot of ground. To the right of the tree was a squat, brown factory-like building with small windows and a brick wall. On the left was the edge of a dull brown house. All the colors—browns, grays, blues, greens—were muted. The whole effect was one of cold, forbidding desolation, no sign of light or life. The painting revealed the bleak and empty soul beneath Speck's euphoria. More than anything else, the picture bore out the truth of Speck's claim that he kept laughing to avoid cracking up.

Speck was pleased with Ziporyn's comments on his technique and with the instruction books, but he lacked the gaiety of the previous week. Solemnly he handed Ziporyn a note to take to his mother. The letter merely introduced Dr. Ziporyn and asked his mother to "tell him everything there is to know about me." There was no personal message in it, though it was signed "Love, Richard."

Ziporyn read the note and said: "Anything else you want me to tell her?"

Speck sighed. "I don't know what else to say. I'm ashamed. I can't face my family."

"Well, I'll try and explain to her what happened."

"How can you explain eight killings?" Speck asked.

"I guess I'll have trouble. I haven't really explained it to you, have I?"

Speck shook his head. His dejection, the first sign of depression in some time, deepened. His narrow jaw sagged between his hunched shoulders. "You know, I can't stop getting into fights with the guards these days. I cussed some of them out and the lieutenant got after me. Then he came in here, gave me some cigarettes. He wasn't looking for trouble. It's not them, it's me. It's all my fault."

He stared at the floor for a moment and went on: "People always used to say I was like two people." He was making no connection with Ziporyn's own observation about the Jekyll and Hyde of his personality; this came from the depths of his rambling memory. "This Maggie—she used to say it all the time. Like two people, she said I was. Maggie was a whore I lived with, last year. Her husband's the one who gave me this scar." He pointed at a deep depression at the edge of his left cheekbone.

"He gave you that because you were living with her?" Ziporyn asked.

"Hell, no. He knew about that. I was just liquored up one day—talked out of turn. See, Maggie and him and me, we went to Houston. He was going to kill somebody. I just went along for the ride. You see, he had a couple of girls working for him and somebody took them away, so he wanted to kill him. Anyhow, I got smart and he took out a pistol and hit me right here in the face. I went down and when I started to get up, he whacked me right behind the ear. Next thing I knew, Maggie was washing the blood off me. I wasn't out long—just a little bit."

"Another knockout," said Ziporyn with a shrug at what now seemed an endless pattern in Richard Speck's life. "When was this?"

"Just before I came up here to Chicago. It was January—just three days before I knifed that guy in Dallas. My mom pawned her wedding ring to bail me out of that one."

"You have a close family, don't you?"

"We stick together." At the mention of his family, Speck became suddenly optimistic. "That reminds me. Doc, after the trial, when I come back here, there's three things I want: that parakeet, and I'd like a TV, a color portable, and I'd like to pay my brother-in-law back all the money he sent me here."

Here was a typical mixture of childlike self-gratification and concern for others who had shown him any affection or attention. He went on to explain that he had kept a written record of all the money his brother-in-law Eugene Thornton had sent him while he was in Cook County Jail. Speck asked again about how long a jail sentence might be, where he might be sent, whether Ziporyn would visit him after the trial. He seemed genuinely hopeful that he was no longer automatically doomed to electrocution.

"Well," said Ziporyn, "I'll tell your mother you're feeling well. And I'll tell her the last time I saw you before I left, you were wearing the shirt she sent you."

Speck managed a wan smile and said: "Yeah, I like these shirts. I like yours, too."

The psychiatrist was wearing a gray sport shirt and remarked that he did not like wearing the white shirts typical of the professional man. Speck nodded his agreement. "Yeah. You know I never wore a tie before this. Now I just wear it for court. I was never fancy, you know. I'd stay home three, four days in a row—with Shirley or Mom. Then the boys would come, pull me out. They'd go joyriding or drinking or stealing. It was never my idea."

This seemed an unconvincing attempt to deny all responsibility for his wayward life, unconvincing because it was overstated; but even his most uninhibited tales of bravado never indicated initiative or independence on his part. Enough of his exploits started out with "the gang"—in which he never emerged as a leader—to show that he was in fact very much prone to follow the example of "the boys." In an adolescence without a strong father figure, it became natural for him to seek the companionship and guidance of a group of males bent on asserting their masculinity with a wild life of drinking, brawling and whoring. It was probably wrong to claim, as Speck himself did, that he had always to be "pulled out" by the gang, but his observation of the powerful influence that they exerted on him was certainly valid.

He turned to the painting-instruction book that Ziporyn had

brought him. Speck asked several technical questions, how to mix colors, how to clean brushes. Ziporyn did his best to answer the questions and referred him to appropriate sections in the book. As Speck was leafing through the book, he came to some illustrations of abstract art. He stared a while and then looked at Ziporyn blankly and said, "What's this?" Ziporyn made an attempt to outline briefly the concept of nonrepresentational art, but Speck could not make the leap from the concrete to the abstract.

"What's it look like to you?" he asked, showing the psychiatrist a composition of Wassily Kandinsky.

"Nothing," said Ziporyn, "but . . ." and launched into another explanation of abstract art. Speck nodded, but the dubious look in his eyes suggested he was humoring the psychiatrist more than understanding him. Enough of art for the moment; he turned to a magazine about the Old West.

"Now those were good days," he said. "Wish I had lived then. I would have been a hermit."

His thoughts were like butterflies now. He turned to a men's adventure magazine and found an article about "Jack the Stripper."

"What's this about?" he asked.

Ziporyn read it through quickly and explained that it was about a madman terrorizing London prostitutes, stripping them naked and then strangling them. So far he had killed six girls in this way.

"They'll get him," said Speck. "Hope they do."

"He's a sick guy," said Ziporyn. "In his sick mind he probably even figures they're bad girls and deserve to die."

Speck glowered. "Nobody deserves to die."

"Cabin in the Hills," Richard Speck's first free-hand oil painting after two efforts with numbered diagrams.

An abstract painting in oils by Richard Speck.

Dallas

DALLAS WAS FULL OF NECKLESS GIANTS WHEN ZIPORYN ARRIVED for his interview with Speck's mother and sister Carolyn. It was December 30, preceding the big football game in the Cotton Bowl between the Dallas Cowboys and the Green Bay Packers, and every footballer, ex-footballer and fan seemed to have gathered in Dallas for the game. In the crowded lobby of the Sheraton Hotel, Ziporyn waited with Gerald Getty's assistant, James Gramenos, for two people who, more than anyone else, would know what influences had formed the man charged with the murder of eight nurses. After dinner on that Friday evening, Gramenos searched among the throng of sports fans for Speck's mother, now Mrs. Mary Margaret Lindbergh, and her daughter Carolyn. He had not seen them before and was worried that they might not come—they had refused to give him their home address and had backed out of an arrangement to meet him the previous morning. He had telephoned again to tell them that Dr. Ziporyn would be with him.

It was Ziporyn who spotted the two women first, one middle-aged and the other in her twenties with a distinct family resemblance to Martha Thornton, the sister he had visited several times in Chicago. Ziporyn went over to them as they stepped off the escalator. The mother was of medium height, thin and angular, with gray hair. She wore a black fur-trimmed coat. Her daughter, also very slim, was a pretty brunette, her hair done in bouffant style. She, too, wore a fur-trimmed coat, in blue. The faces of both Carolyn and her mother were sharp-featured, and as the psychiatrist looked more closely at them he could see that his patient Richard Speck shared the pointed nose and narrow facial features with the female side of his family.

"Hello," said Ziporyn, as Gramenos came up behind him, "we're the people you came to see."

The daughter stared at Ziporyn suspiciously. Gramenos said: "I'm the man who talked to you on the phone. I'm from Mr. Getty's office. You're Richard's family?"

They nodded, but said nothing. Ziporyn sat down with the two women in the lobby while Gramenos went off to find a vacant conference room for their discussion. The psychiatrist reached into his jacket pocket for Speck's letter to his mother.

"I have a note here from Richard," he said.

Still they said nothing. Carolyn reached for the letter, read it quickly and turned her head away from Ziporyn as her eyes filled with tears. Ziporyn waited for her to give the letter to her mother, but instead she thrust it abruptly back at the psychiatrist, who pocketed it without comment. At that moment, Gramenos returned and took them all to a large conference room, where they arranged four chairs around one end of the table and set up a pitcher of water with glasses. The mother declined the glass offered to her, explaining that she did not drink water.

Gramenos began by saying that, for legal and psychiatric reasons, he and Dr. Ziporyn needed to obtain independent confirmation of some of the things Speck had told them. In return, they would tell the mother and daughter anything they wanted to know about the case.

"What I want to know," Carolyn burst out, "is why everybody listens to that dirty girl." The lawyer and the psychiatrist both stared at Speck's sister.

"Who?" Gramenos asked.

"That nurse—that's telling all those lies."

"In the first place," Gramenos replied firmly, "she is not a dirty girl. Perhaps she is making a mistake in what she says, but it's certainly an honest one."

"Anyway," Carolyn went on, fiercely indignant, "I don't believe my brother did it. I don't believe it and I never will."

"That's quite understandable, but it won't get us any place. Maybe Dr. Ziporyn can begin by telling us what he wants to know."

Ziporyn told the women that Speck was in good physical health and had been very pleased with the birthday cards, Christmas cards and the sports shirt, which he now wore regularly. He then explained that he first wanted to know whatever they could tell him about Richard's head injuries. After it had seemed that Carolyn was going to dominate as family spokesman, the mother suddenly began to speak. Carolyn had quickly created an atmosphere of tension with her hostile, suspicious and ferocious manner. By contrast, the mother was calm and carefully controlled. The tension eased considerably. With help from Carolyn in establishing a date or place, Mrs. Lindbergh related six separate incidents in which her son Richard sustained head injuries:

1. At the age of three or four, when they were still living in Monmouth, Illinois, a shotgun fell and hit him on the head. This gave him a bad dizzy spell, but did not knock him unconscious.
2. At five, still in Monmouth, he hit himself on the head with a claw hammer while pulling some nails out of a wooden frame. Again this made him dizzy, but not unconscious. (It was not unnatural, Ziporyn noted, that Speck had attached a greater significance to this childhood memory than either his mother or sister had.)
3. At ten, in Dallas, he fell out of a tree on his head. Carolyn was a witness. He twitched and foamed at the mouth and was unconscious, according to Carolyn, for at least one, possibly two hours.
4. At eleven, in Santo, Texas, he ran headlong into a steel awning rod, but did not lose consciousness.
5. At fourteen, at White Rock Lake, Dallas, he again fell on his head from a tree, and again lost consciousness.
6. At about the same age, while he was still in junior high school, he ran into a parked car while riding his bicycle. For the third time, he was knocked unconscious.

Without any suggestion of humor, at the conclusion of her mother's recital of these injuries, Carolyn observed: "I should tell you this. My brother is accident-prone."

"I gather that," said Ziporyn. He asked them about an episode that Speck had told him occurred when he was sixteen, of being hit on the head by a policeman, but he was not surprised that they did not recall this. Speck had made a point of concealing his many encounters with the police from his family. His mother did recall, however, his assault on her when she came to collect him from the juvenile home.

In a soft, measured voice, she said: "He was swinging and kicking; he kicked me in the hip—he was just wild."

"Did he know what he was doing?"

"No, he was just out of his head."

"Did he ever remember the incident?"

"No, we told him about it the next day. He wouldn't believe it."

"Any more injuries you know about?"

"I can't think of any right at the moment, but there is one thing I do think is important. When he was three months old, he got a bad case of pneumonia. He was sick for a month, in the hospital. He had to have an oxygen tent. The doctor said it wouldn't show up then, but he was afraid the brain might be damaged."

(In the neonatal period—the first six months of a child's life—an attack of pneumonia can cause a condition known as anoxia. During the respiratory difficulties created by pneumonia, a child's blood does not carry a sufficient supply of oxygen for the needs of its growing brain cells. This can prevent the brain from developing at the proper rate.)

Ziporyn then turned to the subject of Speck's drinking, asking specifically whether he drank as much as his anecdotes would indicate.

"Usually just on weekends," the mother said. "He would be all right during the week, but his friends would get him on weekends."

"How did he act when he was drinking?"

"He was hateful and cross," said Carolyn.

"What was he like the rest of the time?"

"What do you mean?" Carolyn asked.

"Was he hard to get along with—when he was not drinking, I mean—selfish, cold?"

"He was very good," the mother said emphatically. "He was always generous with his money, and helpful—used to help old ladies with their packages, and that sort of thing. And he was very responsible at work. Even when he was sick, he'd go to work."

"Sick?"

Carolyn threw a fiery look at the psychiatrist and said: "You know—sometimes, after you're drinking, you get sick to your stomach."

"I see."

The mother, growing more and more protective of her son as she saw the picture that was being painted of him, added: "But even when he was out drinking till two in the morning, he'd be up early and go to work."

"Anything else?"

"Richard was always jolly—he liked to play jokes," said Carolyn, smiling for the first time. "And he loved pets. He liked to take care of animals."

She laughed at a memory. "He won a duck once, at the Texas State Fair. You know, he slept with that thing."

"Was he always nice like that, when he was sober? What about when he first got up from bed?"

"Oh no," said Carolyn, "then he was grouchy, but he'd put cold water on his head—he was always doing that, and. . . ."

Ziporyn interrupted her. He remembered the many times he had seen Speck do that in his cell at Cook County Jail, after he had taken an afternoon nap. "Why was he always putting cold water on his head?" Ziporyn asked.

"He had headaches," the mother replied. "All the time, at least a couple of times a week."

She confirmed that he also frequently complained of dizzy spells.

"Was he untidy in his ways?"

"No, quite the opposite. He was very neat."

Ziporyn turned to Carolyn, whose manner had softened somewhat as she followed the quiet questions and answers between the doctor and her mother.

"Tell me, Carolyn, did Richard look after you?"

"Very much so." Her voice was firm, with a note of tenderness. The tension had receded.

"Richard tells me that he used to warn you that some of your friends had loose morals. He says he made you stop going with them."

"That's true. And he used to bring boys around all the time. And if any of them got interested in me the wrong way—you know—he'd just tell them they couldn't come back."

"Did you ever see him violent?"

"No." The answer came abruptly, not an answer so much as a parry.

"Well, Richard says he once took a .22 and shot holes in the door."

The mother joined in the defense. "He never did."

Ziporyn persisted. "He also says he took a Luger and fired three shots at his mother-in-law."

The women exchanged glances. Richard had evidently told more about himself than they had thought. They seemed to find it strange that he would say things that would reveal him in anything but a good light. Each waited for the other to speak. Finally Carolyn broke the silence with a perfunctory answer.

"He said he was going to shoot, but he never did."

Gramenos had been following the exchanges like a bright boy kibitzing at an old men's chess game, watching, but saying nothing. He suddenly interjected in a neutral voice, not wanting to seem to take sides: "The newspaper said he fired one shot."

"No," the mother replied lamely.

"Were you there?" Ziporyn asked. "Maybe he did fire."

"Shirley was there. She said he didn't fire."

Ziporyn moved on. "What about Richard's knifing a man once?"

"He didn't knife anybody," said the mother.

The psychiatrist stared hard at the mother and said: "Now, look. These are things Richard himself has told me, not what other people have accused him of. If they're not true, why is he lying?"

"Oh, he likes to exaggerate things—to make himself look big."

Ziporyn knew that there was much truth in this, that the mother had seen her son's insecurity and need for self-assertion through his bravado, but at the same time it was equally obvious that both the mother and sister were protectively trying to minimize the violence of Speck's past.

"Did he ever throw his stepfather out?" Ziporyn asked.

"His stepfather was handicapped," said Carolyn.

"I know, but Richard says they always fought."

"That's true. That's Richard's problem right there. His stepfather hated him—always did—always called him a gutter rat."

"Why?"

"I don't know. And Richard always wanted a father. I think he really suffered. He used to cry about it sometimes."

The mother nodded her agreement. "I think he ran with the boys so much, just because he needed men's company so much," she said.

"But he never threw the stepfather out?"

"No," said Carolyn. "Of course, that man was leaving all the time. That's why Richard left school. His stepfather took off and we had no income. Richard had to go to work. He hated school, anyway."

Ziporyn could not be sure whether the incident of the drunken fight between Speck and his stepfather was true or not (Speck had told the same story to one of the panel psychiatrists). But even as a fantasy it showed Speck's deep hostility to his stepfather.

"Was he good at school?"

"No, only in shop and mechanics," said Carolyn. "He was bad in English and arithmetic and everything else." The mother tried to deny that Speck had ever failed in these subjects, but this time Carolyn insisted on the truth.

Speck's academic failure was of course no news to Ziporyn, but it was interesting to see that his manual dexterity had always been apparent, something that might have been constructively developed in a better adjusted life.

"Now let's talk about Shirley," said Ziporyn. "Richard has told me he disliked her."

"Disliked her?" said the mother, incredulously. "I never knew that."

"Well, he says he was always fighting with her."

Carolyn confirmed what her mother did not want to believe. "That's true, they always did fight."

"Did he ever hit her?" Gramenos asked.

"No, but she used to slap him. And he was funny about that—he didn't like to get hit in the face. Once he and I were reading—that always made her mad—and she said she was bored. They started arguing and she walked up and really slapped him. He got so mad. He said he was going to kill her if she ever did that again. But he never touched her." Carolyn paused, and then added angrily: "That's what makes me so mad. All these lies everybody tells about my brother. Drifter, they call him. But he was always here. And girl-killer. He was nice to girls." She did not want to make the distinction between what the newspapers had said about her brother and what he had told Ziporyn about himself. If she and her mother were doing so much to protect him, she seemed to think, how could he indulge in such self-incrimination? It just could not be true, so she put it out of her mind and coupled it with the newspaper "lies."

"He tells me he used to give girls money," said Ziporyn.

"That's true," the mother commented. "There was this Maggie. . . ."

"The one he went to Houston with?"

"Yes, he just went along for the ride. She went with her brother-in-law."

Speck had told Ziporyn it was her husband. Once again, it was not clear whether Speck had embroidered the story to appear more of a lady's man who had moved in on a married couple with the husband's compliance, or whether his mother preferred to camouflage this unpleasant fact. The latter seemed more likely from the way in which she now quickly glossed over Ziporyn's question.

"Brother-in-law?"

"Yes. Well, when Maggie got sick, Richard moved in and took care of her."

"I know my brother," said Carolyn in a positive voice. "It's obvious —if he killed eight nurses, he must be a mental case."

"I agree with you," said Ziporyn, "but the law in Illinois isn't quite that simple. It's not enough just to be a mental case, you have to be a particular kind of mental case."

Carolyn's barely controlled patience was at an end. "Illinois law, huh?" She snorted scornfully and stood up. "Excuse me, I'll be right back." With tears in her eyes she rushed out of the room. While she was gone, Ziporyn turned to the mother and said:

"I still have your letter, you know."

"Are you going to give it to me?" the mother asked.

"Of course. It's your letter. But Carolyn gave it back to me when I offered it the first time."

"She just wasn't thinking. She's upset."

Ziporyn handed over the letter from Speck and she put it in her purse without reading it. The psychiatrist asked whether she wanted to write a note to her son and she nodded, but Gramenos said: "I don't know if that's wise. Any written note might be damaging. For example, if you say: 'I know you couldn't help it,' that's an admission of guilt."

"Right," said Ziporyn. "Still, Richard was unhappy because you hadn't written."

The mother explained that Gerald Getty had told her not to. Carolyn returned to the room and started to write a note to her brother from the two of them. She wrote three lines and burst into tears. "I can't write this," she sobbed, and ripped up the paper. It was then decided that they would send Speck gifts, but no written message. It was after 11:00 P.M., and Carolyn and Mrs. Lindbergh prepared to leave. They declined an offer to take them home, since they still wanted to keep their address a secret. The mother agreed to arrange for Gramenos to see Speck's former wife.

As Carolyn went out of the door, she said: "Tell Richard we love him very much and we miss him." The mother said nothing.

Gramenos stayed behind with Ziporyn to discuss the meeting. They agreed that the value of the information that his mother and sister had provided had to be considered in the light of their constant efforts to whitewash Speck's past and to brand all adverse suggestions about him as lies, even when they came from Speck himself. Ziporyn noted that Speck's sister in Chicago, Martha Thornton, had shown a similar reaction—protective toward her brother and hostile to everyone else. Shortly before coming to Dallas, Ziporyn had spoken to Mrs. Thornton briefly on the telephone. She had commented on the court hearings about Speck's mental competency, saying how "all those doctors lied on the stand about my brother." Speck himself, Ziporyn added, was constantly complaining of lies contained in newspaper and magazine articles.

"Sure," said Gramenos, "he even says you're a liar."

Ziporyn was taken aback. "He does? When did he say that?"

Gramenos went through his files and pulled out a report. "See. In October, the State's Attorney sent Dr. Norcross in to him. And here's one item: Norcross said, 'Dr. Ziporyn claims you have given him information you didn't give anyone else.' Speck replied: 'He's a liar.' "

The psychiatrist nodded. Norcross must have been referring to a report Ziporyn had submitted to Cook County Jail on his interviews with Speck, possibly to a comment that Speck himself said he had not been telling the panel psychiatrists all the incidents of head injury that he had told Ziporyn.

"It wasn't a very fair question for Norcross to ask, but that's a very typical reply," said Ziporyn.

The psychiatrist and lawyer parted with the shared opinion that the problem of establishing the truth in this case was complicated by the fact that its chief characters were themselves indulging in prevarication and half-truths while accusing everybody else of lying.

The next evening, Ziporyn met Gramenos at a Mexican restaurant. Over dinner the lawyer talked of his day's investigations.

"I'm really having bad luck," he said. "I can't find his friends Rod Kenney or Al Butts. I've been to one of his old hangouts, Ginny's Place, but I can't find Ginny. And the manager of the 7-Up plant where he used to work wasn't there, either."

"Did you see Shirley?" Ziporyn asked. There had been no hope of seeing her himself.

"Yes, she's no help."

"What's she like?"

"Confused. Of course, her new husband stood right there with her. I asked her if Richard ever got drunk. She said: 'No, he just used to pretend to be drunk.' "

"Pretend?"

"Yes. He'd come home, fall on the floor, roll out on the porch, pound on the door, cry, carry on. Just pretending, she says. She also says she can't remember where she met him. I said: 'I heard you met at the Texas State Fair,' and she said she didn't remember that. She 'thinks' they got married in 1963."

"What about Robbie?"

"The husband was called to the telephone, so I took the opportunity of saying that Richard claimed Robbie wasn't his child. She said: 'As far as I'm concerned, he's the father.' "

Gramenos shrugged. The smoke screen had grown thicker, but through it, Ziporyn could perceive that the basic, important facts of Speck's story as he himself had told it remained true. He had an impressive childhood history of head injuries, with possible brain damage further complicated by the bout of pneumonia in infancy. The hatred of his stepfather and the lack of a strong male figure in the family were both confirmed. The extreme protectiveness of his mother and sister, suggesting as it did a close, coddling relationship, attested to the power of their influence on the positive side of his Madonna-Prostitute complex. The hostility of his relationship with his former wife, born of real or imagined infidelity, was drawn clear, unmistakable. Speck's drinking and fighting were accepted as facts by his family; the whoring was understandably ignored. Whatever element of exaggerated bravado was present in Speck's bragging of these was explicitly confirmed by the mother, even if she used it to explain away more of her son's exploits than was strictly necessary. There remained the picture of the boy who never came close to becoming a man.

"That Will Never Be"

SPECK WAS EXCITED ABOUT ZIPORYN'S RETURN FROM DALLAS ON the second day of the new year and wasted no time in preliminaries before asking: "Did you see my mom?" Ziporyn told him that he had found her and his sister Carolyn both in good health, that they sent him their love, but could not write to him because Getty advised against it. Speck wanted to know more.

"Your mother's a nice woman. I like her. Carolyn seems to have a chip on her shoulder. For example, she called the nurse that survived the murders 'that dirty girl.' "

Speck seemed amazed. "Why is she mad at her?"

Ziporyn explained that Carolyn felt that since Corazon Amurao had accused him, she was to be considered the enemy.

"That's Carolyn, all right," said Speck with a broad grin. "When we were kids and I got in a fight, she'd join in."

To bring the investigation full circle, Ziporyn decided to confront Speck with the new information he had learned in Dallas and with the incidents which the mother and sister had said were untrue. The psychiatrist told Speck that his mother said the shooting incident at home with the .22 had never happened. Speck was indignant.

"Never happened! I hate to call Mom a liar, but she's telling a lie."

"And then shooting the Luger at your mother-in-law? They say that Shirley was there when you had a fight with your mother-in-law and that that shooting never happened either."

"Shirley wasn't there when I shot those three blasts. The boys were with me." The little boy in Speck was defending his boasts; there was a note of petulance in his voice, and the trace of a pout around his lips.

The psychiatrist told him that his mother had denied that he had ever knifed anybody. Speck smiled and talked more easily, man to man again.

"She didn't know it was a knifing. All she knew was that I was in a fight. There's lots of things I didn't tell her. I guess nobody likes to have their mom know bad things about them. Know what I mean? What else did they say?"

The family pattern was clear where Speck's wild youth was concerned: a pattern of concealment of the truth from each other and from themselves. Ziporyn thought it wise to turn to lighter subjects.

"They told me about your pets."

Speck chuckled. "Oh yeah? Did they tell you about my duck? That was crazy. I won it at the State Fair, even slept with it. And did they tell you about my snakes? I kept about twenty of them—grass snakes, you know. My mom wouldn't even come in the room. Say, are they coming up for the trial?"

In his good mood he made the trial seem like Graduation Day.

"Well, your mom may be here for it."

"She will?" His eyes sparkled with excitement.

"Yes. It's set for February, you know."

"No, I didn't know that."

"Didn't you hear about it? I heard it on the radio in Dallas."

"Are they talking about me all over Dallas? Huh! I wonder what Shirley thinks.

Ziporyn explained that James Gramenos had visited her and that she had told him that Speck had only pretended to be drunk, falling down, pounding on the floor, "just faking." Speck roared with scornful laughter.

"She also said she couldn't remember where she met you."

"Was her husband around?"

"He wouldn't let her out of his sight."

"She was just afraid to talk, then."

"Well, he did go to answer the phone, and Jim Gramenos asked her whether Robbie was your child. She said that as far as she was concerned, you were the father."

He shook his head, exasperated. "No, I know the father. I even know his name. Anything else?"

"Carolyn said Shirley used to slap you and get upset when you wouldn't pay attention to her."

Speck was solemn now. He stared ahead of him through the bars of the cell, seeming to retrace the span of his brief, unhappy marriage. "Yeah, she used to say she wanted me to love her more than I did my mom. I told her, 'That will never be.' Then she'd get mad."

Only implicitly, in his tales of outlandish exploits, had Speck ever given any indication of why he thought his wife had turned away from him. Now, with the slightly pompous phrase, but one which from the depths of Richard Speck's rigid personality carried a completely convincing ring—"That will never be"—he revealed just what lay at the roots of his rotting marriage. He had committed himself, as surely as a monk to his order, to the worship of his Madonna, and contemptuously consigned his wife to the realm of the Prostitutes. It was no paradox that he was himself to wander among those worthless creatures, those women who would never measure up to his mom; for his dealings with them always involved hatred, disdain, impotency, and drove him to acts of self-righteous hostility.

The psychiatrist and his patient sat in silence for a few minutes. Ziporyn looked at Speck and saw that tears were welling up in his eyes. Speck turned his head away as he brushed the tears from his cheeks. Ziporyn paused a while longer and then said:

"Incidentally, I got pretty mad at you in Dallas. Jim Gramenos showed me a report of your interviews with Dr. Norcross. Do you remember him asking whether you told me things you didn't tell anybody else? And you called me a liar, right?"

Speck giggled. "Aw, I didn't mean it the way it sounded. It just slipped out like that."

The psychiatrist told him it was important to distinguish between lies and honest mistakes; he did not go into the details of the specific point on which Speck had said Ziporyn lied.

Speck was apologetic, and anxious not to antagonize the psychiatrist. "I won't call you a liar again," he promised. "I didn't even mean it then. I was really mad at Norcross. He said he was writing a book about tattooing, and he was asking me a lot of questions about my tattoos. I don't like to talk about them, so I was just hot and said anything that popped into my mind."

Norcross had taken the place of Getty as the foil which Speck could use to show that his real friend was Ziporyn. He was eager to placate and distract the psychiatrist and went over to the shelf where he kept his mail.

"Look at this card I got."

It was from New Jersey, signed by two girls. They told him that in spite of their parents, they were all for him, because he was "the neatest guy that ever lived." A prudent postscript for the censors of Speck's mail said: "Cops! Richard doesn't know us!"

Ziporyn smiled. "Pretty cool."

"Cool, hell!" Speck snorted. "Those girls have got to be sick, writing like that to me."

There had been other times when Speck's vanity was titillated by such attentions. Evidently he was still filled with the righteous thoughts which talk of his mother had inspired. As another token of friendship, Speck offered Ziporyn some cake and coffee and they chatted amiably about the forthcoming trial.

Speck was evidently as intrigued as Ziporyn with the whole problem of the authenticity of his anecdotes about past exploits. After taking his daily shower in the jail hospital unit, he met the psychiatrist making one of his other calls.

"Are you coming back to see me later?" Speck asked eagerly. "I've got something to talk to you about."

Ziporyn was puzzled by Speck's conspiratorial air, but put it down to a desire to make an ostentatious show of their special doctor-patient relationship. In the cell an hour later, Speck lost no time in clearing up the mystery. He drew his purloined chair close to Ziporyn, sitting on the bed, and began:

"That woman that I attacked in Dallas—I didn't even know her." (He was referring to a knife assault he had made on a woman he had once before described as a prostitute in debt to him.)

"You didn't know her?" said Ziporyn, rapidly collecting his thoughts and recalling the episode.

"No, and I wanted to get it off my chest. I've been meaning to tell you. See, it was really true about Bertha—that's the whore that owed me money. She really did. Well, I had a few drinks and I started getting mad at her, the thought of her, I mean. So I went to where she usually hung out—near where she lived. I saw this woman, looked sort of like Bertha, so I jumped her. She screamed and I saw it wasn't Bertha at all. So I said that if she screamed any more I'd kill her. But she did anyway, and they put me in prison."

"Why did you lie about it at the time?"

"When they brought me back to prison, the captain asked me about it. I figured it wasn't any of his business, so I gave him the other story. I told that story so many times, I got to believing it myself. But this here's the truth. I'm glad I can tell you."

"Maybe you're doing the same thing with the murder of the eight nurses—telling a story you're beginning to believe yourself."

"No, Doc, I don't remember a thing about that."

"Maybe so, maybe so. But why did you decide to bring this up now?"

"I saw Getty and Wexler today. They say that people are claiming I killed that woman in Monmouth [a charge leveled at him since his arrest after the nurses' murder]. I swear to God I had nothing to do with that Monmouth thing—and I can prove it."

"What's that got to do with it?"

"Well, I want to get everything straight and tell the truth. I'm in enough of a mess as it is, without being blamed for what I didn't do."

Speck was still not denying that he had committed the murders of which he stood accused. He was concerned only to stress that his amnesia for the period involved was genuine. To prove he was telling the truth about this one point, he was willing to admit that many of his other stories had been lies. This eagerness to set the record straight may also have stemmed from the questions raised in Dallas. Or was Speck trying to distract Ziporyn from making too close a scrutiny of the blackout story itself? Whether the amnesia was feigned or real would perhaps never be established, but either way (and Ziporyn still had no reason to believe, like some of his colleagues, that the blackout was faked), Speck's personality pattern, the clue to his possible actions on the night of the murders, remained unaltered.

"What else did Getty have to say today?" Ziporyn asked.

"He said his guy Gramenos got to see Ginny in Dallas and she had nothing but good things to say about me. Imagine that. After all the troubles I caused her. And even Shirley—know what she had the balls to say? She said, 'I think the world of Richard.' "

Speck laughed bitterly. "Getty was wondering whether I had any enemies at all. He said everyone in Dallas liked me."

"That's important to you, isn't it—to be liked?"

"Yeah. You know Nurse Goodloe at the hospital here? Used to hate me. She's getting friendly with me, and I'm getting to like her, too, now she likes me. It's a funny thing for me to say, in my position, with the whole of Chicago hating me, but it's true. I do like people to like me—gets me upset when they don't."

Ziporyn wanted to come back to this.

"What else did Getty have to say?"

"He told me not to talk to anybody at all except him and you."

"Well, that's understandable—you have talked more than is good for you. For example, the thing we talked about the other day—when you told Norcross I was lying."

Speck flushed. He assumed immediately that Ziporyn was still angry with him. "I told you how that was," said Speck quickly. "I just. . . ."

Ziporyn cut him short. "No, you don't understand. I'm not complaining. We settled that. The point is this—there's a lot in your dealings with people here that you don't have the training to understand. In a way, people could use you, manipulate what you say. Look, everybody knows the panel says you're a sociopath. I've told you what that is. Well, one of the things about being a sociopath is that they don't keep friendships. Now here we are—I see you twice a week for months, and then you call me a liar. It makes you look like somebody who can't be close to anyone. I know that that's not true, that that is not what you intended, but that's what it looks like. And the more you talk, the more ammunition you supply. So Getty wants you not to talk."

Speck stared sulkily at Ziporyn, but made no comment. The psychiatrist decided to examine further the sources of Speck's rages. He recalled the Dallas assault on "the wrong woman." "You told me you were drinking and you started to get mad at Bertha. Does that happen often when you drink?"

"Yeah, I get to feeling people are trying to push me around. When I'm sober, I let them. It doesn't bother me so much. But when I drink, I won't take it, I won't let them get away with it."

The paranoid core of Speck's personality had been glimpsed at times in the expression of his fears and suspicions of the world around him, but this was the first time that Ziporyn had heard his patient express his paranoia so overtly. It was particularly significant because it pointed up one of the cardinal characteristics of an organically abnormal brain condition, namely the phenomenon of accentuation. This means that basic personality characteristics are accentuated and made more recognizable under certain conditions of stimulation, artificial or otherwise. When Speck drank, the effect was to create an acute organic psychosis. The paranoid core of his personality, his obsessive worry about the mostly imagined hostility of others, was accentuated by the stimulus of intoxication, and emerged from the unconscious into an actual paranoid state. And in that state—for instance, with the woman he mistook for Bertha—he felt prompted to act. In Speck's case, this organic psychosis developed very easily because the underlying brain damage has as one of its basic symptoms a reduced tolerance of alcohol—that is to say, an increased tendency to develop acute organic psychosis under the influence of alcohol or, for that matter, drugs.

Ziporyn explored another aspect of the paranoid area of Speck's personality. As Speck had already indicated on several occasions, his attitude to jail life, particularly to the thought of moving to another jail than Cook County, was distinctly paranoid. Speck was convinced that the other prisoners would gang up on him. As he proceeded to put it, "I won't take it. Somebody will kill me or I'll kill them. Those guys will all want to get me. It'll help their reputation, to be the ones who got Speck, the guy that killed the eight nurses. I'll never see the streets again."

The psychiatrist decided to forestall the growing signs of depression by talking to him about his skills, his potential for developing a constructive future. This turned Speck's mind quickly to thoughts of his artistic interests. He brought out his latest creation, a well-executed and colorful cartoon of a Donald Duck figure. It was a broad attempt at satire, with the words "Judge Paschen" and a little arrow pointing at the duck. The duck's eyes were red and he held a dagger in one hand and a test tube in the other. The caption was: "Speck's Court, here I come." Speck explained that the test tube contained liquid which would transform the defendant from Dr. Jekyll into Mr. Hyde. He wanted to send the painting to the Judge, but Ziporyn suggested it might not be wise, and he agreed in the end to give it to his lawyer, Getty, instead.

He had also completed a folio of nude sketches from the art instruction book Ziporyn had given him. Many of the figures were copied over and over again, as Speck explained, to correct minor errors—a leg not thick enough, a shadow in the wrong place. His criticisms of his work were precise, meticulous, as earnest as any art student.

He glanced over the sketches once more and said: "Do you think these are dirty?"

"Of course not."

"I thought they were, but Clancy said they weren't—that it's all right for an artist to work on this."

"Sure it is."

The artist was reassured. "Could you get me some more supplies—another tube of white paint, a book on drawing people, another drawing pad and some colored pencils?"

"Will do."

"I'm gonna try some of these . . . what do you call them?" Speck pointed to the Kandinsky pictures in the instruction book.

"Abstracts."

"Yeah, abstracts. I'll try those—just anything that comes to mind?"

This was, to Ziporyn, as useful a definition of abstract painting as any he had heard. He nodded. "Anything."

Speck grinned. "Okay. As long as I get to stay put here, might as well try it."

"You wouldn't want to be out—it's cold outside. Wish I was back in Dallas," said Ziporyn.

"Me, too. Sure wish I was in White Rock. Did you see the lake there? I used to love it there." A wistful, gentle look came to Speck's eyes, soothed by the memory of an easier time, the easier past he shared with every Tom Sawyer America had ever known. "I'd go fishing there—once I saw a big snake in the water. There was a fast current there." But none of the happier memories he had confided to Ziporyn was ever entirely unclouded, and even in this tranquil moment Speck conjured up a grimmer thought. "I saw a kid drown in that current. I warned him not to play by the bank, but he didn't listen. A few minutes later, we heard a scream. We ran back, his sister said he had fallen in. He drowned."

Speck sighed. Violence and death haunted his every conscious moment, in a continuous chain going all the way back to his earliest childhood memory—the automobile accident he and his sister had observed from the window, with the woman injured and screaming in the street. Such moments of violence were the psychic signposts that had led him to the maximum security block in Cook County Jail. But for the time being, Richard Speck was still the little boy in Texas. "Yeah, that current is swift. I got caught in it myself, once. I caught on to some branches and pulled out, but I was really scratched up."

"I guess your sister was right about you. You really are accident-prone."

"What's that mean?"

"You get hurt a lot."

"You're right. I was playing with an old .45 slug when I was a kid, just pounding it on the ground, for kicks, know what I mean? —and it flew up and hit me in the shoulder. There was a million things like that."

"That figures. Didn't you ever try to become a cowboy, ride a horse?"

"I'm no good at it. There was a rodeo once and me and the boys went to see if we could be rodeo stars. I tried riding this little calf, not much higher than my knees. He dragged me all over the ground. That did it for me."

In this relaxed mood, Speck was quite prepared to cast himself in a less than heroic role. Self-mockery was as much a part of him as bravado.

"You've had quite a life," said Ziporyn.

"Yeah, I had some good times." Speck was the prematurely old man again. "Some bad ones, too. But it's all over now."

A Turtle-Neck Sweater

ZIPORYN WAS LADEN WITH PACKAGES ON HIS NEXT VISIT TO SPECK'S cell, bringing two books on figure drawing, a large sketch pad, and other painting accessories. Speck gave them only a cursory glance. He had something on his mind and came straight to the point.

"Hey, remember you was hot at me because of what I said to Dr. Norcross. Well, I was hot at you Monday. You said I was using you. I never used anybody in my life!"

The psychiatrist was taken aback. He knew that Speck was prone to react defensively to the slightest hint of criticism, but he was not always prepared for Speck's complete reversals of what had been said. Speck was managing to turn the most innocent remark against himself. He displayed this marked tendency of the paranoid now with a dark, brooding hostility.

"No, Richard, I didn't say that," said Ziporyn quietly. "I said that people were using you, using what you said against you."

"Oh, well, all right." His glowering look slowly receded. "I just want you to know I'm not like that. I don't use people."

"I know that. I just said that the issue was whether you could have a friendship with someone. The idea that was being spread around, from what you had said, was that you weren't my friend."

"You are my friend," Speck insisted. "You ask Mark Clancy how I feel about you!"

Ziporyn let it go at that. It would not have been wise to make the distinction between the rapport he sought to maintain as a psychiatrist and the concept of friendship as Speck understood it. To suggest at this point that there was a distinction would probably have made Speck retreat into his shell and feel even more alienated. As it was, Speck was satisfied with the explanation and turned happily to his new acquisitions. Reciprocally, he showed Ziporyn two abstract paintings he had completed—two pinwheels of kaleidoscopic color. Their effect was dazzling. Ziporyn complimented him on them.

"Yeah, but it made my head spin. Saturday night, when I was working on them, my head started to throb so bad I had to quit."

It did not seem too far-fetched to see these frenzied whirls of color as a projection of the jangling aches inside Speck's head. The headaches and the colors seemed to have struck a responsive chord in a manner that made it hard to determine which was the chicken and which the egg.

Speck turned to his very first effort, the squat brown building in the bleak landscape. "See what I did with that first painting? I enlarged the windows." It did make the building a little more attractive, but Speck was not satisfied.

"That's really a mess, ain't it?"

"Well," said Ziporyn cautiously, "it's a good first attempt. It's just that the tree has no leaves, and. . . ."

"Hell, it's winter!"

He talked on happily about his paintings. He had done a new folio of nude figures in sitting and reclining positions. "Those I'm really proud of." Ziporyn told Speck he had shown his wife one of the paintings and she had asked whether Speck might be able to do a painting of their son Evan, from a snapshot.

Speck took the photograph and studied it. He shook his head. "No, I can't do no face. See, I'm working on figures right now." And he pointed to the nudes again. They were technically well executed, but very straight and unspectacular, showing no quirks that might suggest any attitude Speck had toward the naked female body. His own recent comment about whether it might be considered "dirty" to draw nudes had obviously been an afterthought. There was neither a lurid nor an overly modest tone to his drawings. They were a piece of craftsmanship, pure and simple.

"I'm impressed," said Ziporyn. "I think you should change the name of this cell to the Richard Speck Studio of Fine Art." In a weird manner it was beginning to look like that anyway, with the paintings and sketches spread around the walls.

Speck beamed now. His sulking was forgotten. He looked around at his work.

"Say," he said suddenly, "I got a letter today from the woman who sent me the sweater."

"The one in Montreal?"

"Yeah, she—you know, you've got a memory like an elephant—she sent me a picture. You know something, she's sick."

"Why?"

"Look at this picture. Her husband's in it, her mother-in-law or mother, three kids—and she's writing to me! I'm not going to write to her any more. She must be out of her mind."

"But even married women get bored and want a little variety and excitement in their lives."

"Makes no difference." Speck was indignant. This offended his sense of propriety. "She shouldn't be writing to me. And she's got nice-looking kids, too." The mention of the children reminded him of the photograph of Ziporyn's son. He brought out the picture again and said: "Well, I'll try it. I'm no good on faces, though. I can't promise anything."

"Okay. But when you get to be a famous artist, I want you to tell people it was my idea to get you started."

Speck laughed. "That's a deal. Being a famous artist isn't all that great, though. They have their troubles. Look at this guy Peter Hurd, that did a picture of the President. Saw about it on TV. Imagine that cheap bastard Johnson not paying him. I think it was a good picture, myself. But even if it wasn't, the man put in 30 hours of work; he deserves to get paid."

As always, the rights and wrongs of the matter were starkly clear in Speck's mind.

The psychiatrist told Speck he had known Peter Hurd many years ago in New Mexico and was impressed now by the fact that Hurd and Speck had many physical qualities in common, particularly their large hands. Hurd was a robust man who liked to play polo on week-ends, Ziporyn said.

"How about you?" he asked. "Did you ever play any sports? Basketball, for instance?"

"Yeah, when I was about fifteen. I played for the East Dallas Baptists."

"Were you good?"

"No." And then at a tangent: "Know something, I always kept a long-sleeve shirt on when I played. So my tattoos wouldn't show. Imagine, fifteen and the only kid with tattoos."

Speck's front of manliness—the reason for the tattoos—had never been a constant feature with him. He was repeatedly showing an awareness of how shaky that façade was—something that he preferred not to expose too often.

Talking of his youth again, Ziporyn brought up the question of his schooling.

"Carolyn says you flunked a grade in school, but your mother said you didn't. Did you ever fail?"

"Yeah, I failed eighth grade, spent an extra year there."

"Why did you fail? Did you have trouble with the teacher?"

"Yeah. I was shy. And I couldn't talk in class. Once I had to make a speech or else I'd be suspended. So I just went home for three days. I'm still afraid of people and crowds. You know, when I go to court, it's terrible for me. To go through that door into the courtroom, and in front of all those people, I just freeze up."

"Were you like that in earlier grades?"

"No. I don't think so. I just changed."

Ziporyn recalled that the first really serious head injury had occurred when Speck was ten. "Did you change after you fell from that tree the first time? I mean, did you seem to be different?"

Speck held his chin in his hand and thought awhile. "I think so. I did get real touchy. It wasn't just at school, though. For instance, I remember getting into a big fight with my cousin. We really got rough. I think I said I was gonna kill him. I was never like that before the fall."

"What was the fight about?"

"Grant and Lee."

"Grant and Lee?"

"Yeah, see I was from the North, a Yankee. So we fought about who was better. I was rough. I did seem to be different than before."

Ziporyn could not be sure that Speck was not feeding him what he thought the psychiatrist wanted to hear. But on balance it seemed that the impression about the influence of that tree fall was right, though obviously many other factors were involved. As Ziporyn prepared to leave, he noticed Speck's black turtleneck sweater on one of the shelves. He made several admiring remarks about it and then Speck interrupted him.

"You like it? You can have it."

He swooped it off the shelf and handed it to the psychiatrist. "Here, take it."

"No, Richard, I didn't mean. . . ."

"Here, take it," Speck insisted. "You want it, it's yours."

Ziporyn explained that he had admired the sweater but had not meant to imply that he wanted it. Speck would not accept his refusal.

"Take it."

Ziporyn temporized. "Let's wait till you go to Peoria. Then I'll see."

Reluctantly, Speck put the sweater back on the shelf. By not accepting the sweater, Ziporyn had come close to hurting Speck very deeply. Speck evidently realized that their relationship, which he saw as a friendship, was a quite fragile link, and he felt apparently that the cement of a gift was needed to sustain it. Ziporyn went out and saw more evidence of this in the next cell. Mark Clancy had a handsome towel set hanging on his bars.

"You're pretty fancy," said Ziporyn to Clancy. "Where'd you get those towels?"

Clancy grinned and pointed a thumb through the bars at the middle cell, where Speck was smiling sheepishly. "From Richard," said Clancy. "He gave them to me. Pretty nice, eh?"

Something to Live For

THE PSYCHIATRIST PAID A BRIEF CALL ON GERALD GETTY ON JANUARY 13 and brought the Public Defender the painting of Judge Paschen as Donald Duck. Getty accepted Speck's gift with mixed feelings. He was obviously pleased with the thought that Speck would want to give him something and he was also impressed by the skill with which the painting was done, but he was irritated by his client's disrespect for the judge.

Getty then asked Ziporyn to review his clinical assessment of Speck. The lawyer listened hard as Ziporyn went over what he called a "chronic brain syndrome associated with cerebral trauma," analyzing the technical intricacies of electroencephalograms and the obstacles in the way of a definitive diagnosis by EEG tests. He repeated previous statements about the flaws in EEG testing and concluded: "They are helpful, but unreliable, you see?"

Getty nodded his head but looked doubtful. "Yes, but I've got some studying to do."

They then reviewed the doctor's analysis of Speck as a man with brain damage, given to hostilities that regularly spilled over into sadistic behavior. They compared Ziporyn's ideas with the conflicting diagnosis of the panel psychiatrists, who were prepared to accept the EEG readings as showing Speck to be normal. Getty did not appear confident of successfully opposing the panel's views with the theory held by Ziporyn. The lawyer put a formal question to him:

"Is it your opinion that, by reason of mental disease or defect,

Richard Speck was not responsible for his actions on the night of July 13 to 14, 1966?"

Ziporyn replied: "It is my opinion that Richard Speck had a mental defect which prevented him from governing his actions or being responsible for his conduct at that time."

Getty then formally asked Ziporyn whether he was prepared to testify, and the psychiatrist agreed to do so if a subpoena was issued. The psychiatrist then explained that he had another appointment later that afternoon, with Getty's trial opponent William Martin, and left. As he went out the door, he heard Getty switch off the tape recorder he had used—with Ziporyn's consent—for each of their conversations.

Between visits to the two lawyers, Ziporyn stopped in to see Speck.

"I've been up to see the Warden," said Speck.

"What about?" asked Ziporyn.

"Gambino. I told the Warden if they don't get him off my back, I'll kill him. He's just no good, that Gambino. Lot of little things he does, always starts trouble. The Warden says Gambino is just looking for publicity. He says I shouldn't pay any attention to him. He says I've been a moral prisoner and I should stay that way."

"You mean *model* prisoner?"

"I guess so."

"By the way, I've just seen Getty and he wants to know whether there was anyone with you at the time of the murders. Was there?"

Speck sat staring at Ziporyn for a full minute before replying. "As I sit here now, I don't remember anything about it, so I can't answer you. But I'll tell you this; if I did remember, and there was someone else with me, I would not tell you about them. I'm not that kind."

The feeling of resentment clouded his face a moment longer and then his features relaxed. He spoke very softly, almost in a whisper. "But I don't see how I could handle eight girls alone. Could you do it?" His tone was pleading, begging for clarification.

Ziporyn could only hazard a guess at what seemed likely to remain forever an insoluble mystery. Why had the girls not resisted the man who was to murder them one by one? Was it the reassurance they derived from his "gentle" manner, even to the point where the idea of murder never occurred to them? The feeling of safety in numbers, ruling out the possibility of rape? The obvious immobilizing effect of the gun? The understandable belief that the man would certainly be interested only in robbing them—the tying-up was natural enough—and not in killing them? All these were the logical conclusions of pure speculation. One also had to take into account the imponderable elements of illogical behavior caused by an abnormal situation. Ziporyn went over these points with Speck and then asked suddenly: "Does any of this bring something back?"

Speck's eyes were narrowed to slits, his gaze steady. "Not a thing," he said slowly. "I don't know what it feels like to kill."

Speck stared at his feet a moment and added: "Know something? When I get back here, I'm going to make them kill me. I can't live like this, like a robot. I'm going to wait till after the trial, because I don't want to mess up Jack Johnson. But I'm not going to do any time."

The old, all-too-familiar depression had seeped back into his consciousness; the discussion of the murders pricked the thin membrane of calm he had carefully let grow across his pained mind. Ziporyn put a hand on his shoulder and told him he had to leave for a meeting with Martin, but would be back soon.

Speck drew himself up from his slumped position on the chair and said: "All right. I'll have the coffee on."

"Doesn't he have any remorse?"

The questioner was William Martin, as earnest as ever, more intense than Getty and, appropriate to his role as prosecutor, more skeptical of Ziporyn's diagnosis.

"Remorse?" said Ziporyn. "Yes, lots of it. He's constantly expressing regret, saying the whole thing was so unnecessary. . . ."

"But he still claims not to remember. Do you believe him?"

"I do."

"Why?"

"If he is trying to deceive me, why would he tell me something incriminating like the blood he found on his hands the morning after the murders? Also, he knows how important the head injuries are. Why didn't he tell all the psychiatrists on the panel about them? Some, like Cleckley, came away knowing nothing about them."

Martin nodded gravely. He discussed other aspects of Speck's lack of interest in protecting himself, all pointing to the blackout as genuine, and then asked: "Do you think he could have been coordinated enough to do these things after passing out?"

If Martin could not grasp the meaning of the blackout, Ziporyn saw little chance of succeeding with a jury. "Let's get it clear," said the psychiatrist. " 'Out' means mentally unaware. He never said he collapsed physically. There are dozens of other examples of his being 'out' and performing coordinated, if often wild and violent, actions."

"Do you think he could have blacked out on alcohol alone—or were the drugs essential?"

"If he had enough alcohol, that would have done it."

The point was crucial. The defense could prove that Speck had consumed alcohol but there was no evidence of drugs beyond Speck's own word. As it was, a case built around the blackout could still be made on the basis of alcohol alone, because of the decisive factor (as Ziporyn saw it) of Speck's brain damage. For the rest, Martin's interest in Speck's mental condition covered the same ground as Getty's inquiries earlier that afternoon—he wanted to know what Speck's possible motivations were, in terms of both his personality and the circumstances of the murder night. Martin listened respectfully as Ziporyn went over his theories but, like Getty, the young prosecutor was happier considering the circumstantial evidence and asked Ziporyn for further tidbits about Speck's past, his movements in Chicago. Finally, Martin asked:

"Will Getty call you as a witness?"

"He says he wants to. Whether he will or not, I don't know."

"I don't see he has any other defense," said Martin, firmly, with persuasive confidence. His associates, as youthfully eager as himself, nodded in agreement. They had been present at each of Ziporyn's meetings in the State's Attorney's Office. The psychiatrist was more skeptical.

"Perhaps. But you see, I view Speck as a total entity, with good and bad features. Getty wants to hear about the good, but he doesn't want me to tarnish Speck's image by talking about his past acts of violence. For me, that violent past provides part of the explanation of why I feel Speck, if he did commit the murders, was not responsible for his actions at the time."

"What would *you* do with Speck?" Martin asked.

"You mean, if I were the judge and knew what I know now?

Well, the chair is out of the question. I firmly believe this was not a deliberate, planned, premeditated act. Now, if we consider the law as it reads, then I feel he's not guilty, because he acted in a way he could not control. But that is unrealistic; it is the law, but the law could probably not be followed in this case. Since he is not psychotic, if he were placed in a mental hospital, ordinarily a man with his condition would be quickly released. Such a close adherence to the law would undoubtedly infuriate the law-abiding people. So, as usual, pragmatic compromise would be necessary. I guess I'd give him a long prison term, 199 years or something like that. He's a nice guy when he's sober, but he says himself he can't quit drinking and he doesn't trust himself. So I guess prison is the solution."

Ziporyn knew his answer would not be entirely satisfactory either to a lawyer or to a psychiatrist. That, he thought with the rest of society, is what we have judges for.

When he returned to Speck's cell, his patient was as depressed as ever. Speck handed him some coffee and began to talk, in a torpid monotone.

"I've been thinking since you left. There's no use in living, somebody like me. I want it over with. Know what I want? When I'm burned, I want my mom to get my body out of here fast, so Clancy can't get at it."

"Clancy?"

"Yeah. He says he's gonna mess my body up."

Clancy had always had a unique sense of humor, but however outlandish it might appear, it always managed to exploit Speck's gullibility, especially when Speck's resistance was low in moments of depression. Ziporyn tried to convince him that there was no point in taking Clancy's remarks seriously.

"It'll be a long time before you die. Clancy will be in a wheelchair by then!"

Right now, nothing was going to console Speck. Everything was black.

"I don't want that," he said. "Think I want to spend my life here, like this? This is like the living dead. I can't take much more."

"Listen, Richard, if you get a prison sentence, you probably won't stay in a cell like this. Jack Johnson might put you in a tier, even have you take charge of it."

"I don't want to take charge. I had plenty of chance in prison to run things. I don't run things. I follow orders."

Ziporyn sighed. The precariousness of Speck's condition was made more evident than ever by this reversion all the way back to the darkest moods of his first weeks at Cook County Jail. The remorse Martin had asked about was now sunk deep in his general despair.

"All right," said Ziporyn. "Let's start again. You figure you have nothing to live for, is that it?"

"That's it."

"Well, you're wrong. The past is done with, you have to look to the future."

"I don't have any."

"Yes, you do. If you have destroyed life, you also have the chance to do something in return. That guy Leopold—you know, he and Loeb killed the little boy, a cold, deliberate murder—well, he spent over 30 years in prison. He taught, volunteered in scientific experiments. He tried to give value back to the world. And when he got out, he went into social work. Now he's married and he's a useful member of society."

"Where'd he get the money?"

"His family was wealthy."

"See?" Speck was not in a mood to be persuaded.

"That's not the point. The point is he tried to give back something important to the world."

"He only took one life. I took eight."

"But you still have something to give. You might have real artistic ability."

"Aw, look at those pictures—they're rotten."

"They're primitive, that's true, but you've only been working three weeks. For three weeks' experience, they're remarkable. Let's see what you do after five years' work. It could be quite an exhibit."

They both laughed. Speck said: "Should make money, anyway. You sell them and keep the money."

"No. They're your paintings, you get the money."

"What do I need it for?"

"You could put your nieces through college, for instance."

"That's true." Speck relaxed back into his chair and the lines in his face softened slightly. Ziporyn picked up one of the art books he had just brought Speck. It contained reproductions of the old

1-13-67

I understand Dr. Ziporyn is writing
book about me. I'an glad he is doing this,
because he is the only person who know's
anying thing about me. I want the world
to know what I am really like, and I
fell he is the one who can tell about me.

Richard F Speck

A photograph of the second signed statement by Richard Speck concerning this book. In September of 1966 he signed a formal release, which was witnessed by a jail guard, granting permission to write this book. The above statement was written later, as a confirmation.

masters. As they leafed through it together, Speck became more and more lively. He particularly liked a primitive by Henri Rousseau, "The Snake Charmer." Ziporyn showed him a Monet and gave a brief explanation of what Impressionism was. Speck seemed fascinated, especially by a brilliantly colored Pissarro. He whistled as Ziporyn told him about the multiple effects aimed at by Pissarro's pointillism. "That has to be a lot of work," said Speck admiringly.

"You see," said Ziporyn, "some of these paintings are hundreds of years old and are still giving us pleasure. You can sit here in this cell and feel good because of something done centuries ago. In the same way, you feel bad that you have destroyed life and beauty, but you have a chance to create life and beauty as well. You have the chance to give the world some pleasure. It's a debt you owe the world."

Speck stared hard at the psychiatrist. He seemed to be struggling with the obviously difficult idea that he had something to offer that people might welcome. Ziporyn left him still pondering.

Three days later, Ziporyn saw Speck only briefly, but long enough to see that his patient had largely overcome his depression. He proudly showed the psychiatrist his newest painting—a Western scene. Against a background of a mountain range, Speck had painted a white stallion, rearing back at the sight of a coiled rattlesnake on the ground. Using one of the instruction books on horse figures as a guide, Speck had achieved a really lively effect. But, as usual, he was less interested in the overall effect of the picture than its minutiae, a characteristic already noted in the detailed figure drawings he had made for the psychologists on the court panel. This typified his obsessive-compulsive personality mold.

"If you look close," he said, "you can see the rattles. Made the whole thing up out of my own head."

After horses, he said, he would like to turn to big cats, tigers and lions. The theme of strength and power evidently appealed to him.

"Remember what you said the other day," Speck went on, "about how important art is? I've been doing a lot of thinking about that."

"And?"

"And I think you're right."

Monkey at the Typewriter

SPECK WAS WEARING WHITE PAJAMAS WITH BLACK POLKA DOTS when he received Ziporyn on January 20. He grinned broadly as he said: "These came from my mother. Like 'em?" He strutted up and down the cell, a gangling fashion model. His grin soon dissolved. "I saw my old pal Thedford today. He's still crying."

"He's scared," Ziporyn observed.

"Well, he's a cop killer. That's a bad thing, a serious thing. I told him he done it, now he's got to take his medicine."

Speck's eye-for-an-eye attitude prompted Ziporyn to say: "But that doesn't go for you, does it?"

Speck's response was immediate. "Sure it does. I'm guilty and I should be punished. The thing I did—I'm ready to die for it."

His old reaction was unshaken. For the hundredth time, Ziporyn said: "I've told you over and over. I believe you weren't responsible. You didn't know what you were doing—or did you?"

"I swear on my mother's grave, I didn't know anything about it."

Proudly wearing the pajamas his mother had sent him, Speck made this eery oath with an insistence that defied doubt. But Ziporyn continued.

"Do you remember now?"

"May all my family drop dead if I remember anything," Speck said, his voice rising almost to a shout. "And you know how I feel about them. I wouldn't say a thing like that, if I didn't mean it."

"All right. So you weren't any more responsible for what you did than a man is responsible for sneezing."

Speck shook his head. "I'm guilty for three reasons: one, I had a job. I should have waited to get it, not mess around; two, I knew my mother had told me not to drink; and three, my sister Martha gave me the money to live on, not to waste it on girls and whisky."

"But even if I agree you shouldn't have been drinking, the fact is you were. Now suppose you were blind drunk and driving a car and hit somebody walking. Would you still feel you should be killed for what you did?"

"If somebody killed my child that way, I'd want to kill them. How would you feel if it was your daughter?"

"I agree with you, emotionally. Sure, I'd be mad. But there's more to a human being than just plain primitive reaction. We build civilization on thought and reason and understanding, not just plain revenge. I'd *want* to kill the guy, of course, but my sense would tell me it was an accident, it wasn't planned, it wasn't done on purpose."

Speck nodded. He seemed to see the argument, but it did not change his mind. "A guy I knew in Dallas, Roy Anderson, he was drinking beer one day and his little girl was playing on the lawn. This drunk drove by, out of control. The car wound up on the lawn, just missed the little girl by a foot. Boy, was Roy mad. He came charging down, yanked that guy out of the car, really belted him good. I'll tell you this, he really slapped him good."

He paused and looked at the psychiatrist, defying him to disagree.

"All very natural," Ziporyn commented, "but you can't make me believe a man should be executed for doing something he couldn't help doing and didn't even know what he was doing."

"I want the chair, Doc. I wish Getty would plead me guilty. You know, that guy Witherspoon [a convicted murderer] just got his appeal denied. I saw it on TV. He said he'd go to this court and that court and they asked him where he would go after that, and he said: 'To God, I guess.' "

Suddenly it was clear why Speck had resurrected all his old fears. The news of Witherspoon's predicament had mobilized the fears and prompted the usual defense mechanism: he insisted to himself that he really wanted what he was afraid of. It was the false bravado of whistling past the graveyard, all over again. Ziporyn tried to allay Speck's anxiety by affirming that neither Witherspoon nor he would ever go to the electric chair.

"I hope he don't, and I hope I do. But I hope I'm the last one to sit in the chair." Add to the bravado the heroic stance. "If only," he went on wistfully, "if only I had stayed out of trouble, got that ship. You know what I wanted? Work and some money, and I'd have opened a lounge. You know—a nice respectable tavern, on the Texas-Oklahoma line. But I drank too much, too much."

"More than in Texas."

"Yeah. You see, in Texas you can't buy it by the shot, you have to buy a whole bottle. I never had enough money, so me and the boys would split the liquor. Sure, sometimes I went wild, but here in Chicago, I just kept putting those shots away. That last day, I must have had at least half a dozen, some of them double shots."

"That's as much as you remember. How about after you were 'out.' That was still early, wasn't it?"

"Yeah, it was getting dark, but was still light. I don't know what I did after that. One thing does come to me, though. Something about a broken leg. I don't know what it was, it's like a dream, but I do remember a broken leg that night."

The vagueness of this memory, like an exception that proves the rule, seemed to support the validity of Speck's blackout that night. It was a chink of light that made the surrounding darkness all the blacker.

At their next meeting, three days later, Speck was again wearing his new pajamas, in the middle of the afternoon.

"I get tired of wearing my clothes all the time," Speck tried to explain, but his attachment to his mother's gift showed in his beatific smile as he straightened out the pajama top as meticulously as if it were a new dinner jacket.

With the inspiration of a new art book which Ziporyn had brought him, on jungle cat illustrations, Speck's latest painting—half finished—was a rather skinny leopard prowling through the jungle. The psychiatrist could not help comparing it with his patient walking around the cell in his polka-dot pajamas. Suddenly the loose-limbed Texas leopard pounced on a sketch pad in the corner of his lair and took from its pages three cartoons he had cut out of *Playboy* magazine. He explained that Tony Gambino, who had left Cook County Jail for the Joliet prison after receiving sentence, had given him the magazines.

"This one really cracked me up—laughed all night about it."

Speck showed Ziporyn a cartoon depicting three villainous-looking masked cowboys holding up a train. In front of them stood an ugly little old lady, stunted and scrawny, stripped to her old-fashioned chemise and bloomers, impatiently waiting for the bandits to do their dastardly worst. One of the embarrassed desperadoes was insisting: "Honest, lady, we didn't come to rape or molest nobody—just to rob the damn train." It seemed more than an accidental irony that this particular cartoon appealed so much to a man accused of what everyone felt sure was a monstrous sex crime, but a crime that had apparently started out as nothing more than robbery to get some money to go to New Orleans.

The other two cartoons were less subtly related to his present situation. One showed a defendant and his lawyer appearing before a Dracula-like hooded judge, with the caption "It's really a shame we happened to draw this judge." Speck pointed to the figures and said: "That's me, that's Getty and that's Judge Paschen." The second was of a jury foreman demonstrating the verdict with a pantomime of hanging himself by his necktie. Speck commented: "That's what I'm going to get."

"You really are set on the death penalty, aren't you?" asked Ziporyn.

"I don't want no long term, I know that. Would you?"

Ziporyn said he would certainly prefer it to the electric chair, but Speck was scornful, full of his familiar bravado.

"Not me. I'd be scared for maybe five minutes, then it would be all over. I don't want to go to prison. I'd never make it. I can handle myself man against man, but if they come at you, four to five guys, it's terrible. I saw a man killed in Huntsville that way. Bunch of cons got him in the yard—hit him, kicked him, put a pencil in his eye. He was lying there gasping, bubbling. He died."

Speck shuddered. His own vivid description had clearly scared him.

"Is it the memory of that which made you so frightened when you first came to Cook County Jail?" Ziporyn recalled Speck's arrival in the jail hospital and the threats of his fellow inmate, from a nearby bed. Speck nodded but said nothing. He said again that he was convinced the other prisoners would consider it a special mark of achievement to "get Speck," and was not impressed by Ziporyn's assertion that other notorious prisoners in Illinois jails—William

Heirens, Paul Crump, Roger Touhy—served their sentences without anybody "getting" them.

"I got worked over in prison once," said Speck calmly. "I hit a guard accidentally. See, I got into a fight with a guy in a shower and the guard tried to break us up, and I hit him. They put me in the hole and then the guards really gave it to me."

Ziporyn did not place too much significance on the story. It sounded manufactured to make a point. And, sure enough, Speck proceeded to contradict himself. Ziporyn asked him: "Are you really that scared of getting hit?"

"No," Speck protested, seeing his masculinity questioned. "I'm not scared. Why, my whole life has been fights." He then launched into a twenty-minute flood of words, recounting endless episodes of violent battles with other youths back in his Dallas days. Besides the customary braggadocio, significant points did emerge from his narrative. Each of the battles was distinguished by the fact that he had been drinking or had taken drugs beforehand. Although he never emphasized this aspect, he did reveal the effect of this intoxication, saying in bitter recollection: "I could just feel myself starting to get mean."

One episode, which started out sounding like all the other brawls he had ever retold, ended with an addition for the psychiatrist's dossier of Speck's mental condition. "I was with my buddies, Randall and David," said Speck breathlessly. "They got into a fight together —we were all drinking. I went to help David because Randall's a big guy, with muscles out to here. He started pounding me, and then David went after me too, for mixing in. So I figured to hell with them both. I ran and dived through some bushes. I hit a brick wall, head-on. I saw it coming. Then, colors—green, white, red— then, out. They said I didn't come to for thirty minutes."

"Another concussion!" Ziporyn marveled, but Speck attached no importance to it whatsoever, going right on with his next big battle, after a wild car chase with "some Piedmont boys." It was evidently not Speck's own intention to construct a careful history of head injuries to provide himself with a defense of brain damage. If the clinical information emerged from his tales of wild living, he would not conceal it, but he did not go out of his way to highlight it. And he was telling these stories to the jail psychiatrist, not to a member of the Public Defender's Office charged with his defense.

These tales also brought to light another girl in Speck's life. During a fight at a drive-in movie, Speck was hurt, bleeding from face injuries. As he hid from his pursuers, he heard a girl call his name.

"It was Carol Walker. She was an old girl friend of mine. You know, I really liked her. She was really my first girl. I still like her and I should have married her. I wanted her real bad, but the boys got in the way." He looked ahead of him sadly. "I never touched her. She was a nice girl, you know. I had too much respect for her, so I never touched her."

In the simplest and clearest terms, Speck was pinpointing the basic attitude that his Madonna-Prostitute complex had created—the view that the purity of a good woman, a Madonna, must never be defiled by any sexual act, and that sexual acts themselves are necessarily acts of defilement.

"This would really have been different if I'd married her," Speck went on. "But I was too wild. I wanted excitement—I sure got it. But that was my life, fighting, pilling, joy riding, drinking. Now I've got to pay—and I'm glad. I want the chair."

Ziporyn asked him whether it was the appearance of the Witherspoon case on the television news that had started him thinking again about the death sentence. Speck confirmed that this was so and sat staring gloomily through the bars. To divert his attention from this subject, Ziporyn asked Speck once more about the drugs he had taken before he blacked out on the night of the murders. Speck reiterated that he had received narcotics from the sailors. He could not remember who they were, but did recall for the first time what they looked like.

"One was a little Puerto Rican-looking guy. Then there was a chubby guy. But I don't know their names."

"What did you mean when you mentioned a broken leg? You mean you saw a leg broken, or a man with a leg in a cast?"

"In a cast. It seems like I had a fight that night with a man with his leg in a cast. Shoved a gun and knife in his face."

"You remember this now?"

"Sort of, but foggy."

It seemed possible that, piece by piece, the whole of that blackout period could be reconstructed, but the haphazard way Speck recalled the events of that night made it likely that it would take as long as for the proverbial monkey at the typewriter to compose *Hamlet*.

Ziporyn shook his head. "Richard," he said, "what are we going to do with you?"

"You don't have to worry, Doc. Mr. God and his twelve disciples will take care of that in Peoria."

"It's All Imitation"

SPECK HAD FOR SOME TIME BEEN RECEIVING THREATENING LETTERS. They came from the magazine *U.S. News and World Report,* warning him that if he did not pay them the $2 for the subscription he had been receiving, he would be in serious trouble. Evidently, the subscription computers had not been programmed for the kind of practical joke someone had played by ordering a subscription on behalf of a man awaiting trial on eight murder charges.

Speck gave Ziporyn the threatening notes to read when the psychiatrist paid his first visit to the jail in eight days, having been kept from his normal Friday visit on January 26 by Chicago's mammoth snowstorm, the worst in living memory. As he chuckled over the payment demands, Ziporyn apologized for not appearing Friday.

"Didn't expect you," said Speck. "Only an idiot would have driven that day. It's been wild here, too. One of the guards died, and you know something? I saw a fight in the hospital—two guys, it was a real battle." Speck grinned with pleasure. This had been the stuff of excitement all his life. "They got coffee all over Nurse Goodloe."

Seeking the appropriate question, Ziporyn asked: "Who won?"

Speck's answer was typically sardonic: "The guards." He handed Ziporyn a cup of coffee and the thought passed through the psychiatrist's mind that his relationship with Speck could as easily be measured in the gallons of coffee they had shared, as in the number of hours of interviews.

"Have you got my sister Martha's telephone number?" Speck

asked. "I'd like you to call up and see how they are. I heard 47 people died in this storm. I'm worried about the family and I wonder if the kids got to school okay."

Ziporyn agreed to telephone. He looked around the cell as he drank the coffee and noticed that, for the first time in many weeks, there was absolutely no change, no new piece of furniture, no new picture. Even the skinny leopard was no nearer completion.

"Given up painting?"

"I figure I'm being moved any day, so I didn't want to have any wet paintings."

In the midst of all the legal maneuvering that had gone on as the Peoria trial approached, Speck had not been told that the start had been postponed again. It was now set for February 13. Ziporyn explained to Speck that this postponement was due to pretrial motions presented by Getty.

"I wish he'd quit that. Let's get it over with," said Speck.

The psychiatrist again argued against his patient's fatalism and his false bravado. This time, Speck was prepared to be more frank about his hopes.

"I really would like to go to a nut house. But I ain't going to act crazy to get there."

"Nobody's asking you to."

"Well I ain't crazy. I'm just me, just plain no good."

The psychiatrist tried to persuade his patient that he shared a highly aggressive, combative nature with all mankind. The urge to kill was not Speck's alone. Speck's defect, Ziporyn said, was not that urge to kill, but his failure to control the urge. The failure was an inevitable result of the drugs, alcohol and brain damage in combination. Speck would not accept this.

"I don't feel like no killer," he said, "but I know I'm no good. I've drunk, got pilled up, and you know I've messed around with whores."

Whatever chances Ziporyn had of convincing him about the meaning of the violent side of his nature, he knew that Speck would remain intractable in his attitude to sex. His strict puritanism in this regard was a common trait of sex criminals. Their moral sense rebels against natural law and regards most of sex as filthy, disgusting, wicked and evil. Sex criminals are not hedonistic sensualists, believing that "all is permitted." On the contrary, they are inhibited Puritans who have attempted so arduously to repress their natural and normal impulses that when, for any reason, they lose control, there is an explosion of emotion, impulse and action. Speck would never cease being what he was, nor would he begin to realize what he was, until he was ready to accept his sexuality fully and freely. At present, his inhibitions loomed as large as ever. Sex was still the devil.

As the trial date approached, Speck had to spend more and more of his time in Judge Paschen's chambers for the hearing of his lawyer's pretrial motions. Getty was working feverishly to exclude as much as he could of the physical evidence, such as alleged murder weapons and clothing, on the grounds that they had been improperly obtained by police without a warrant. A gun and knife had been successfully eliminated. On February 3 at 4:30 P.M.—the usual time for Ziporyn's visits—Speck was still away from his cell. The psychiatrist chatted with Mark Clancy about his forthcoming prison sentence, which he expected to be about ten years, and his future after that.

"You've got no problems," said Ziporyn ironically. "You'll just go back to cowboying." This was jail slang for the romantic, adventurous criminal who roamed the country in cavalier fashion, robbing banks and jewelers at the point of a gun.

"No, I don't think so," said Clancy, looking less lively than usual, rather weary, almost solemn. "I'm through with that."

"You have creative ability, Mark. You should use it."

"I'm not creative. For that matter, nobody is. I think the only creative thing anybody does is cry when they are born. After that, it's all imitation. That's why I think you are wasting your time with Richard. What makes you think he can create anything?"

"I don't know if he can or not, but I want him to try—and he's got the manual dexterity. I want him to think constructively and positively about the future, not brood on the past. I want his energies and feelings and thoughts focused on what he can accomplish, and on his strengths and good qualities, not on his misdeeds and weaknesses."

Clancy remained the earnest skeptic. "Yes, but can he do it?"

"We'll see. Remember, he's self-taught, and has only been painting one month. Ask me in three years. Don't you like his work?"

"It's got promise, but he tends to get into cartoon style."

"That's true. The scrawny leopard he did reminded me of the Pink Panther. Do you know that character?"

Clancy shook his head. A prisoner, for all his access to newspapers and television, necessarily has a narrower frame of reference than outsiders, and even a regular visitor like Ziporyn tended to forget this at times.

"No," said Clancy. "I haven't seen it. We just get the old ones on TV. Speck watches them on the kids' shows every Saturday morning. You know what his favorite is? *The Road Runner*. Wow, does he love *The Road Runner!* He'd rather miss a meal than that cartoon."

For sheer, unrelenting sadism, the *Road Runner* cartoon was hard to equal. The endless series of bone-shattering, flesh-pulping collisions and disasters offered the ultimate in stylized violence. This was Richard Speck's favorite cartoon.

At that moment Speck returned, and was led to his cell by two guards.

"Boy, am I glad to be back here," said Speck, as Ziporyn followed him into his cell. The prisoner busied himself at his usual household chores, preparing coffee, tidying the shelves around the cell, all in an almost ceremonial manner, to establish himself back in his own home. "They only gave me a lousy sandwich at noon. I been thinking about this nice, quiet cell and some good hot coffee for hours."

He winced and jerked the back of his head as if he had cricked his neck. "And I got a terrible headache."

But the headache, normal for his days spent at court hearings, did not make him less talkative than usual.

"I had a dream the other night," he said—he had never recalled a dream before. "I dreamt that I went to a nut house forever. I really do want to go to a nut house. In a nut house, I could work and paint, and have some freedom. It's not like a prison, is it? What's it like?"

The psychiatrist explained that the main difference between mental institutions and prisons was in the former's more attentive attitude to their inmates. He said that the prison staff's preventive approach made them less accommodating.

"That's what I want," said Speck. "I couldn't take prison. You know what a prison is like. Do this, do that. If you say one different word, you get arrested. You're just a slave in a prison. And I can't take that. I've got to be free. And I'd get out of line, sure as I'm sitting here, and I'd get beaten up."

It would be pointless to question his justification, in his present predicament, for complaining about the prospects of a prison sentence. Ziporyn was thankful enough for the time being that Speck was at least not focusing on the death penalty.

"You really feel so strongly about that?" the psychiatrist asked.

"Hell, yes. Do you think I got any chance of getting sent to a nut house?"

"It's hard to say. But that reminds me—Getty is sending another psychiatrist in to see you, a Dr. Ner Littner. Now don't play games with him. You should tell him everything, and don't leave out your head injuries."

"Okay. I got plenty. You know, if they shaved my head, they'd see so many scars they couldn't count them—and there's a dent in my skull, here." He pointed to the top of his head.

"Maybe you should shave it," Ziporyn suggested.

"Only if I could stay in my cell till the hair grew again. I don't want anybody to see me without hair."

"You could wear a cap."

"No, I don't look good in a cap."

His vanity was still stronger than any sense of self-preservation. Having those head injuries visible for everyone to see was less important to him than "looking good." And he was not particularly interested in ingratiating himself with the judge. He told Ziporyn he had given the ghoulish courtroom cartoons from *Playboy* magazine to Judge Paschen. The judge had returned them without comment.

The psychiatrist stood up to leave and asked Speck, since he would not be seeing him for another week because of the scheduled court hearings, whether there was anything he needed. Speck examined his paint box and decided his supplies were sufficient. He said he was being permitted to take his paints and radio to Peoria.

As the guard closed the cell door behind Ziporyn, Speck walked to the bars and said: "Do me a favor, Doc. Try and keep my relatives away from the trial."

The doctor explained that as far as he knew, at least Speck's mother and sister Carolyn would be testifying, since Getty had told him he wanted them to establish facts about Speck's injuries and illnesses if he decided on an insanity defense.

"Okay," said Speck. "But try to keep the others away. Say, the next time you do come, could you bring me some hot peppers? I got a craving for them."

Ziporyn nodded and moved to the door, but again he was stopped.

"Hey, Doc. What about that sweater of mine, don't you want it?"

It was obvious that Speck was sensing that their relationship was approaching an end. He wanted to maintain a link, however tenuous, by means of the tangible gesture of a gift. Ziporyn promised that they would talk about it.

"If a Black Mamba Bites You"

ZIPORYN WAS IN COURT ON FEBRUARY 10, TESTIFYING IN ANOTHER case, and met Jerry Wexler, who was shortly to go into private practice but was at present still with the Public Defender's Office. The psychiatrist asked him how the hearings in chamber had gone.

"Not bad," said Wexler cheerfully. "We made some points—we got the gun, the knife and now the clothes ruled out. But you should see the scene. See, they sit at a long conference table. It looks like the Board of Directors' meeting of General Motors. There are about twelve guys, and they're wisecracking and smoking cigarettes—and Speck's right in there along with them. He sits at the table and lights up, and Judge Paschen says: 'Hi, Richie, how are you today?' It's all very casual. It's like these guys are discussing a sales promotion campaign or something—only in fact, they're deciding how to burn this character."

Ziporyn found the scene ghoulishly amusing and was not too pleased to find himself chuckling. He recalled Oscar Wilde's aphorism: ". . . A community is infinitely more brutalized by the habitual employment of punishment than it is by the occasional occurrence of crime."

Back in his cell after the hearings, Speck was not bothered by such thoughts. He was exuberant and in high spirits when Ziporyn arrived. He was obviously pleased by the termination of the hearings—the trial date was now put off another week to February 20—and happy to be back, for a short time at least, in his cozy cell.

"Did you see the papers this morning?" he asked the psychiatrist. "Really put my foot in it. I was leaving court yesterday and this guy asked me when I was leaving for Peoria. I thought he was a bailiff, so I said: 'How the fuck do I know! I haven't got my bus ticket yet,' and walked on."

Clancy was listening from next door and hooted with laughter.

"Turned out the guy was a reporter," Speck went on, with a wide grin, "and he put it in the paper this morning—without the language, of course."

"That will teach you to talk to strange men," said Ziporyn. "One more strike against you."

"Makes no difference. That judge—he's said nothing but 'no, no, no,' to everything Getty asked. He's got it in for me and I hate him with a purple passion."

"But I talked to Jerry Wexler and he said Judge Paschen was friendly with you."

"Friendly? Ha! Like a snake. He's nice as pie to the prosecutor. But to me. . . . You know that guy you were with in Dallas—what's his name? Jim Gramenos—he told him to keep quiet—'Keep quiet, young man.' That's how he talked to him."

Ziporyn let Speck play himself out. His observations sounded like the usual complaints he heard from other prisoners after their day in court. And Speck added his personal ingredient. "I'm glad it's over. Every day I've had headaches. I been mean, fighting with the guards. Wish the whole trial was over."

He lifted his head as something on the television screen on the guard's desk caught his attention. It was a progress report on a little Chicago girl who had suffered 60 per cent burns over her body and was listed in critical condition.

"I want to see the Warden," said Speck firmly. "They say she needs blood and I want to give her blood. And they're talking about skin grafting. I'll give her my skin. Think they'll let me?"

The psychiatrist suggested that the offer might be interpreted as a play for sympathy.

"No, no, no," Speck said vehemently. "I don't want anybody to know it's from me. And maybe they can get blood from other people, but where they going to get skin?"

He proceeded to make a long dissertation on skin grafting—where the donor sites were, what the chances of success were, how it was done. He had apparently listened to the television accounts of the case with avid interest. He emphasized over and over again that he wanted his offer to remain anonymous. Ziporyn promised to relay his wishes to the Warden.* Speck seemed satisfied and returned to the subject of his day in the court building.

"You know what Getty showed me? There's a book out about me. It's called *Justice, U.S.A.*†

"It's about you?"

"Yeah," he said with some pride. "Me and Errol Flynn and Sam Sheppard and a bunch of other guys. Getty showed me where it said how I showed a bartender a knife on the Thursday after the murders and told him I killed a bunch of people with it. That's a damn lie. I never did such a thing. I'd like to see that bartender."

"Did you know what you were doing Thursday?"

"Off and on. I was drinking again—whisky and coke—and I kept blacking out."

"So maybe you did it while you blacked out."

"Well, let's put it this way. I don't remember doing it, and anyway, I didn't have a knife Thursday."

Ziporyn told him he would buy a copy of the book and check into it. Meanwhile, he admonished him not to be so quick to brand as a lie everything he did not agree with. Speck smiled ruefully.

In mock earnestness, Ziporyn went on: "What would you say if I told everybody that you are always violent and attack me, and I have to fight for my life every time I come in here?"

Speck laughed but pointed out that there was a serious side to Ziporyn's joke.

"Hell, you're the only one who comes into my cell. Well, you and the priest. Everybody else, they stare at me, but you couldn't pay them a million bucks to get near me."

For the man that all the newspapers readily called a "loner," almost as if he had deliberately sought that role, his treatment as a complete outcast, even within the confines of the jail, had left him considerably embittered. It made his contact with the psychiatrist and the priest in his cell, and with the Warden in his office, all the more valuable. Whatever his attitude to the prison staff in general, Speck retained a warm affection for Warden Johnson. The nickname "Big Daddy" had stuck.

* Nothing ever came of the offer.

† Howard Felsher and Michael Rosen, *Justice, U.S.A.* (New York: Crowell Collier and Macmillan, Inc., 1967).

Speck was relishing his last week at Cook County Jail before the trial. "I'm going to watch a lot of TV. They got some good shows coming up—the kind I like. For instance, there's a couple of Westerns and war movies, and stuff like that—especially 'Machine Gun Kelly'—but there's also some Bible pictures. I like them a lot. You know, like the one where the lightning hits the rock and the people are worshipping the Golden Cow. And the ones where they're throwing people to the lions. This guy Victor Malone is in them a lot."

"You mean Victor Mature?"

"I guess so."

The Freudian slip of replacing the film star's name with the maiden name of Speck's former wife reminded Ziporyn of Speck's interview with the latest of the psychiatrists to see him, Dr. Ner Littner. (Dr. Littner practiced general psychoanalysis, but was best known for his work in child psychiatry.) Ziporyn asked Speck how the interview had gone with Littner.

"Fine. He's a nice guy."

"Did you tell him about your head injuries?"

"No."

"Did he ask you?"

"No, he just talked about my childhood. I just sat and drew—stuff like 'Speck the Wreck' and 'Born to Live in Hell.' He asked me for my drawings. I asked him why he wanted them. He said he collected stuff like that, so I gave it to him. But I couldn't really talk to him. You know I can't talk to strangers."

Speck was no closer now to protecting his own interests by informing psychiatrists about his past than he had been when Ziporyn first talked to him more than six months previously. Whatever lies Speck had told Ziporyn himself during these months of intimate conversation, it did not seem likely that Speck had been trying to present a picture of himself more favorable than the reality. His behavior with all the psychiatrists had been passive and guileless.

Speck tried to prevent Ziporyn from leaving, but acquiesced when the psychiatrist told him he had to go out that night with his wife.

"Who's going to look after the kids?" Speck asked.

"My mother."

Speck smiled contentedly. "Moms are wonderful, ain't they?"

That much he would never hide from anyone.

Ziporyn's last interview with Speck was on February 13. The cell was in total darkness as the psychiatrist approached, and for a moment he thought Speck had already left—security surrounding the departure for Peoria was so strict that only the most high-level authorities knew when it was to take place. But Speck was still there, lying on his bed. When Speck switched the light on, Ziporyn saw that his face was suffused with fury. The psychiatrist glanced around and saw the reason. The cell had been stripped of all the trimmings with which Speck had made it into a home in the past six months. The shelves were gone, the books, the playing cards, the paintings, the pie-pan "mirror," the neat piles of clothing and towels, all were stuffed into three cardboard boxes, piled one on top of the other in one corner. The walls were bare to their sickly cream color once again. Just another prison cell, bearing witness to its present tenancy only with the slogan painted in white on the door: RICHARD SPECK, BORN: DEC. 6, 1941, DIED: ?

"So you're finally moving?"

"Yeah," said Speck bitterly. "The Captain came in at 3:30 today, told me to pack. He said I might go tomorrow. And they lied to me. The Peoria Sheriff and the Warden, they said I could take my radio and my paint stuff. Now they say I can't take nothing. They say the State will give me everything I need. I can't even take my shaving and washing things."

"Maybe when you talk to the Warden again, you'll find it's a mistake."

"It'd better be, or I'll go wild there. I can't just sit in a cell for seven weeks or however long it's gonna take, with nothing to do but stare at a guard—I'll attack him or something. It's not like solitary—at least it's dark there. But do you know what it's like to just sit in a cell, just sit? And another thing—I want that suit to go to court in. It's tailor-made for me. And I won't go to court without a shave and shower."

"They'll give you all that. I'm sure they have a barber."

"I can shave myself. But they broke their word. They promised me, right in front of Sheriff Woods."

Ziporyn tried to reassure him that things would not turn out to be as strict as they sounded. Speck was obviously feeling depressed by the prospect of moving and was seizing at every opportunity to fret. (As it turned out, he was allowed to take his paints and his suit with him. It was never clear whether it was he or one of the guards who had misunderstood the final instructions, or whether the authorities relented and observed their original promises. Either way, the persecution was more imagined than real.)

Speck's demeanor relaxed. He had had a chance to ventilate his feelings and could now turn to the one vestige of his familiar jail life, one last cup of coffee for the doctor.

Ziporyn took from his briefcase the book Speck had been talking about, *Justice, U.S.A.*, an investigation of the prejudicial obstacles with which a free press can impede the right to free speech. The psychiatrist had first to convince Speck that various sensational claims quoted in the book about Speck's activities before and after the murders were not made by the book's authors themselves, but by the press they were criticizing for publishing these claims before Speck went to trial. The particular passage to which Speck had objected was one quoting *Life* magazine as reporting in its issue following the murders: "Thursday morning, only a few hours after the killings, Speck was in a tavern eleven blocks away from the nurses' apartment. As usual, he had a knife. Suddenly he put his arm around the bartender's neck and stuck the knife edge against his throat. 'This knife has killed several persons,' he said. Everyone except the bartender joined in the laughter."

When Ziporyn had finally persuaded Speck that the book itself was not stating this as a fact, Speck was still anxious to prove it a lie.

"I was asleep in my room Thursday morning."

"Maybe it happened before you went to sleep. But that's not the point. Let's suppose, for the sake of argument, it is true. Suppose you did flash the knife. Don't you see what it means?"

"No."

"Well, it proves to me you were out of your mind at the time. Don't you see? Look, suppose a perfectly sane person kills eight people. Does he run around in bars, saying: 'I did it'? Of course not. He would look for the fastest way to get out of town. Only somebody out of their mind would kill eight people and then brag about it in a bar hours later. See the point?"

Unconvincingly, Speck replied: "I guess so."

"You guess so? Well, it's clear to me. *If* you flashed that knife and said what they claim, you must have been completely out of touch with reality, because even the slightest awareness of the world would make a killer shut up, hide and run. That business with the bartender, if true, would be conclusive proof that you were insane at the time, because it is clearly an insane act, an act apart from the ordinary rules of reason, logic or experience."

Speck remained unimpressed and continued leafing through the book. The concept of his mental irresponsibility was too complex for him and he preferred to grasp at something simpler.

"Has your wife seen this book?" he asked.

"Yes, she thinks it's well done."

"Does she ever ask you about me?"

"Occasionally. I talk about you to her. She knows that I think that this was not your fault, and she knows I like you, so she's prepared to like you, too."

The idea of Ziporyn's wife liking him pleased Speck enough to bring a brief smile to his lips, but he would not accept the psychiatrist's argument. "It *was* my fault," Speck insisted.

It was Ziporyn's last chance to try and impress on Speck the true nature of his responsibility, or lack of it, for the crime he was accused of committing.

"Richard, I believe you did not choose to be a killer. I believe that what happened was not the result of your conscious decision. We don't ask to be born. We have nothing to say about the color of our eyes, or the shape of our heads, or the construction of our brains. If the next guy is smarter than you, it's not to his credit, he didn't earn his brains—they're a gift of nature. And if he didn't fall on his head, that's his good luck, too. And if he had a father who lived, parents who taught him, or good friends who encouraged him, that again is his good luck. We have nothing to say about our anatomy or what we inherit or the things that happen to us in spite of ourselves. After all these things mold us, then we react the way we were made. To hold you responsible is like holding a leaky jar responsible for the water it loses—rather than the materials from which the jar was made and the way it was manufactured. Sure, some jars leak and some don't. The leaky jars were made wrong or they were damaged. Like every other human being, you, Richard, are the product of your heredity and your environment. *You* didn't pick either one. I can find what you did terrible. I do, and you do, too. But I can't honestly find you responsible for your actions. Do you understand?"

Richard Speck did not answer. He held his head in his hands and sobbed. He looked up and tears were streaming down his face as he shook his head, still unable, unwilling to comprehend his situation. His tension was proving intolerable and he looked around the cell for distraction. He snatched a men's magazine from one of the cardboard boxes in the corner and held it out to Ziporyn.

"Do you believe this?" he asked.

Ziporyn looked at the article. Typically, it was a lurid description of a black mamba killing four people on horseback.

"Sure, why not?"

Speck laughed with a faint note of hysteria in his voice. "I like what it says here—if a king cobra bites you, the best thing to do is lie down and die comfortable. If a black mamba bites you, there's not even time for that."

He laughed again and the laugh rang hollow in the stripped prison cell. Ziporyn made one more effort. "As you've been told many times, you have real brain damage. You just can't control your feelings. It's not your fault that you didn't get real medical care."

"What good would it have done? You know what would have happened if I'd been brought to you on the outside. I'd have listened politely, agreed with what you said, and then gone away and laughed at you."

"Of course. You've done that here, too. Don't you think I know that you haven't always been truthful with me? But that's the point—even the wrong things are the *result* of your brain damage. I can't hold your *symptoms* against you, and in your case your personality and actions are the symptoms of mental defect. I can't hold them against you any more than I can blame a guy with tuberculosis for coughing."

He had listened intently to these last remarks and sat deep in thought. The psychiatrist took his leave, promising to see him again in Peoria.

"I hope so, Doc. Will you bring your wife, too?"

"Of course. Meanwhile, think about what I've told you."

"I will, Doc, I will."

Ziporyn left the cell and stood by the outer door of the maximum security block, waiting for the guard to unlock it. Speck stood by the bars of his cell and waved his long-fingered hand.

"See you in Peoria, Doc."

Peoria

RICHARD SPECK WAS WATCHING "MACHINE GUN KELLY" ON TELEvision when the Sheriff's deputies came to take him from his cell at midnight on Tuesday, February 14. He had been looking forward to that movie for several days and he was annoyed that the deputies had interrupted him in the middle of it. As prisoner 387443 took his leave of the maximum security block, he asked his good friend Mark Clancy to be sure to write and tell him what happened to Machine Gun Kelly in the end. The date was February 14, 1967, exactly seven months after eight nurses were killed in their house on the South-East Side of Chicago.

The man accused of their murder was placed between two armed deputies in the back seat of an unmarked car, the second of three that slipped through the gates of Cook County Jail into a dense fog to make their way along Route 55 to Peoria, Illinois, 150 miles southwest of Chicago. Speck had noted with satisfaction that with him went his cherished paint set (minus a palette knife, under renewed security measures), some Western paperbacks, the radio and his dark blue tailor-made suit. The lead and tail cars of the caravan were filled with more deputies, armed with shotguns and machine guns. At 2:45 A.M. they deposited their prisoner in a cell on the fourth floor of the Peoria County Jail, across Hamilton Boulevard from the modern, L-shaped five-story County Courthouse where his trial was to begin in six days.

Back at Cook County Jail, a few days after Speck's departure, Ziporyn went down to the maximum security block to talk to Mark Clancy. With both Speck and Gambino gone, Clancy was left with only a guard for company. For entertainment he preferred poetry. When Ziporyn arrived, Clancy was relaxing on his bunk, reading a ballad by the French poet François Villon.

"Hi, Doc," he said affably. "You know something, this guy Villon is great. He really speaks my language."

Of all the poets Clancy might have chosen, this lyrical fifteenth-century rogue, who uniquely raised crime to the level of an exquisite romance, was certainly the most appropriate to his situation.

The bunk Clancy was lying on was covered with a handsome new bedspread in red and black plaid. It made his otherwise dingy cell positively glow. The psychiatrist asked him where he had got it. Clancy laughed.

"Richard gave it to me when he left. He got it from that broad in Montreal who was writing to him. Sharp, huh? Poor old Richard, they pulled him out halfway through 'Machine Gun Kelly.' Wait till I tell him Kelly turned out to be a fag. At the end, Kelly was whimpering, crying, begging for mercy, just a punk. Richard'll flip when I write and tell him."

Clancy's voice had been a mixture of disgust at the humiliation of Machine Gun Kelly and amusement at the effect the news of this would have on Speck. Clancy's affection for his former cell mate was unconcealed.

"You like the guy, don't you?" Ziporyn asked.

The smile on Clancy's handsome, square-cut face disappeared as he said, after a moment's thought: "Yeah. I do. He's not bad at all. I've had worse cellies, I can tell you. I hope he's okay now."

"You talked to Richard a lot, Mark," the psychiatrist said. "What's your opinion of the whole case?"

Clancy looked flattered that the doctor had asked him for his view.

"Really want to know?"

Ziporyn nodded.

"Well—I'm no psychiatrist, of course—but, just as a friend of his, I think if he did it, he must have been drunk or out of his mind. I can't see him doing it deliberately—he's just not made that way. The way I figure it, he was drunk or on pills and went in to rob the joint, and something happened to snap him. I don't think he remembers. I don't think he knows any more about it than we do."

Ziporyn had known Clancy for more than a year. He knew him to be highly intelligent, intensely loyal to his friends and naturally hostile to authority. But Clancy had not spoken now, Ziporyn felt, to protect a "cellie." Clancy knew that the psychiatrist was sympathetic to Speck's position, so that there was no need to "sell" him on it. At the same time, Clancy had expounded his ideas to Ziporyn as if they must be coming as fresh information to the psychiatrist. He had no notion of the detailed theory Ziporyn had already built up, since Ziporyn had never previously discussed Speck's case in depth with Clancy. The psychiatrist found it interesting that the one person who had been even closer to Speck than he himself since the summer of 1966 had independently arrived at an identical conclusion. Clancy's views obviously did not add professional weight to Ziporyn's theory, but this personal impression on the part of a sensitive individual was certainly not without value.

Speck had waited seven months for his trial to begin. One more week, even in the strange surroundings of the Peoria County Jail, in a cell four feet narrower than the one in Chicago, apparently did not prove to be the intolerable burden he had expected. He spent the time quietly painting and sketching—restricted to soft, harmless crayons, instead of the lethal pencils he had been used to. On the morning of Monday, February 20, he dressed in his "court" suit, with a handkerchief bearing the monogram "R.S." tucked neatly in the breast pocket. He wore a slim dark tie and white shirt. Freshly shaved and barbered, he was ready to go. Two sheriff's deputies clipped handcuffs on each of his wrists and led him to a closed police truck which drove him over to the courthouse.

It was 11:30 A.M., two hours later than the scheduled start of the trial, but the machine was slowly grinding into action and nothing would stop it till a jury reached a verdict. The police truck backed up close to the rear entrance of the courthouse and Speck was bundled out through a gauntlet of press and television cameramen into the building and up to the second-floor courtroom. (To avoid future security risks, it was decided to keep Speck for the rest of the trial in a cell on the ground floor of the courthouse.)

The twenty-seven reporters who had been given the coveted accreditation to what the Chicago newspapers had been pleased to call the "crime of the century" were briefed on how they were expected to behave by Judge Herbert Paschen a short while before Speck's arrival. It had been said that the Chicago press had treated the Speck case with immense reserve, compared with their traditional blood-and-guts reporting of murder most foul. By comparison with previous efforts this may have been true. But still the public was not deprived of comprehensive coverage, including a special eight-page supplement on the case in the *Chicago Tribune* shortly after the murders, that appropriately corresponded to the sensational nature of the crime. With fresh memories of prejudicial press behavior during the Cleveland murder trial of Dr. Sam Sheppard, Judge Paschen had issued fourteen directives to avoid anything similar in Peoria. These directives included bans on using cameras, tape recorders and even sketch pads inside the courthouse; on discussing the case with any witnesses, prospective or chosen jurors, lawyers and court employees; even on buying the daily transcript until after the verdict. The directive had come in for sharp criticism from the press, and the *Chicago Tribune* brought suit in the Illinois state legislature to have some of the directives removed.

Judge Paschen's fear of prejudicing Richard Speck's case was perhaps best illustrated by a passage in directive 9: "Nothing except that which happens in open court, adduced only in evidence and argument in open court, will be disseminated. The news media are placed upon notice as to the impropriety of publishing material not introduced in the proceedings. The news media must be content with the task of reporting the case as it unfolds in the courtroom—not pieced together from extra-judicial statements."

The judge, aged 61, a silver-haired patrician with a soft, warm voice, mellow as a bassoon, made clear his intentions when he assembled the accredited reporters in his chambers to soothe their bristling tempers. Calmly, he told them: "The eyes of the world are on this trial. We don't want a reversal on this case, as we've had on other cases in the recent past, because of anything that's been published that is prejudicial to a fair trial for Richard Franklin Speck. We're not going to change the directives now.* We want to see if there are going to be a few bastards among you before we do anything."

The reporters laughed and the judge rose to put on his robes for the trial, announcing—somewhat incongruously—to the newsmen as they left his room: "Okay boys, let's get this show on the road."

* Shortly after the trial began, in response to the *Tribune*'s suit, the judge allowed the sale to the press of daily transcripts once the jury was selected and also agreed to the publication of the names of prospective jurors after they had been excused and of the jury itself when all twelve (plus two alternates) had been chosen. By general agreement among those covering the trial, the other directives never had an unduly restrictive effect.

The Trial Begins

"THE COOK COUNTY GRAND JURY OF JULY, 1966, CHARGES THAT on or about July 14, 1966, in said county, Richard Franklin Speck committed the offense of murder in that he intentionally and knowingly strangled and stabbed and thus killed Suzanne Farris.

"The Cook County grand jury of July, 1966, charges that on or about July 14, 1966, in said county, Richard Franklin Speck committed the offense of murder in that he intentionally and knowingly strangled and killed Nina Jo Schmale.

"The Cook County grand jury of July, 1966, charges that on or about July 14, 1966, in said county, Richard Franklin Speck committed the offense of murder in that he intentionally and knowingly strangled and killed Patricia Ann Matusek.

"The Cook County grand jury. . . ."

The litany, with its eight almost identical verses, took Judge Paschen twelve minutes to read. Couched in the colorless, horribly simple, judicial language of the indictments, the enormity of the crime, its substance and import, was perhaps more effectively conveyed than in all the reams of newsprint devoted to that summer night on the South-East Side of Chicago.

Gerald Getty had won what was felt to be an important victory for his client Richard Speck by having all eight murder charges combined together in one trial with one verdict and one sentence. Prosecutor William Martin had fought hard to have each murder tried separately, so that a failure to convict on the first charge might be reversed in the trial on one of the subsequent charges. But Getty's victory was not unalloyed. The repetition of the eight indictments, even though the judge had insisted to the prospective jurors that it carried no implication of guilt, had an unavoidable hypnotic effect, associating the name Richard Franklin Speck again and again with "the offense of murder . . . intentionally and knowingly . . . strangled . . . stabbed . . . killed. . . ."

Richard Franklin Speck himself sat through it all holding his chin in his right hand, his eyes staring glassily ahead of him, not at the judge, but through him. Before Judge Paschen opened the trial, Speck, accompanied by two deputies, and now unmanacled, had walked slowly to his swivel chair at the defense table between Getty and James Gramenos, with another defense attorney, James Doherty behind him. His jaws chewed slowly on some gum. He looked neither tense nor relaxed, just numb. When his name was called out, he had to be prompted by Doherty before he reacted by rising and bowing slightly to the judge. Speck's trial had begun.

If Speck had needed any concrete proof that the pretrial publicity had left no one without some kind of opinion about his role in the nurses' murders, such proof was provided by the six weeks it took to find an apparently fair and impartial jury. Getty and Martin had to question 610 veniremen before they could agree on the twelve jurors and two alternates. In the process of jury selection, prospective jurors were "excused for cause" if they revealed any bias for or against the defendant or if they were unwilling to accept the death penalty. In addition, defense and prosecution counsel had at their disposal peremptory challenges with which they could dismiss a prospective juror they did not want, without having to state their reasons. Although Getty had managed to consolidate the eight murder charges into one trial, he was able to have the murders considered separately when it came to allotting the number of peremptory challenges. Thus, since Illinois law permitted 20 peremptories for a murder charge, each side in the Speck case was entitled to 160 peremptories to get rid of prospective jurors it felt might jeopardize its chances of success. This gave Getty wide scope in uncovering latent prejudices which pretrial publicity had nurtured in the minds of the Peoria veniremen summoned to decide on the fate of Richard Speck.

While bias remained a subtle and elusive element—and Getty had to muster all his great trial experience to pin it down—Martin's task was more straightforward. Admittedly, bias could work against the prosecution, but in this case of the murder of eight young nurses it was highly unlikely. Martin's primary objective was to find jurors who did not oppose the death penalty. In pretrial hearings, defense counsel had successfully argued that it would have been improper for the judge himself to ask prospective jurors whether they were against Illinois's death penalty, since this would tend in the jury's mind to associate the judge with the prosecution side. As a result, the question was left to the prosecution.

Judge Paschen told the veniremen before they were subjected to individual questioning by prosecution and defense counsel that at least three verdicts would be presented for their consideration in this case: not guilty, guilty with the sentence to be a term of imprisonment fixed by the judge, and guilty with the death penalty. As each venireman sat by himself in the jury box for interrogation, out of hearing of the other prospective jurors, Martin would pause at the end of some perfunctory questions about the venireman's background before saying: "You understand that there will be three separate verdicts presented in this case. If we fail to prove the defendant's guilt beyond a reasonable doubt, you would sign a verdict of 'not guilty.' If we succeed, you might choose to sign a verdict of 'guilty' in which the defendant would be sentenced to serve a number of years in the state penitentiary, the number being fixed by His Honor. A third verdict would be death, which in this case the State will ask. With those three verdicts in mind, do you have any conscientious or religious objection against the death penalty?"

Hundreds of times in those six weeks of jury selection, this question was asked, identically worded, with the same intonation, flat, matter-of-fact, totally undramatic. Yet every time it brought a hush to the court room quite unlike the shuffling silence that accompanied other questions. At this point, both Martin and Getty would stare fixedly at the prospective juror watching for any flinch, half-smile, intake of breath, hesitation, shrug or blink that might precede or accompany the answer. A "yes" was simple and immediate cause for dismissal, but a "no" did not automatically satisfy Martin. It was a vital question, one that went to the very depths of a man's feelings about life and death. The man's reaction could reveal how firm, resolute, confident he was in reaching a decision. The personal responsibility involved was hammered home immediately with Martin's next question: "If you felt that this was a proper case, would you sign a verdict of death?" There was never any emphasis in Martin's voice on the word "you," but the weight the word carried by itself was unmistakable. Most of the veniremen who accepted the death penalty in principle also accepted the *personal* responsibility of signing such a verdict, but enough of them yielded to the second challenge to make it worthwhile for Martin to pursue his two-pronged attack.

No one watched the veniremen more closely than Getty while the question of the death penalty was raised. On a number of occasions, Getty's subsequent peremptory dismissal of a prospective juror might be traced back to a moment when the person hesitated at Martin's first question, about his attitude in principle, and then glanced quickly at Speck before answering with a firm "yes."

Speck's own reaction remained impassive. The intricate psychological battle was being waged over his head. It did not seem to have much to do with him. He looked bored.

Getty was constantly on the lookout for weaknesses in a venireman's answers which Martin might have hoped to gloss over. An elderly, gray-haired control clerk at Caterpillar Tractors, the dominant Peoria industry, told Judge Paschen in preliminary questioning that he had read about the Speck case in the newspapers, but had no fixed opinion. The judge asked him if he could be a fair and impartial juror. The man answered: "I believe so." To Martin's questions, the man gave satisfactory, neutral-sounding answers. The prosecution seemed happy with him. Getty was not so sure.

"Now then," the Public Defender began, smiling affably, "you told His Honor you 'believe' you could be a fair and impartial juror, that you have read about the case and have no fixed opinion. From what you read of the case, tell me what you recall exactly."

"I was a little shaken up at the time, but I don't recall any details."

"Shaken up?"

"Well, naturally, I mean. . . ."

"You heard that eight girls were killed. Anything else?"

"That, and one of them under the bed."

"Do you recall anything of the defendant's background?"

"He's supposed to be an ex-con, isn't he?"

"Is *that* what you remember? Knowing this, might it have an influence on you in this case?"

"I really don't know."

"The fact that you read it in the papers—you're certainly going to take that into the jury box."

"Well . . . I couldn't erase it, no."

"That's right. We don't have any magic erasers here. It might never come out in evidence, but you'd have it with you?"

"Yes."

"Therefore it could influence you?"

"I suppose so."

"At the time you read about it, did you form any opinion?"

The man did not answer. Getty raised his voice.

"You didn't have an opinion that this man was innocent, did you?"

The man blushed and stammered: "You m-m-mean, the defendant?"

Getty replied in a harsh staccato that seemed like a parody of all the popular attitudes toward his client: "Yes, this man Speck." Speck himself looked up sharply, glancing from his lawyer to the increasingly embarrassed venireman in the jury box.

"I couldn't say," the man mumbled.

"But you did remember that he was an 'ex-con'?"

The man stared ahead of him, his eyes registering, perhaps for the first time, the realization of an untapped bias in the depth of his mind. Judge Paschen quickly excused him, "for cause." Getty commented later, outside the courtroom, "Here was a perfect case of a man I knew at my fingertips to be a 'killer' and I got him off the jury, got him off for cause." For Getty, in this capital case, with his proud record of never having lost a client to the electric chair, all potentially dangerous jurors were "killers."

In contrast to Martin's solid, earnest manner, Getty was avuncular, folksy, making a man-to-man appeal with the simple farm and laboring people of Peoria. His own round, smile-wrinkled face minimized any alienating effect a big-city lawyer might have had. One of the points he constantly sought to make with prospective jurors was to convince them of the difficulty of his task—"Look, I'm charged with defending this guy," he told a red-faced laboratory assistant, "and I don't want twelve persons in that box with fixed opinions, do I? What kind of shape would I be in then? All I'm looking for is a fair trial, so I want to know if you have a fixed opinion."

Getty continued in this vein, just short of wheedling. He reviewed at some length the principle that the law presumes a man innocent until he is proved guilty. The venireman understood all that, didn't he? He had heard the judge make that point, hadn't he?

"And you," Getty finally asked the man, "would you have difficulty in presuming Richard Speck innocent?"

Having nodded himself into a state of dormant acquiescence, the venireman dutifully said: "No."

"Of course not. And you wouldn't want to just listen to the State's witnesses and make up your mind and say: 'That's it, I don't want to hear any more,' would you?"

"No."

"Wouldn't you want to be the kind of juror who'd be prepared to weigh all the evidence before making up his mind?"

"Yes," said the man, as if hypnotized, "that's the kind of juror I'd want to be."

"Of course you would." Getty then went over the possible verdicts, asking him whether he was prepared to sign a "not guilty" verdict if he had a reasonable doubt, and whether he was equally willing to consider signing a "guilty" verdict that carried with it only a prison sentence as he would be to give the death penalty. The man's answers came as pat as ever, but Getty was not convinced. He repeated his questions and suddenly the man made a turnabout and said he would accept the death penalty as the only possible verdict. Judge Paschen excused him "for cause."

Another "killer." How had Getty sensed this? Later he commented simply, with his hands fluttering in the air: "Fingertips, fingertips."

Neither Getty nor Martin, in the prolonged process of jury selection, gave much indication of what their eventual trial strategy would be. Occasionally Getty would ask whether the prospective jurors knew anything about fingerprints, whether they gave any special weight to testimony made by police officers, pointing to the circumstantial aspect of the case. He also made the point that besides the three verdicts listed by Judge Paschen, "other verdicts" were possible. This was taken to refer to a verdict pronouncing Speck "guilty but insane," but Getty never spelled this out.

At the end of six weeks of maneuver, bargain and compromise, Martin and Getty finally chose a jury of seven men and five women who had convinced the prosecution that they would be prepared "in a proper case," to sign a verdict carrying the death penalty, and who had convinced the defense that they would not bring to the trial a fixed opinion based on a knowledge of the case gained from copious newspaper, radio and television coverage. It was perhaps too much to say that Getty was absolutely convinced he had got a jury without fixed opinion, something he felt was an impossibility in the circumstances, but this was the closest he thought he could get.

Throughout the monotonous process of selecting that jury, Speck sat and waited, impervious to the legal haggling going on around him. The wheels of the machine were moving without him. It scarcely seemed to matter whether he, Richard Speck, was there or not. In his courthouse cell he painted and sketched and read his Westerns. As ever, he was complaining of headaches. His eyes hurt him and he was taken to an ophthalmologist and fitted for glasses. After resisting the idea of wearing glasses since boyhood, Speck finally yielded, but his vanity would not yet let him wear them in public. As he walked into court each day, he would slip the glasses off before sitting down at the defense table.

Dr. Ziporyn did have one more talk with Speck, but only brief and inconsequential, at the invitation of Getty. The Public Defender telephoned Ziporyn on Thursday, March 16, asking him whether he would like to come to Peoria. The following Wednesday, Ziporyn had to go to the state capital, Springfield, to testify before a House committee on drug addiction. On his way back to Chicago, he stopped off in Peoria to see Getty, who told him he had not yet decided whether or not to go for an insanity defense, preferring for the time being to "play it by ear." After dinner they went over to the courthouse to visit Speck. Getty and his assistant, Gramenos, accompanied Ziporyn into the cell.

Speck was surprised to see Ziporyn and seemed a little shy. His cell was large and well lit, and the psychiatrist noticed that the change of scene was not having the feared bad effect on him. Speck looked comfortable and well fed.

"You're getting paunchy," Ziporyn teased him.

"Yeah, the food's better here than in Chicago," said Speck, patting his stomach with an appreciative grin. He saw Ziporyn looking round the room and up at the light in the center of the ceiling. Speck had tied the light cord in the form of a noose.

"That's my appeal," Speck commented wryly.

With the lawyers present, Ziporyn did not see any point in making more than light conversation. Speck gave him some Easter cards to mail to his mother and sister Martha, and Ziporyn took his leave. Speck's "Good-bye" was friendly, casual, the tension of their last meeting in Cook County Jail completely forgotten.

The Perpetrator

RICHARD SPECK HAD APPARENTLY COMPLETELY FORGOTTEN HIS last conversation with Dr. Marvin Ziporyn in Chicago, and the point Ziporyn had tried to make: that Speck was not legally responsible for the murders—even if he had committed them—because of mental incompetency caused by brain damage and drugs or alcohol. But as far as his trial in Peoria was concerned, this made absolutely no difference; Speck was not the only person who had disregarded Ziporyn's arguments. As Gerald Getty told the jury in his opening statement on April 3, "The theory of the defense is that Speck, this defendant, is not the perpetrator of this crime."

Getty had finished "playing it by ear" and decided to base his case on the claim that Speck was not in the nurses' house on the night of the murders. If the question of insanity was to be raised at all, it could now only serve in mitigation of sentence if Speck were found guilty. Getty had apparently decided that Speck's mental state was the second and weaker of two cards he had to play.

"The only issue here," Getty told the jury, "as in every criminal case, or I might say in most criminal cases, [is that] the State must prove that the crime actually happened. And then they must prove who is the perpetrator who did it. In this case, before we ever started out, I told you that this crime happened. The State does not have to prove that the crime happened. Yes, it did happen. Eight girls were killed. Martin has outlined his theory of what he expects the evidence to prove. And I knew every bit of that evidence, and that is why I told each and every juror here about that before you even started.

"The theory of the defense is that Speck, this defendant, is not the perpetrator of this crime. The State will have to prove this beyond a reasonable doubt. And their evidence will be an eyewitness, whom you will have to test—whether that witness is actually an eyewitness. [Martin] also indicated that he expects the evidence to show three fingerprints. And, of course, he assumes these are the defendant's. But after you hear all the evidence, it is not Martin telling you what the evidence is, it is not Getty telling you what the evidence is, it will be up to you jurors to test the witnesses from the witness stand and arrive at your verdict from your own mind and your own conscience."

William Martin had presented in his opening statement a detailed account of how the State believed Speck came to be in the neighborhood of the townhouse; how he had entered the house at 11 P.M. on Wednesday, July 13, 1966, had herded the six girls present in the house into one of the bedrooms, adding the other three as each of them came home, and then murdered them one by one, raping the last victim, Gloria Davy, and leaving only one survivor, Corazon Amurao. The State's case, as outlined by Martin, was circumstantial —Speck's presence in the neighborhood, the discovery of three fingerprints corresponding to his own, *two* T-shirts of the same size he normally wore and, above all, the identification by Miss Amurao. Getty's reply—equally circumstantial—was to fight the evidence, piece by piece. The issue was a man's fingerprints, his facial features, his clothing, his movements. His nature, his psychology, his conditioning and his ultimate responsibility—all this was deemed irrelevant.

The prosecution established with their first two witnesses, sailors Dante Bargellini and George Mackey, that Speck had tried unsuccessfully to get a job aboard a Great Lakes tanker on the day before the murders and then expressed the wish to go to New Orleans. Getty did not shake this testimony in cross-examination and was content to establish that Speck's hair at the time "was long and combed back over his head." Bargellini and Mackey also testified for the State that Speck had been in the vicinity of the nurses' house the day before the murders.

Bringing Speck closer and closer to the scene of the murders, Martin spent the second day of testimony painstakingly tracing the defendant's movements, at the Shipyard Inn—where witnesses, one of them with his leg in a cast at the time, saw Speck with a small black gun and a knife with a three- or four-inch blade. He was also seen at the gas station diagonally opposite the nurses' house, and at the National Maritime Union, only half a block from the house. From cross-examination of each witness, Getty extracted that the man they saw had long hair, combed back, a pock-marked face, and wore a red polo shirt. From the manager of the Shipyard Inn, he established that the bed in Speck's room on the Thursday morning after the murders had been slept in. (In his opening statement, Getty had claimed that Speck spent the night of the murders in that bed.)

Having established Speck's presence in the murder neighborhood, Martin was ready on the third day to present his star witness, Corazon Pieza Amurao, to describe the night of the murders and identify the man she saw at the time.

The young, bespectacled prosecution counsel gripped the sides of his wooden lectern, his knuckles showing white as he asked in a dry, metallic voice: "Now, Miss Amurao, if you see that same man in the courtroom today who came to your bedroom door on Wednesday night, July 13, 1966, would you please step down and point him out."

It was the time-honored question of all classic murder trials. In the trial of the People of Illinois versus Richard Franklin Speck, the question bore practically the whole burden of the prosecution's case. Now the question was addressed to the sole survivor of a night of mass murder for which endless retelling had rendered the word "horror" most horribly superfluous. Corazon Amurao, the Filipino nurse from San Luis Batangas, stared intently and unflinchingly at William Martin as he asked the question. Without any word of acknowledgment, she rose slowly as a bailiff opened the gate of the witness stand. In a starched white short-sleeved blouse, dark blue culottes modestly reaching to below the knees of her black-stockinged legs, and flat brown shoes, she walked a dozen short steps to the polished oak defense table. Clutching a white handkerchief in her left fist, she held her tiny four-foot-ten frame erect and steadily raised her right hand to within six inches of Richard Speck's ashen face. "This is the man."

Her small features remained expressionless as her accusing hand hovered by Speck's left cheek a split second longer following her statement. Her four words seemed similarly to hover in the air for that hushed split second. Speck's eyes flickered momentarily toward Miss Amurao and then resumed their glassy stare at the judge's bench behind her. She returned to the witness stand while Martin's mechanical tones resumed the business of the prosecution case: "Identifying for the record, the defendant, Richard Franklin Speck."

This hushed, almost dreamlike sequence seemed to be the very core of the case against Speck. Speck's lawyers immediately acknowledged the acute effectiveness of the moment by branding it, in a huddle with Judge Paschen out of the hearing of the jury, as an "ostentatious display for the sole purpose of prejudicing the jury." Getty backed up this accusation by his assistant James Doherty with a motion for mistrial, which Judge Paschen promptly denied.

The impact of Miss Amurao's testimony in pointing to Richard Speck as the murderer of her eight fellow student nurses was intensified by her demeanor throughout Martin's three-hour direct examination. Her manner was at once determined in precise responses and highly charged with emotion as memories of her ordeal moved her to tears and sobs. She was the perfect prosecution witness—businesslike with the facts, but not cold and dehumanized with their personal implications.

Tracing the events after Miss Amurao had gone up to bed for the night, Martin had no need to prompt her in more than a perfunctory way—a favorite style of this eminently cool lawyer—to get the simple, vivid realities as she saw them, emphasized by unsophisticated, heavily accented English.

"What did you do after you arrived in your bedroom?"

"I lock our bedroom door and then I'm about to put off the light but Miss Gargullo told me not to, because she told me she is going to say her prayers first."

"What did you do after Miss Gargullo asked you not to turn the light off?"

"Then I went up to my bed and I sleep."

"Did you wake up at any time later, Wednesday, July 13?"

"Yes."

"And would you tell the court and jury how you happened to wake up?"

"I heard a knock in our bedroom. It was about four knocks and the knocking was done in a normal manner."

Miss Amurao's answers came at first in a quiet, level tone but, as the moment of her confrontation with the intruder approached, her voice faltered. "I went up to the . . . I went to the door," she said, fighting back tears, swallowing, and then continuing, "and I unlocked it and I started to open it and at once there's somebody who's pushing the door." She broke down and wept as she added: "Then I saw a man."

Getty proposed that Miss Amurao take a few minutes to compose herself. She regained a firm hold on her feelings and repaid the Public Defender's concern for her well-being with a devastating description of the intruder, uncomfortably close to that of the man Getty was defending.

"I saw a man standing on the center of our door," she said, "with a gun in his right hand pointed toward me and I noticed that he had marks on his face, the clothes was dark from the shoulders to the foot and his hair was blond, hair combed toward the back and some hair in the front."

The description shook one of the pillars of the defense which, according to Getty's opening statement, would throw doubt on the identification of Speck because the police sketch and police reports circulated after the crime described a man with hair in a crew cut, not combed back like Speck's, and made no reference to any pockmarks on his face. Getty was also seeking to establish that there was not enough light in the house at the time of the intrusion for Miss Amurao properly to identify the man. Martin, however, elicited testimony from Miss Amurao that the man stood in the light from her bedroom when she first saw him. It was after this that the prosecutor asked her to point out the man if she saw him in the courtroom.

After she had identified the man in court, Miss Amurao unfailingly referred to the intruder as "Speck" throughout her testimony. The repetition of the name took on all the aura of a proven fact. She recounted how he took the six girls present on his arrival to the house's large south bedroom, making them sit on the floor at the point of his small black gun.

"One of the girls," she said, "asked Speck: 'What do you want?' And then Speck answered: 'I want money, I'm going to New Orleans.' "

Her account revealed that he did not have to rummage through the house for the money, since the girls fetched money for him from their purses; that they remained unbound for about an hour after his arrival; that he carried on conversations with the American girls, which she did not understand; that when he did finally bind their hands and feet with strips meticulously cut from a bed sheet, there was no reference to gagging them as well. These new elements in the story deepened the mystery of how he managed to persuade the girls to cooperate with him without undue resistance or attempts to shout for help.

"And then," said Miss Amurao, "when Speck was tying Miss Davy's ankles, Miss Davy (who had come home at 11:30) said: "Why are you doing this? We are student nurses.' Then Speck answered: 'Oh, you are a student nurse,' and Speck was smiling during this time."

None of his actions, as described by Miss Amurao, was harsh up to this time. "When he was tying one of the girls, he told us: 'Don't be afraid, I'm not going to kill you.' "

At that point, Miss Amurao recalled, a doorbell rang downstairs. He had just finished tying Patricia Matusek's ankles, but had not yet tied her hands. He took the remaining untied girls—Miss Amurao and Merlita Gargullo—downstairs to see who was at the door, leaving the rest in the bedroom, unguarded. Miss Amurao's story left unanswered the question of why, with her hands still free, Miss Matusek did not try to free the others while the intruder was downstairs.

There was no one at the door. (Subsequent testimony revealed that it had been another student nurse, Tammy Sioukoff, who had come to borrow some bread for a sandwich but left again when she could get no response to her ringing.) The man Miss Amurao said was Speck then took her and Miss Gargullo back upstairs and tied them up like the rest. Miss Amurao said that she smelled alcohol on his breath, that he inexplicably asked Miss Gargullo, "Do you know karate?", that he nervously clicked his gun on the floor as he sat talking to the girls and was constantly looking out the bedroom window.

In the midst of this tense behavior, Miss Amurao testified, he stood up and walked over to Patricia Wilkening, untied her ankles and led her from the room.

Then began a stark counterpoint between Miss Amurao and Martin, recounting each of the eight murders. With the aid of the gray wooden scale models of the townhouse specially built by the FBI, Martin asked Miss Amurao to explain how each girl, represented in the model by a wooden block, was taken from the south bedroom, never to be seen alive again. Or, as Martin put it in his typical formal manner: "Let the record show that I have removed the wooden block bearing the name 'Wilkening' from the south bedroom." Miss Amurao's own account made a poignant contrast.

"After Speck had taken Miss Wilkening from the south bedroom, did you hear anything?"

"After about one minute, I heard Miss Wilkening say 'Ah.' It was like a sigh."

"Did you hear anything after the noise you just described?"

"No, I didn't hear anything."

After this, Mary Ann Jordan and Suzanne Farris arrived home. Miss Amurao said that Speck followed them up to the bedroom where the other girls were lying. He took them out of the room at gunpoint.

"I heard a noise as if Miss Jordan and Miss Farris were resisting. I just heard a noise as if. . . . They were talking in a low voice, but I don't know what they were talking. As if they were yelling, but in a low voice." And then: "Before he came back to the south bedroom I heard water running in the bathroom, as if Speck was washing his hands."

And the next. "After about one minute, I heard Nina Schmale say 'Ah,' just the same like Miss Wilkening." To which Martin intoned: "Let the record show that I have removed a wooden block with the name 'Schmale' from People's Exhibit 13 for identification." And again Miss Amurao added that before Speck returned, she heard water running in the bathroom.

A period of 20, 25 or 30 minutes passed between each girl's disappearance from the south bedroom and the man's return. During one of these periods, Miss Amurao stated, she and three other girls tried to hide behind and under beds, but all except Miss Amurao were discovered when the man returned. The morbid story resumed.

"Did you hear anything after Speck had taken Miss Pasion from the south bedroom?"

"After about two minutes, I heard Miss Pasion say 'Ah' more loud than the two other American girls." More water running in the bathroom, another 20 minutes passed.

"What happened after you saw Speck carrying Miss Gargullo from the south bedroom?"

"Then after about five minutes, I heard Miss Gargullo say 'Masikit.' "

"Could you tell the court and jury what 'Masikit' means in your native language (Tagalog)?"

"It means 'it hurts.' "

Detail was piled upon pathetic detail. Miss Amurao reported Patricia Matusek's last words: "Will you please untie my ankles first?" Then, as Martin removed Miss Matusek's wooden block from the south bedroom in the townhouse-model, Miss Amurao arrived at the most harrowing part of her story—the ordeal as she lay across from the bed which once belonged to Miss Wilkening, on which the man now approached his last victim, Gloria Davy, the woman Richard Speck said reminded him of his wife, Shirley.

"Speck stood up and I saw that he was removing Miss Davy's jeans."

"What happened next?"

"Then I heard a pants being unzipped."

"And what happened after that?"

"Then, when I look at them, I saw that Speck was already on top of Miss Davy."

At that point, Miss Amurao again broke down and wept. Judge Paschen called a brief recess. Sympathetic, but showing his unperturbed professionalism, Martin resumed after the recess with the question: "Miss Amurao, you were describing what occurred when you saw the defendant, Richard Speck, on top of Gloria Davy. Will you tell us what you saw or what you heard?"

"I saw Speck was on top of Davy. Then, when I saw he was right on top of Davy, I put my face down. And then I heard the bedsprings moving. . . . After a few minutes, Speck asked: 'Will you please put your legs around my back?' "

"Where was your head at the time?"

"My head was facing down on the floor."

"Could you estimate how long you heard the bedsprings move in Miss Wilkening's bed at that time?"

"I heard it for about 20 or 25 minutes."

"Was your head down during that time?"

"Yes."

"When did you next look up?"

"About five minutes after the bedsprings stopped. I looked up and I saw that Davy and Speck was not there anymore."

Proof of the total impact of Miss Amurao's testimony was frozen in the face of every juror and every spectator in the court as they listened to this account of the rape of Gloria Davy.

After a pause, Miss Amurao resumed her testimony and told the court that it was 45 to 50 minutes before Speck returned after removing Miss Davy—"the longest time he was out"—but she knew nothing of what had passed in that three-quarters of an hour. Everything that followed—the man's departure, her rescue and recuperation in hospital—was necessarily anticlimactic, but the effect of her appearance in court that Wednesday, April 5, was indelible, in Getty's own private words, "devastating."

His cross-examination the next day was short but by no means defeatist. Unsurprisingly, he found Miss Amurao considerably less cooperative with him than she had been with Martin. He showed her the same kindly, avuncular manner he had employed in his examination of prospective jurors, but her response to him was consistently cold. The first point Getty sought to make—that the American girls at the townhouse were in the habit of coming home with their boy friends after dates—was achieved without difficulty. But from then on, her memory began to fail her. After remembering in minute detail the answers to the previous day's prosecution questions about events leading up to and following the murders, she was suddenly unable to remember whether the evening was warm or not or whether the house's one air-conditioner was on or off. She quickly established a leitmotiv for her cross-examination: "I can't recall."

Seeking to weaken her identification of the intruder, Getty tried a little trick with the question of the bedroom light, which she said was shining on the intruder when she opened the door to him.

"You say you saw the man there with a gun?"

"Yes, sir."

"And who turned the light off, then?"

"The light was already on."

"Well, who turned it off?"

"I don't know who turned it off."

Getty recognized that he was not going to get her to say the light was off when she first saw the intruder and so he dropped the line of questioning. Her answers had been firm and without any sign of wavering. He had to content himself with making the point that the south bedroom, in which the intruder kept the girls, was not lit until the very end, when the man returned to see if anyone was left and did not notice Miss Amurao under the bed.

Evidently trying to soften her up, Getty attempted several little jokes and humorous remarks in exchanges with her, with the judge and with Martin, but Miss Amurao gave him not so much as a smile.

A major part of Getty's battle against Miss Amurao's identification of Speck lay in the discrepancies between police descriptions of the intruder, which police said they compiled from Miss Amurao's description of him, and Speck as he actually looked at the time. Miss Amurao insisted, however, that she did not say anything about a crew cut, although this was in the police reports, and that she did make a point of saying the intruder had "marks on his face," although this was absent from the reports.

Getty's next assault on the identification procedure was more successful. Following many I-can't-recall's, Miss Amurao acknowledged that after Chicago police had shown her a book of over 100 photographs of wanted men in which she picked out one as "similar" to the intruder, she was then given three or four loose photographs to look at. From these she chose one as "more similar"—that of Richard Speck. The photograph, from the records of the U.S. Coast Guard, showed Speck with hair combed back and pockmarks visible on his face. While Miss Amurao was picking out this photograph, the police artist, Otis Rathel, was composing a sketch which police later said had come from Miss Amurao's description. The sketch showed a crew cut and no pockmarks, even though the artist had access to Speck's picture while he was drawing. Getty appeared content to have scored two points: the book of more than 100 photographs was irrelevant to police claims that the picture identification was a fair process, since Miss Amurao's final choice was taken from the three or four loose pictures; the police would not be able to verify Miss Amurao's description of the intruder, since her version now was at variance with the one they claimed she gave at the time of the murders.

Pleased with his progress, Getty suggested Miss Amurao might be "a little tired," but accepted her offer to continue with a third point that successfully added to the confusion over the whole process of police identification of the murderer. Rathel's sketch, which had been praised at the time of its publication in the press for its likeness to the subsequently arrested man, seemed to have nothing to do with Miss Amurao's description. Yet Miss Amurao insisted that she told Rathel, as she had told other police officers, that the intruder's hair was combed back and his face pockmarked, but that Rathel disregarded her remarks. Though she recalled emphasizing these two features to the artist, Miss Amurao added that she could not recall any of the man's other features.

Suddenly, as Getty itemized lips, nose, eyes, eyebrows, ears, Miss Amurao's habitual answer of "I can't recall" seemed about to come home to roost. She found herself finally resuming for Getty in one sentence the point he had apparently been aiming at all along.

"I can't recall about the man, about his ears, about his nose, or about his eyes, I can't recall."

Getty went over the points once more for good measure, seeking and getting an "I can't recall" to each, and then adding with a smile: "Now, any time you want a rest, Miss Amurao, you just tell me."

The Public Defender ended his cross-examination in a little over 90 minutes. He had scored his points, but they were points of detail. They did not seem to counteract the electrifying effect of Miss Amurao's positive identification of Richard Speck the day before, or the sureness of her account of the events she inexorably attributed to the pockmarked man with his hair combed back.

The State resumed its methodical case with police witnesses to describe what they found in the townhouse after the murders, the state of the bodies, the discovery, on the morning after the murders, of a wrinkled, sweat-soaked T-shirt, size 38-40 medium, BVD brand, and then the discovery two weeks later of a second T-shirt, size 38-40 medium, Hanes brand, wrapped inside Gloria Davy's purple and white jeans and white panties on one of the bunks in the south bedroom. Neither T-shirt had any blood on it and there was no explanation offered for why there were two.

Under protest from Getty, because the testimony "might further inflame the jury," the State called Dr. Eugene Tapia, autopsy surgeon who examined the girls' bodies. He found Pamela Wilkening, stabbed in the left breast and strangled; Suzanne Farris, stabbed eighteen times, in the chin, the neck and the back, and strangled; Mary Ann Jordan, stabbed in the neck, breast and in the eye; Nina Schmale, stabbed in the neck and strangled; Valentina Pasion, stabbed in the neck; Merlita Garguilo, stabbed in the neck and strangled; Patricia Matusek, strangled and kicked in the stomach; Gloria Davy, strangled. The clinical recitation of these facts augmented the emotional impact of Miss Amurao's description of the girls' last sighs and muffled screams. The seven men and five women of the jury sat pale and tense through the testimony, the strain telling on their drawn faces.

Martin then traced Speck's movements on the day following the murders, from tavern to tavern with his seaman friend, Robert "Red" Gerrald. Gerrald testified that in the Ebb Tide, "there was a lady and a man and they had brought up about these nurses being killed. So Richard, he made a statement to the bartender, 'Whoever did it must have been a sex maniac.' "

From the South Side taverns the prosecution witnesses trailed Speck to the North Side, to Skid Row, and finally to his attempted suicide and arrest in Cook County Hospital. The remaining piece of the State's jigsaw puzzle was the fingerprints, for which Martin presented three witnesses.

He first called Chicago Police Crime Laboratory technician William Scanlon. A total of 34 fingerprints had been found in the townhouse. Thirteen of these prints were identified as belonging to the nurses and one of the investigating policemen; 18, including six palm prints, were unidentified, leaving three that the State said belonged to Richard Speck. William Scanlon testified as to where the three vital prints had been located. On the door of the south bedroom, Scanlon said, he found one of the prints three and one-half inches above the knob; a second, two inches to the right of the knob, and the third, 16 and one-half inches from the bottom of the door and two and one-half inches from the door's outer edge.

Lieutenant Emil Giese, 18 years a fingerprint expert in the Chicago Police Department and Commander of its Identification Section, was called to the stand to identify the prints. He compared the prints found on the door with Richard Speck's fingerprints taken for registration with the U.S. Coast Guard in April 1966, and then again after being admitted under arrest to Cook County Jail hospital, three days after the murders. Analysis of ridge characteristics known as whorls, deltas, cores and bifurcations of the prints persuaded Giese that "these fingerprints are identical" to the right index, right middle and left middle fingerprints on the hands of Richard Speck.

Giese testified that ten to twelve characteristics were sufficient for identification of a fingerprint and that he had noted ten characteristics in common with Speck's right index, 17 with the right middle and 17 with the left middle prints. After 50 minutes of testimony, Giese concluded (referring to photographs of the prints on the door and of Speck's prints): "After examination as to basic ridge detail in both prints, it is my opinion that these fingerprints or impressions were made by the same individual"—Richard Speck.

Following a brief recess, Giese was subjected to more than two hours of cross-examination by Getty's chief assistant James Gramenos, who attempted to show that the fingerprints were too smudged to be positively identified, and that if they were anyone's, they were as much like those of victims Suzanne Farris and Gloria Davy, as those of Richard Speck. But Giese remained adamant. There was, in his opinion, ample evidence to show the prints were Speck's. At the end of the day, Gramenos heaved a long, dissatisfied sigh and said: "It is late in the day and I'm through." He had battered at the fingerprint evidence from all angles, but it still stood. Another prosecution fingerprint expert, this time one without police connections, Belgian-born André Moenssens, was brought in the next day to back up Giese's testimony. In cross-examination, Getty tried to suggest that it was possible that the prints (which he preferred to call "smudges") had been planted on the door by the Chicago police. Moenssens admitted that such "lifting" was possible, but it was his opinion that it had not been done in this case. The fingerprint evidence still stood.

The weakness of Getty's case against those fingerprints could be gauged by the fact that he did not put a fingerprint expert of his own on the stand in rebuttal when he began the defense case on Wednesday, April 12. Instead he brought eight members of Speck's family—his mother, five sisters, a brother and brother-in-law—as witnesses. The testimony of Speck's mother and five of her children was evidently only a perfunctory effort to portray the defendant in more human terms than had been possible in the grisly and technical detail that had preceded the defense case. The prosecution did not bother to cross-examine. Speck's younger sister, Carolyn, wept as she took the stand to testify how she had put Speck on the bus from Dallas to Chicago in March 1966. She was followed by her gaunt, thin-lipped mother, who blew a kiss to her son as she took the stand.

Speck half-smiled in acknowledgment. She testified that Speck's father had died when the defendant was just six years old, but otherwise contributed nothing new to the court record.

Before the rest of the family rose to offer similarly inconsequential personal testimony, Getty called to the stand the one sister, Martha, who lived in Chicago and had seen Speck a few days before the murders. She testified that her brother's hair had not been in a crew cut and that police had handed her notes to ask specific questions about his whereabouts when he telephoned after the murders. She remained protectively noncommittal in her answers under cross-examination concerning the brand of T-shirts Speck wore, as the prosecution attempted to match them up with the B.V.D. and Hanes T-shirts found at the townhouse. (Through a later police witness, the State established that Martha had been more communicative when questioned by the police and had named BVD and Hanes as two of the brands her brother wore.) Questioning of her husband followed a similar pattern, and then the rest of the family gave tearful testimony to their connection with the man sitting at the defense table in front of them.

The family was followed by Michael Compateso, a witness who offered circumstantial testimony that he had played pool with Speck an hour before Speck, according to Miss Amurao, knocked on her bedroom door.

With nothing to defeat the fingerprint evidence, Getty's case looked weak. He had promised to show that Speck was sleeping in his hotel bed at the time the murders were committed, but there had been nothing to show that this promise could be made good. What was left?

What was left was the bold, dramatic gesture of offering an alibi that placed Speck a mile and a half from the murders at the time they were committed, an alibi for which bartender Murrill Farmer swore: "I'll stake my life on it." The life that was in fact being staked was Richard Speck's. The bartender testified that Speck was in the South Side tavern where Farmer works, Kay's Pilot House, at midnight on July 13—the time that Corazon Pieza Amurao had sworn that Speck was preparing to remove the first of eight murder victims from the south bedroom of their townhouse, 12 blocks away. Farmer's testimony was backed up by his wife, Gerdena, who worked as a short-order cook in the same tavern.

The Farmers were on a list of prospective witnesses questioned in the summer of 1966 by the prosecution. The list was given to Getty under a provision that the prosecution's evidence and names of witnesses must be made available to the defense. The police and the State's Attorney's staff had questioned the Farmers repeatedly but were unable to shake their claims that Speck was in Kay's Pilot House from 11:30 P.M. to about 12:30 A.M. on the night of the murders. Now they were Getty's trump card.

Murrill Farmer testified that Speck had first been in the tavern, one block from the Shipyard Inn, about 8 P.M. on the night of July 13. He ordered a VO bourbon and Coca Cola. He was wearing a short-sleeved red shirt. He left after half an hour and returned at about 11:30 P.M., this time wearing a short-sleeved black shirt. "Speck told me he had spilled a drink on the red shirt and changed it," Farmer said. He noticed that on one of his arms was a tattoo, "a crude marked 'Shirley.' "

"What time did you see him?"

"It was very close to midnight."

"And how did you fix the time that he was in there?"

"At 12 o'clock, Arco Door Company [with headquarters nearby] has their break and they [Arco employees] were in for about ten minutes and they drink as much as they can in that time. I put a hamburger down [on the grill] for him [Speck] and I had to get the wife to finish it."

"Can you tell us what time he left?"

"Between 12:15 and 12:30."

Gerdena Farmer confirmed this story.

Cross-examination by prosecutor Martin was aimed more at suggesting that Farmer and his wife were mistaken about the times than that they might be telling outright lies. Martin seemed less coolly sure of himself than he had been throughout the gruelling trial, but he never showed any sign of panic. Both husband and wife remained firm and unrattled by the cross-examination. Gerdena asserted she knew what time it was because Speck appeared at the time she routinely washed the dishes each night—shortly before the midnight arrival of the Arco workers.

Having spent six weeks maneuvering to find a jury, Getty rested his case after just two days, presenting only 11 witnesses, compared with the prosecution's 42. He was obviously gambling everything on the chance that the quiet conviction of the bartender and his wife was strong enough to withstand the impression left by Corazon Amurao's testimony and the thorough scientific evidence of Speck's fingerprints being found on the door of the south bedroom of the townhouse.

The gamble failed. After only 49 minutes of deliberation, the jury returned with their verdict. On all eight charges they decided: "We, the jury, find the defendant, Richard Franklin Speck, guilty of murder in the manner and form as charged in the indictment, and we fix his punishment at death."

Richard Franklin Speck sat motionless in his chair at the defense table, showing not the slightest emotion. Judge Paschen adjourned the court, preparatory to hearing post-trial motions, after which he would pronounce sentence in Chicago. Speck stood up between two policemen and left the courtroom. As he was going through the door behind the judge's bench, the courtroom door at the front was opened and a deputy announced the verdict to a crowd of spectators waiting downstairs. Cheers and applause arose from the crowd, mainly girls and middle-aged women, cheerful in gay, casual clothes for one of the first warm days of spring. Speck turned his head at the noise. His mouth dropped open, uncomprehending eyes stared across the courtroom. One of the policemen beside him put his hand on Speck's shoulder and the boy who was born to raise hell disappeared.*

* On June 6, 1967, Judge Herbert C. Paschen sentenced Richard Frank Speck to die in the electric chair.

Afterword
by Marvin Ziporyn, M.D.

"None would will to be wicked, none would not be blessed."
Anonymous
(Quoted in Aristotle
Nicomachean Ethics, 1117)

THE YEAR OF 1966 WAS MARKED BY A WAVE OF MURDERS THROUGHout the United States. The first to catapult into public awareness was the July 14 killing of eight nurses in Chicago. Less than a month later, Charles Whitman killed thirteen people from a clocktower overlooking the University of Texas campus. In November a high-school senior coolly shot and killed four women and a little girl in a beauty parlor in Mesa, Arizona. What was particularly disturbing was that the victims were taken at random; that there was no relationship between killer and victim, no apparent motive. The acts were clearly outside the bounds of ordinary reason and experience.

The destruction of human life is always repugnant and unacceptable. However, when murder can be linked to the rational in some fashion, it can be faced and coped with in some emotional form. In the mass killings of 1966, the irrational and incomprehensible were so pronounced that rational society demanded an explanation.

Time magazine presented the public view in a commentary appearing on August 12, 1966. After spelling out the general necessity of comprehending the mass murderer, the magazine stated: "Far too little is known about the mass murderer because he erupts infrequently—and even less frequently survives. Psychiatrists firmly believe that Richard Speck, accused of the nurse killings, ought to be studied intensively rather than be punished by society."

In another expression of this opinion, psychiatrist Theodore Isaac Rubin, in the context of a query concerning the Chicago nurse murders, wrote in *McCall's* magazine of October 1966: "We cannot be effective [about murder] unless we have the opportunity to see and if necessary treat the patient. Also, there are still gaps in our knowledge of human behavior. This includes our knowledge of violence. Vindication and punishment do not advance our knowledge or close these gaps one iota. It is a pity that much that can be learned from the very sick 'criminal' is often lost to the electric chair."

As this book makes clear, I became Richard Speck's treating psychiatrist after he was placed in the Cook County Jail. Speck was that rarity: a surviving accused mass murderer. He was verbal, cooperative and capable of establishing good rapport. It soon became clear that I had a unique situation—the opportunity to treat over a lengthy period an enigma that was of vital importance to society and the opportunity to study in depth the complex makeup of such an individual.

I felt that it was mandatory for me to share my findings with society at large. Merely to study Speck and conceal my findings from the world or to share my observations with a few selected individuals would, in my estimation, amount to a complete abdication of my social responsibility. The knowledge I had gathered was too important to be restricted in any way. It belonged to the collective awareness of all mankind.

This principle dictated the manner in which the book was written. My first impulse was to write an article for one of the medical journals. Brief reflection, however, showed the total inadequacy of this technique. Medical journal articles are short descriptions, five to ten pages in length, really designed to provide future experimenters with the guidelines to repeat a study and verify conclusions. However, in this case the study was a unique one—it was not a case of obtaining ten more subjects and painstakingly following a protocol. Further, in ten pages, I could do no more than make a few general comments and give my conclusions. There would be no space for the specific facts which constitute the raw data of this study. These facts are in this manuscript and furnish everyone with the same material previously available only to me. If I have misinterpreted or misconstrued anything, the error is put down in black and white for anyone to observe and correct. For this reason, I decided I would put into it every aspect of our relationship, even those that might be construed to reflect poorly on me. These took place frequently, and for several reasons. First, in the early stages of our relationship, the patient was defensive and manipulative, that is, he sought to guide our conversations along lines that suited him. I was groping in the dark for a clue, but often I did not know treasure when I found it. Second, I often proceeded on assumptions that were later proven false or mistaken. Nevertheless, I have put in everything exactly as it took place—if I were not completely honest, the book would be worthless as a study. There were times when I misunderstood the import of what Speck said, but the material is an exact reproduction of my impressions, however fallible they may have been at any one time.

A word on technique might be of interest. I saw Speck twice a week from July 29, 1966 to February 13, 1967. Each session lasted from one to three hours. On leaving his cell, I would sit down and write details of the visit. I would like to emphasize that the dialogue in this book is verbatim, not an imaginative reproduction polished for literary effect. In keeping with my desire to present the raw data, I wanted to let Richard speak for himself. My thought was to give all interested parties the same opportunity I had—to study Richard's exact words and formulate their own opinions and theories. If I had not given the exact words he used, then I would be a roadblock, an artificial filter; Richard could only be seen through my eyes. I hope in this book he can be seen almost directly. Of course, I realize that no written exposition can exactly reproduce the jail atmosphere, the Texas drawl, the dramatic pauses, the tonal inflections, the nuances, the looks, the timing, the nonverbal communication. The book, as it now stands, comes as close as any written account can, but it is literally true that the way something is said is often more important than what is said. This book is like an orchestral score—it requires the interpretive powers of the reader. But it is intended simply as a document of truth. My aim is not to hurt anyone or to expose anything: it is simply to present things as I saw them.

After I wrote my notes I turned the material over to Jack Altman, my collaborator. Mr. Altman, an experienced journalist, has given the work a professional refinement that I could not hope to achieve.

As we worked on the manuscript, it quickly became apparent that he was adding a new dimension to the work. He saw the problems from a layman's point of view, raised questions and demanded explanations for things that I took for granted. It became obvious that I was much too close to my subject. So much of the work emanates from this factor that it was decided to write the book in the third person. It was my relationship with Speck as understood by a third party. Thus, Speck's dialogue is recorded verbatim, and the non-dialogue is written by Jack Altman.

One persistent question that has bothered me about this book is the ethical consideration. Of course, as I have already indicated, society demanded that those who knew Speck share their knowledge. But what about the doctor-patient relationship? Is it not sacrosanct?

I have obviously decided that it is ethical to reveal this material. Perhaps a few comments on my reasons for reaching this decision are in order.

The Austin killings touched off a wave of discussion in professional circles on this issue, because Charles Whitman had made certain comments to his psychiatrist indicating that he was in a very disturbed state of mind. Should this have been revealed? The issue was put very squarely: If the public interest and the individual's right to privacy are in direct conflict, which shall prevail? A growing body of opinion, both in the American Medical Association and the American Psychiatric Association, held that the public welfare was primary and that it pre-empted individual rights. However, no rigid guidelines were set. The American Medical Association Principles of Ethics, Section 9, says "A Physician may not reveal the confidences entrusted to him . . . *unless* it becomes necessary to protect the welfare of the community" (italics mine). Well and good, but when does it become necessary?

The American Psychiatric Association attempted to clarify this question in a paper dated January 13, 1961, stating that "confidentiality, like freedom, is not quite absolute." It points out that there are indeed situations that may require a breach of confidentiality. As a working formula, the paper states that "in the final analysis, the physician must turn only to God and his own conscience for guidance."

In discussing these statements in the specific context of the Austin and Chicago murders, Dr. Henry A. Davidson, editor of *Mental*

Hygiene, the professional organ of the National Association for Mental Health, wrote in an article in the *Medical Tribune* of August 27-28, 1966, "The dilemma of confidentiality . . . can't be programmed into a computer. There is still no substitute for personal judgment, the acceptance of responsibility and the path-pointing of the human conscience."

All this means simply that each doctor must decide in a given case where the public interest lies—his decision is his own and need not be presented to any organized body for confirmation. Therefore, this in itself would resolve the ethical question. Clearly, the public interest in the Speck case demands full and complete revelation of anything and everything that could shed light on his actions. Fortunately, in this particular instance, there has been no conflict between public and private interests. It has always been taken for granted that a patient can voluntarily waive his privilege and authorize his doctor to reveal information about himself. Speck has at various stages of our relationship given me this authorization, both orally and in writing, to reveal the content of our conversations.

In September 1966 I told him that I wanted to write a book and that I needed his written permission. He told me, "Write anything you want to" and gave me a written release. Later, in November, he told Dr. Norcross (one of the panel doctors) that I was writing a book. Dr. Norcross reported this officially so that both the State's Attorney and Public Defender were aware of my intention. Speck's consent would be meaningless were he not sane, and I was convinced that he was aware of the import of events in his life. Speculation on this point ended when he received a formal competency hearing and was adjudicated legally competent.

Even though I had a formal release, I still would not have violated his confidence or proceeded against his wishes. Consequently, in mid-January, when it became obvious he would soon be transferred to Peoria, I asked him again whether he objected to publication of a book. His answer of January 13, 1967, reproduced on page 193, speaks for itself.

My concern over Richard's feelings calls for clarification, and I should like at this point to make my personal and philosophical position clear. Many people have asked me for my subjective feelings about Richard Speck. The answer is simple. I like him. He can be courteous, thoughtful, generous and witty, and he has considerable charm. I know Richard in a way most people do not—as a human being. It would be difficult to spend over 100 hours of intimate discussion with another person, listening to his reminiscences, sharing his hopes and anxieties, guilt and remorse, without developing an empathy and understanding. To me, Speck was not the monster the press depicted; he was Richard, a confused, tense, frightened, insecure young man, seeking desperately to be loved and knowing he was an outcast among outcasts, despised, scorned, cursed, rejected and, as he always felt, hopelessly doomed.

I realize that my position in this matter will shock some readers and seem incomprehensible. I found it interesting to observe my own reaction when Richard was taken to Peoria. As the weeks went by, and my only news of him was through newspaper and radio, my own feeling of closeness waned. I too began to see him as "Speck," a name in a headline rather than my friend Richard, the poor, frightened human being in the dark middle cell in the maximum security block of the Cook County Jail. Therefore, I can readily understand the general feeling that Richard Speck is an inhuman fiend and that many will think that I too must be abnormal if I like him. Nevertheless, I have come to know Richard Speck and this makes a significant difference in attitude. This is a phenomenon I have observed many times during the course of my professional duties. A major crime would occur and the perpetrator be apprehended; I would read about him in the cold print of the press and see him as evil incarnate, a member of a qualitatively different species. Then, the next day I would meet him. More often than not, he would prove to be merely a dependent, love-seeking, emotionally disturbed, miserably unhappy member of the human family.

That I might be fond of Richard does not mean that I condone his crime. For that matter, neither does he. But I cannot escape my philosophy of life.

Let me begin by stating that I am a strict determinist. Determinism is the doctrine that all events are the inevitable result of antecedent conditions and that the human being, in acts of apparent choice, is the mechanical expression of his heredity and environment. Further, I do not believe in man as a being who is essentially a passive altruist. Such a creature would never have had the will or aggression to subdue the environment and conquer the planet. I do not believe in "original goodness." I do not see the problem in terms of explaining why man acts violently—history offers overwhelming evidence that this is a basic and continuous pattern. The real puzzle is how man manages to achieve his occasional moments of peaceful coexistence and cooperation. I tend to agree with Robert Ardrey when he says that "Man is in essence a killer—the most sophisticated killer in the world."

I agree too with Plato's comments on human nature in Book IX of the *Republic,* and the reader who condemns my opinion of Speck should give this passage some thought:

> Certain of the unnecessary pleasures and instincts are deemed to be unlawful; every man appears to have them, but in some persons they are subjected to the control of laws and reason, and the better desires prevailing over them, they are either wholly suppressed or reduced in number; while in other persons these desires are stronger and more abundant. I mean particularly those desires which are awake when the reasoning, taming, and ruling power of the personality is asleep; the wild beast in our nature starts up and walks about naked; and there is no conceivable folly or crime, however shameless or unnatural—not excepting incest or parricide—of which such a nature may not be guilty. In all of us, there is such a latent wild beast.

No less than anybody else, I am saddened by the thought of the eight murdered girls. They are to be sorrowed for as the Abels of the world—pathetic victims.* But I feel pity for the man convicted of their murder as well. He too is a victim of existence. He murdered under the drive of forces he could not begin to understand. It is easy to forgive the innocent; the mark of true humanity is to forgive the guilty.

All men are victims of their destiny. They cannot escape their

* One persistent question that is repeatedly asked relates to the problem of the nurses' passivity and lack of resistance. The issue is usually posed in terms of "why didn't they fight for their lives?" It seems to me that this question is posed in terms of an assumption—the belief that the girls *knew* what was going to happen. In reality, they did not know and there was no reason for them to know. The idea of a mass murder was entirely foreign to them or to anyone else, *prior* to the events of that night. Who would have imagined such an occurrence? In a situation such as that, women ordinarily would be afraid only of rape—and their very numbers betrayed them. Since one man could not sexually assault nine women, they were lulled into security. The future killer was to all appearances an ordinary burglar, armed with a gun and knife. Certainly they would not risk bodily harm for the sake of a few paltry dollars in their purses. Rape, as I have indicated, seemed ruled out because of their numbers. Murder never crossed their minds. When the killer had tied them—a frequent occurrence in burglaries, not an act to call forth suspicion—it was too late.

determining factors. This conception has been well stated by others.*

Laws are founded on the premise that everyone is responsible for his conduct—that if he is good it is because he chooses to be good, and if he is bad it is pure cussedness on his part. I cannot accept this, philosophically or scientifically (though my collaborator, Jack Altman, would not choose to go as far as I do). Man can no more control his personality than he can control his sex or eye color or any other physical property. Given a chance, everyone would choose some form of goodness or greatness—to be handsome, perhaps, or heroic or physically perfect, supremely intelligent beneficent heroes. Who would elect to have a clubfoot or cerebral palsy or blindness? Similarly, who would elect to be stupid or emotionally unstable or a criminal shunned by society? But people cannot help themselves if their neurons do not produce great thoughts; they cannot help themselves if their parents are poor or if they are not fed properly; they cannot help themselves if their central nervous system is poisoned by infection or damaged by injury; they cannot help themselves if they live in an environment dominated by antisocial elements.

It must be remembered that thought and feeling are physiological activities, not qualitatively different from other body functions such as respiration or digestion. It is true they are less well understood, but they are still subject to the inexorable control of the biochemistry of the body. As Freud put it, biology is destiny. As a physician, I have seen countless helpless individuals showing cognitive and emotional changes under the impetus of physiological malfunction. I have seen full-blown psychosis resulting from metabolic changes in the pancreas or liver or hormonal changes in the adrenals; and everyone is familiar with the mental aberrations that often accompany a stroke. In a less dramatic vein, hundreds of thousands of women regularly become

* "We cannot directly will to be different from what we are."

Aristotle *Ethics,* iii, 7.

"Chance is the name of a thing that does not exist. What chance is in the universe, so will is in man."

Francis Bacon, *Novum organum,* 1, 60, *De interpretatione nature,* in Nichol, ii, 118.

"Men think themselves free because they are conscious of their volitions and desires but are ignorant of the causes by which they are led to wish and desire."

Spinoza, *Ethics* I, App.

In Epistle 58, ed. Pollack, Spinoza likens the feeling of free will to a stone's thinking, as it travels through space, that it determines its own trajectory and selects the place and time of its fall.

irascible, depressed, tense and impulsive. They say and do things they later regret and make life wretched for those they love the most. They do not act this way because they *will* to do so; they perplexedly seek psychiatric help. This problem, a hormonal and metabolic one, is called premenstrual tension.

It is very difficult for man to rewrite the laws of nature, especially if he is not aware of the cause of the difficulty. Of course, when we are cognizant of the nature of the problem we can enlist aid; but even then the results are uncertain, limited and not directly related to will and volition. If the reader wants to pit his indomitable will against the dictates of his body, he can make a simple test—let him will to remain awake for a short period of time, say 100 hours.

Even when we can enlist outside help, such as drugs and medications, we can defeat biology only within well-defined and structured limits. We can be less than nature allows—never more. We can will our death but we cannot will to lengthen our life. A man can decide to have only one leg—he cannot decide to have three. No man, by free will, has ever succeeded in flying like a bird. If a man does not wish to have a beard, he can shave it—but even then observe the stubbornness with which nature reasserts itself. And man's will does not grow hair on his bald head. But my point is simply that pure choice alone is a very weak tool indeed when dealing with biological phenomena. And the precursors of action—thought and feeling—are biological phenomena. Personality is simply the sum total of an individual's experiences acting on his basic genetic structure and his constitution.

There is a poem of Henley's that declares:

> I am the master of my fate
> I am the Captain of my soul.

to which Clarence Darrow replied: "A fine captain, a fine master of his fate! He wasn't master enough of his fate to get himself born, which is rather important, nor to do much of anything else except brag about it. Instead of being the captain of his soul . . . man isn't even a deckhand on a rudderless ship." *

Do I then feel that persons such as Richard Speck, not being re-

* Clarence Darrow, "Facing Life Fearlessly; Omar Khayyam and A. E. Housman," *Verdicts Out of Court,* ed. Arthur and Lila Weinberg (Chicago, Ill.: Quadrangle Books, 1963).

sponsible for their actions, should be left at large and their actions condoned? No, I feel that the answer lies in rehabilitation and re-education rather than punishment, and in some cases, such as that of brain-damaged individuals whom we do not know how to rehabilitate and re-educate, perhaps permanent institutionalization until science finds the answer—but certainly not punishment as though the person willed to be a criminal.

The concept of talion punishment—an eye for an eye—is at least as old as Hammurabi. It has not solved the problem of crime in the last 4,000 years, and yet mankind stubbornly insists on applying it. If a person attempted to leave a room through the wall, it would take only a few failures to convince him that his tactic was ineffective and fallacious—he would try a different maneuver. Yet, society has tried punishment for thousands of years, failed completely, and doggedly persists. No one would think much of a doctor who had one treatment for all illnesses. Crime is due to a multitudinous number of factors—yet we have one cure—punishment.

We are so punishment-oriented that we lose our sense of reason. If a man commits a crime, we reject psychological explanations and we reject physiological explanations. If it is denied that a man acts in an antisocial manner because of environment or heredity or because of environment plus heredity, what is the explanation? To say simply he is "bad" begs the question—it clarifies nothing, explains nothing, offers no understanding of the cause or operative mechanism of the "badness." It is a completely meaningless term. Where does the evil come from? Surely the concept of evil as an entity unto itself, operating in a void in the criminal's skull, strains credulity. There must be causation, and it is the eradication of the causative factors, rather than pure revenge, that will eventually achieve the goal of reducing crime. Any other approach departs from logic.

I see Richard Speck as a victim and therefore to be pitied equally with all other victims. Specifically, we are dealing with impulsive behavior. This is analogous to the sneeze of hay fever. Given an inherited constitution and the accidental environment of pollen, the selected individual explodes into a sneeze. He does not wish to sneeze and cannot explain why he does, but sneezes even when consciously trying not to do so.

As I told Richard, he is like Dr. Jekyll and Mr. Hyde. Given the magic potion (drugs and alcohol), this gentle, considerate man turns into a murdering monster. Speck's motor is like everyone else's motor —it is his brakes that fail him. Richard Speck did not wish to kill; the question remains—why did he?

The essential elements are: a brain-damaged human being—impulsive, childish, emotionally labile, racked by headaches; drugs, alcohol and barbiturates which excite him—methedrine to make his judgment poor, catalyze latent hostility and enable him to work with great efficiency; a basic obsessive-compulsive personality, rigid, punitive, puritanical, sado-masochistic, containing unconscious hostility to females because of a Madonna-Prostitute complex; hatred of his wife for suspected infidelity and for divorcing him.

These elements are all present at the scene of the murders. A hopped-up, brain-damaged drunk, looking for anything and nothing, with a gun and knife, stumbles into a girls' dormitory near his union hiring hall. The girls are bound and helpless. One of them resembles his hated wife.

The existential moment has arrived. Fantasy (of revenge on women) is suddenly reality—eight helpless girls are at the mercy of Mr. Hyde, whose damaged, alcohol-, barbiturate- and methedrine-poisoned nervous system cannot brake, control or censor him. He transmutes dream into reality. The result: the murder of eight student nurses on July 14, 1966.

UPI Photo

Corazon Amurao (*right*) leaving the trial with her mother and a Peoria County detective.